Welcome to the *EVERYTHING*® series!

These handy, accessible books give you all you need to tackle a difficult project, gain a new hobby, comprehend a fascinating topic, prepare for an exam, or even brush up on something you learned back in school but have since forgotten.

You can read an *EVERYTHING*® book from cover to cover or just pick out the information you want from our four useful boxes: e-facts, e-ssentials, e-alerts, and e-questions. We literally give you everything you need to know on the subject, but throw in a lot of fun stuff along the way, too.

We now have well over 100 *EVERYTHING*® books in print, spanning such wide-ranging topics as weddings, pregnancy, wine, learning guitar, one-pot cooking, managing people, and so much more. When you're done reading them all, you can finally say you know *EVERYTHING*®!

E FACTS
Important sound bytes of information

ESSENTIALS
Quick handy tips

E ALERT
Urgent warnings

QUESTIONS?
Solutions to common problems

THE
EVERYTHING®
Series

Dear Reader:

You hold in your hands an introduction to some of the world's great thinkers. These are men and women who have changed the world in very different yet very dramatic ways. They are masters and mistresses of their chosen professions, be they messiah or moviemaker, scientist or strategist.

The list is an eclectic one. Some are saints; others are scoundrels. I have taken a sampling from a variety of walks of life. Some of them are obvious inclusions; others are more obscure. You may think there are some important people left out. That is inevitable in a single book. A truly all-encompassing collection would be encyclopedic in length.

What do Jesus Christ, the Marquis de Sade, infomercial king Ron Popeil, and Elizabeth Cady Stanton have in common? Their lives and their deeds stand as a testament to dreams fulfilled and missions accomplished. Some paid an awful price for their choices; others are alive and well and enjoying enormous wealth and acclaim. Some lived to see their dreams become reality; for others it was a posthumous victory.

I hope you can draw inspiration from the lives and works of these great thinkers. Perhaps you may feel compelled to delve further into the personal histories of these amazing people. There is a wealth of information beyond this humble introduction.

Perhaps you too might be inspired to boldly go where you have never gone before and strive to make your own dreams reality. In the immortal words of Rocky Balboa, a thinker who is not included in this book: "Go for it."

James Mannion

THE

EVERYTHING®

GREAT THINKERS BOOK

Exploring the minds of the men and women
who have changed the way we see the world

James Mannion

Adams Media Corporation
Avon, Massachusetts

EDITORIAL
Publishing Director: Gary M. Krebs
Managing Editor: Kate McBride
Copy Chief: Laura MacLaughlin
Acquisitions Editor: Bethany Brown
Development Editor: Lynn Northrup
Production Editor: Khrysti Nazzaro

PRODUCTION
Production Director: Susan Beale
Production Manager: Michelle Roy Kelly
Series Designer: Daria Perreault
Cover Design: Paul Beatrice and Frank Rivera
Layout and Graphics: Colleen Cunningham,
Rachael Eiben, Michelle Roy Kelly, Daria Perreault

An Everything® Series Book.
Everything® is a registered trademark of Adams Media Corporation.

Published by Adams Media Corporation
57 Littlefield Street, Avon, MA 02322 U.S.A.
www.adamsmedia.com

ISBN: 1-58062-662-9
Printed in the United States of America.

J I H G F E D C B A

Library of Congress Cataloging-in-Publication Data
Mannion, James.
The everything great thinkers book / James Mannion.
p.   cm.   —(An everything series book)
Includes index.
ISBN 1-58062-662-9
1. Biography. I. Title. II. Everything series.
CT104 .M36   2002
920.02–dc21   2002009410

Illustrations by Barry Littmann.
Additional illustrations courtesy of Dover Publications.

This book is available at quantity discounts for bulk purchases.
For information, call 1-800-872-5627.

Visit the entire Everything® series at everything.com

Contents

Introduction

WHAT MAKES A GREAT THINKER? You can be an absent-minded professor alone in your basement apartment and generate many deep thoughts within the confines of your ever active cranium, but if you do not share them with the world, it is all for naught.

The men and women in *The Everything® Great Thinkers Book* are also men and women of action. Their thoughts became activities and their doings changed the world. Not always for the better, either.

Many may ask, "How can you include every great thinker within the covers of a single book?" The short answer is "We can't." *The Everything® Great Thinkers Book* is meant to be a sampling of philosophers, innovators, and social and political activists from ancient history through modern times. It is clearly not a comprehensive list; no such animal exists. And not every reader will agree with the choices. Some might see strange additions and others may note glaring omissions. So be it. One person's great thinker may be another person's pompous blowhard.

What this book does provide is an introduction to a cross-section of some of the great minds from antiquity to the twenty-first century. These are thinkers from all walks of life and all schools of thought, representing a smorgasbord of ideas. Some may feel political and military folks are not great thinkers at all, since war wreaks havoc and politics, by its very nature, is ethically suspect. Many an evil person can reluctantly be called a great thinker; many a kind-hearted soul can be deemed not especially intellectually stimulating or gifted.

Some may find it odd and incongruous to include Socrates, Sigmund Freud, Mahatma Gandhi, Madonna, and infomercial king Ron Popeil in the same book. However, as you peruse these pages, you will note that great thinkers are, if nothing else, an eclectic cast of characters. These people embraced their dreams, gave them shape, and made them come true. They were not afraid to use their talents in an effort to change the world. Some had lofty goals, others had more simplistic (or even selfish) motivations, but they all succeeded in their objectives, and their ideas have in one way or another inspired millions.

We hope that this introduction to some of the movers and shakers and shapers of our world will encourage you to delve more deeply into the lives, words, and achievements of this fascinating group of men and women. Perhaps you will be prompted to take some of the great thoughts that have been buzzing around your brain and turn them into a reality that could make the world a better place.

The ideas and deeds of the great thinkers in this book changed the world. And if history has taught us nothing else, it is that individual men and women in the right place and the right time at the right moment can make a difference.

So put on your thinking caps. Go out there and shake things up, rattle some cages, and leave your mark. If Gandhi and Ron Popeil can do it, so can you.

CHAPTER 1

The Great Greek Philosophers

Primitive man was a creature of superstition and his world was a land teeming with gods and monsters that controlled his life and environment. But humankind is nothing if not evolutionary (and often revolutionary), so it was inevitable that a group of men would come along and look at things from a different angle. These men were the first philosophers.

The First Philosophers: Monists and Sophists

Before Socrates appeared on the scene, the Monists and the Sophists were the primary ancient Greek philosophers. The Monists (from *mono,* meaning "one") were first, trying through trial and error to explain the world by means beyond superstition and primitive religious beliefs.

Individually, the Monists arrived at the same conclusion: that one basic "stuff" comprised reality. Thales said that the stuff was water; Anaximenes said it was air; Anaximander said it was something called the Boundless (*ápeiron* in Greek); Pythagoras said it was numbers. Heracleitus said everything was in flux; Parmenides said everything was stagnant.

The other notable pre-Socratic group was the Sophists, and were more like teachers than philosophers. They instructed young wealthy Greeks in the arts of rhetoric and debate, teaching them how to win a debate even if they were wrong, and giving us the wonderful word *sophistry.* Sophists could spin and twist things in ways that would make them the envy of any political spin doctor.

These cagey charlatans were giving philosophy a bad name until one man came along and used some of their methods against them— successfully. Since that time, his name—Socrates—has been associated with philosophy and great thought.

Socrates

Socrates (469–399 B.C.) was a controversial Athenian figure who spent a lifetime in the public square engaging in dialogues with the young men of Athens. He was so fond of dialogues a form of it was named after him: the Socratic dialogue.

A short, squat, and somewhat homely man according to all accounts, Socrates was a rather eccentric loner. He did not put much stock in appearance or material things. Socrates was from what would be considered a middle-class family, son of a stonemason and a midwife. Although we do not know much about his youth, we do know that he was honored for his service in the Peloponnesian War and served the Athenian city-state with complete loyalty. He married a woman named Xanthippe, but the general belief is that his interest in women was not especially strong.

Socrates was a student of natural philosophy, what would later become "science." In fact, Socrates is a character in a comedy titled *Clouds* by the Greek playwright Aristophanes. Socrates is portrayed as a natural philosopher who has his head in the clouds and is oblivious to what is right in front of him. However, this theatrical lampoon does not represent the real Socrates who has come to us through his disciple, Plato.

ESSENTIALS

There is no word for homosexuality in ancient Greek. It was not a concept that they were especially focused on. People were sexual and partnered with whom they chose; bisexuality appears to have been more or less the norm.

Socrates rejected the focus on the exterior world upheld by the Monists and the linguistic legerdemain employed by the Sophists. He was in search of Truth with a capital *T,* and it would not to be found in nature or through parsing words.

His Star Rises

From age forty to age seventy, Socrates was the unofficial philosopher of Athens. He could be seen here, there, and everywhere enjoying the life of a journeyman seeker and philosopher. He eked out a modest living from a combination of the Athenian equivalent of welfare and a family inheritance. This living enabled him to devote himself to philosophizing, for which he never charged and thus never made a drachma.

Socrates enjoyed chatting and debating with the young men of Athens. It was in these lively discussions that he developed and perfected the style of debate that came to be known as the *Socratic dialogue*. The dialogue involved posing questions to his intellectual quarry and eliciting responses. He made the unwitting upstarts think for themselves and they often became acutely aware of their own ignorance in the process. This format of question and answer with a logical debate of opposing views is called a *dialectic*.

Interested in the pure pursuit of Truth no matter what, Socrates made many a Greek earn his education the hard way. Many felt foolish after a verbal fencing match with the master, but it was not Socrates' goal to make them appear ridiculous. His style of dialogue was intended to help the other fellow figure things out for himself, not simply to give him the answer. Socrates did not claim to have all the answers, but he did know how to ask the right questions.

Socrates fancied himself a midwife to ideas. (He probably liked the analogy because his mother was a midwife.) He did not originate deep

Socrates

thoughts, he maintained. Rather, he drew them out of the person with whom he was conversing. He also likened himself to a gadfly—that particularly stubborn, nasty insect that torments horses by landing on them and stinging their buttocks. Using its tail, the horse angrily shoos away the gadfly, but the persistent insect remains undeterred. In the analogy, society was the horse's buttocks, annoyed with the relentless Socrates and his insistence on holding the mirror up to nature and forcing the world to see itself as it really was. A fly can eventually be swatted with crushing finality, and so, too, was Socrates.

A Wise Guy

Socrates modestly laid no claim on wisdom, only on ignorance and an ever-questioning nature. The Oracle at Delphi, a priestess of the prophetic Greek god Apollo, pronounced Socrates the wisest man in the world. Socrates countered that if he was indeed wise, it was only because the truly wise person admits that he really knows nothing at all.

QUESTIONS?

What is a *Socratic dialogue*?
Socratic dialogue is a form of debate, in which probing questions and answers lead to lively, intellectual, educational discussions.

Socrates made many enemies during the course of his philosophizing. Many of the students who were made to appear foolish under his probing were sons of the ruling class and went on to become political authorities. Socrates was eventually charged with "impiety," a serious offense punishable by death. His speculations did not stress the proper reverence for the gods, it was alleged, and such a free spirit was naturally a bad influence on children. Facing charges of impiety and corrupting the morals of the Athenian youth, Socrates was put on trial.

The Apology That Wasn't

During his trial, Socrates defended himself in an eloquent speech Plato preserved as the *Apology*. It contains the essence of Socrates' character and philosophy. He begins with characteristic humility, but the *Apology* was anything but an act of contrition. It was a spirited, defiant defense of his life and work. He stated his case, continued to agitate his enemies, and stayed true to his singular course until the end.

How you, O Athenians, have been affected by my accusers, I cannot tell; but I know that they almost made me forget who I was—so persuasively did they speak; and yet they have hardly uttered a word of truth. But of the many falsehoods told by them, there was one which quite amazed me;—I mean when they said that you should be upon your guard and not allow yourselves to be deceived by the force of my eloquence. To say this, when they were certain to be detected as soon as I opened my lips and proved myself to be anything but a great speaker, did indeed appear to me most shameless—unless by the force of eloquence they mean the force of truth; for if such is their meaning, I admit that I am eloquent. But in how different a way from theirs!

Socrates was accused of being a Sophist. Although he used some of the Sophists' debating methods, he turned them toward the pursuit of Truth. Yes, he had once been interested in the natural sciences, but that interest had declined in the years before his trial. He distanced himself from the Sophists, explaining that he didn't charge for his services nor did he presume to convey any wisdom. He repeated the story of his encounter with the Oracle of Delphi, in which he claimed to know nothing. This claim is called the *Socratic disavowal of knowledge.*

Socrates explained his philosophy of life during the course of the *Apology:* The ultimate goal is not fame or fortune. It should be to live a virtuous life. Doing the right thing should be the motivating force and its own reward. Socrates was convinced that he had lived his seventy years according to this precept. As a result, nothing his enemies did could truly harm him.

The virtuous life, according to Socrates, includes loyalty to the state. Socrates and his disciple Plato were wary of democracies. They did not believe in placing too much power in the hands of just anyone. Since Socrates was about to lose his life through the abuse of power in a democracy, we can understand his viewing this form of government with a jaundiced eye. And as we will see, Plato's *Republic* is anything but a democracy as we understand the concept in modern times.

FACTS

While cross-examining his accusers, Socrates used his celebrated Socratic method to systematically demolish their arguments. While he scored points in logic, he continued to infuriate those who were about to cast judgment on him.

During the *Apology,* Socrates was quite aware that the court would likely vote to convict him, and that the penalty would be death. He expressed no fear of death. If there was life after death, he did not fear damnation. And if there was nothing, he reasoned, then there is nothing to fear?

Socrates was prepared for the verdict. He did not throw himself on the mercy of the court. He faced his accusers unbowed and unapologetic. Had he acted differently he might have reduced his sentence and spared his life, but he elected to follow his path.

It was no surprise when he was found guilty. The tradition of the time allowed the condemned man to suggest his own punishment. Socrates proposed that he be given free room and board and be supported by the state for the rest of his natural life. Needless to say, that idea was rejected. He then proposed a very small fine, then a slightly larger one. Defiantly, he told the court that if he were allowed to live, he would not stop practicing philosophy. Then, he made the statement for which he is most famous, a motto that should be every philosopher's raison d'être. He said, "The unexamined life is not worth living."

ESSENTIALS   Socrates' motto should be the rallying cry of every great thinker. The quote "Know thyself" is also attributed to Socrates. True insight is gained not only from observing the externals but also through introspection.

Socrates was sentenced to death. Socrates met his end like a secular martyr. Word filtered down to him that should he decide to flee the city before sentence was passed, the government would not aggressively hunt him down. Ignoring pleas from some of his followers, Socrates elected to drink hemlock (in those days, the convicted were apparently given the option of killing themselves) and died in the company of his adoring entourage.

His last words were, "Crito, I owe a cock to Asclepius; will you remember to pay the debt?" Thus with this rather banal request ended the life of the world's most famous philosopher.

Plato

Plato (427–347 B.C.) was Socrates' most famous student. We would know nothing about Socrates without Plato as a primary source. As Socrates' protégé, Plato made studious observations and took copious notes, bringing Socrates to the world through many chronicles of his life and philosophy. Since Socrates never committed anything to writing, Plato is the filter through which we view the great man.

Of course the dilemma is this: Where does the Socrates end and the Plato begin? Did Plato accurately report the life and teachings of Socrates, or did he use Socrates as a dramatic mouthpiece for his own ideas? The early Socratic dialogues are generally accepted as a more faithful picture of Socrates, and the later dialogues are thought to be more and more "Platonized."

Plato's Cave

Unlike Socrates, whose classroom was the world, Plato founded an academy that he called, somewhat unimaginatively, the Academy. Plato's philosophy is capsuled in his story, "Myth of the Cave," in which he compares people to prisoners chained in a cave. There is nothing but a small fire illuminating their environment. The cave dwellers see only their own shadows and the shadows flickering on the wall in front of them. This is the only reality they know, and it is a distorted and narrow vision of the Big Picture.

Plato maintains that we wander through the world with a veil over our eyes, obscuring our ability to perceive Truth. In Plato's myth, one of the cave dwellers is freed from the confines of the cavern. Arriving at the surface, he is blinded by the light. His eyes are not accustomed to the brave new world before him. Even though he is free from the strictures of the other cave people, he can still only see a blurry version of Truth because his eyes cannot quickly adjust to what is before him.

ESSENTIALS

The man who leaves the cave, yet still cannot see, is a clear reference to Socrates and a commentary on humanity's tendency to savor their narrow view.

Eventually, though, this refugee will adjust to the new world around him. He will see reality with a clarity that his comrades cannot. This enlightened individual returns to the cave and tries to tell the others what they are missing. How will he be perceived? Will he be welcomed with open arms? Will the others shake off their shackles and strive to join him? Not according to Plato. He suggests that the "prophet" will be killed by his fellow men and women, which history has confirmed. Plato sums up the allegory as follows:

This entire allegory, I said, you may now append, dear Glaucon,
to the previous argument; the prisonhouse is the world of sight,
the light of the fire is the sun, and you will not misapprehend me

if you interpret the journey upward to be the ascent of the soul into the intellectual world according to my poor belief, which, at your desire, I have expressed—whether rightly or wrongly, God knows. But, whether true or false, my opinion is that in the world of knowledge the idea of good appears last of all, and is seen only with an effort; and, when seen, is also inferred to be the universal author of all things beautiful and right, parent of light and of the lord of light in this visible world, and the immediate source of reason and truth in the intellectual; and that this is the power upon which he who would act rationally either in public or private life must have his eye fixed.

Moreover, I said, you must not wonder that those who attain to this beatific vision are unwilling to descend to human affairs; for their souls are ever hastening into the upper world where they desire to dwell; which desire of theirs is very natural, if our allegory may be trusted.

And is there anything surprising in one who passes from divine contemplations to the evil state of man, misbehaving himself in a ridiculous manner; if, while his eyes are blinking and before he has become accustomed to the surrounding darkness, he is compelled to fight in courts of law, or in other places, about the images or the shadows of images of justice, and is endeavoring to meet the conceptions of those who have never yet seen absolute justice?

The Nature of Reality

Plato said that for every thing we see in perceptible reality, there is a corresponding "Form" or "Idea" out there in the ether. Like the cave dwellers, we see only a small fraction of reality. Plato said is it is difficult to perceive the true nature of reality, but he does offer four ways in which we can try:

1. Knowledge from imagination, dreams, and what was later called the unconscious
2. Perceptions of the outside world

3. Mathematical knowledge
4. Philosophical knowledge, which was Big Picture knowledge, an awareness of absolutes, universal truths in the form of those elusive Forms

Plato called the first two forms of knowledge "opinions," because although perception may be reality, things are perceived differently by different people. The second two were True Knowledge; according to Plato, Forms are immutable.

ESSENTIALS

Plato believed that there was an ultimate Form that he called the Good. This Form could be interpreted as God as Plato understood Him. The heavenly realm of the Forms and the Good is the true reality and our world is the illusory shadow world.

Plato, like many Eastern philosophers and mystics, believed in reincarnation. This is, of course, the belief that beings have multiple lifetimes, learning and growing with each passing incarnation. In the period between lives, Plato believed, we will have access to a clear picture of this other world and be able to view the Forms and the Good in their celestial splendor. We must enjoy it while it lasts, however, because when we return for the next life, our memory of the experience is wiped clean. We are left with a vague awareness that we are missing out on something big. That awareness is what makes great thinkers; they are searching for the missing pieces to the puzzle.

Plato's Republic

Plato's best-known work is called the *Republic*, in which he puts forth his political philosophy. Having seen his beloved mentor unjustly convicted by a crooked democracy, Plato has little use for that form of government.

Plato felt that everyone needed to be part of the state and a contributing member of society. So he assigned classes, or more accurately castes, within which citizens would be organized. You probably would not have wanted to live in Plato's Republic, his utopian vision of the perfect society. The rigid caste system offered no chance of upward mobility. You were assigned to a role in life and there you stayed.

Given his chosen profession, it is no surprise that Plato made the Philosopher class the highest caste. According to his system, the

Plato

Philosopher class rules the state; the Warrior class protects the state; and the Producer class serves the state with goods, services, and skills.

This Republic doesn't sound very democratic. A ruling class of philosophical aristocrats would direct the affairs of state, with the famous Platonic concept of the Philosopher-King at its head. The Philosopher class guides the other classes, keeping the military in check and the producers honest, while contemplating the world of the Forms and trying to make reality as Form-friendly as possible.

QUESTIONS?

What about the classical arts?
In Plato's way of thinking, art was a copy of reality, which in turn was a pale representation of the Forms. What value is there in a pale copy of a pale copy? For a citizenry striving for the Ideal, Plato regarded such earthly concerns as frivolous, if not downright destructive.

Plato went so far as to suggest that children be taken away from their parents and raised in state-run foster homes supervised by the Philosopher class. He believed that the state could do a better job of raising (and indoctrinating) children than their parents could. He also believed in community property, and in the communal sharing of wives! Plato's Utopia hardly sounds ideal to modern ears, yet he remains one of the three great sages of antiquity.

Aristotle

Aristotle (384–322 B.C.) was Plato's student at the Academy for twenty years and was considered the heir apparent to succeed Plato. However, Aristotle broke with the maestro on a number of issues so theirs was not the most cordial of relationships. After Plato's death, Aristotle traveled extensively and even spent five years tutoring the celebrated world conqueror Alexander the Great (see Chapter 14).

Aristotle finally formed his own school and called it the Lyceum. He was a philosopher who was as fast on his feet as he was with his mind. He liked to walk as he talked, his neophyte student body keeping pace with, if not his thoughts, at least his gait. His students became known as the Peripatetics, from the Greek word meaning "to walk."

Being and Becoming

Aristotle disagreed with many of Plato's theories. Some in academia may call it bad form to challenge the professor, but Aristotle did so on the Platonic notion of Forms. As we discussed, Plato believed that "myriad" Forms floated about in another dimension in the ether. Truth,

Aristotle

Beauty, Love, and other abstractions were actual entities, which cast their shadows, if you will, in the earthly conceptions of these Ideas. Aristotle did not buy into this undeniably farfetched notion. The theory did not make much sense to him, and it was certainly impossible to prove empirically.

Whereas Plato believed the Forms were separate entities, Aristotle believed that Forms were characteristics embedded in the things themselves. For Aristotle, the here and now was the reality to be concerned with. He called his revised version of the Forms, *Universals*. There were universal truths, but they could be found in our perceivable space/time continuum.

Plato believed that there were Ideals and their pale imitations. The pre-Socratic philosophers Parmenides and Heracleitus believed, respectively, that everything was stagnant and that everything was in flux. Aristotle adapted these opposing viewpoints and came up with his own theory, a radical belief at the time and perhaps his major contribution to philosophy. He called this the theory of *potentiality*. Potentiality means that within everything, including people, there exists a natural evolution toward fulfilling its own potential, in essence becoming its own Form. It is a movement in nature and in humans from imperfection to perfection, or as close as anything can get to perfection. This potentiality, or ultimate potential, is a characteristic of all things and achieving it is an involuntary process. The universe is in a constant progression of being and becoming, working toward its own perfection.

QUESTIONS?

What is a syllogism?
Aristotle is famous for the syllogism: a logical argument that takes two truths, connects them, and arrives at a third truth. The most celebrated syllogism is "All men are mortal. Socrates is a man. Therefore, Socrates is mortal." Aristotle believed that the syllogism was the most effective, logical means of leading the mind to absolute knowledge.

Aristotle identifies four causes in the process of being and becoming:

1. Material cause: an external force that is creating or initiating the new thing
2. Efficient cause: the process of creation
3. Formal cause: something in its natural state
4. Final cause: what it can become when it fulfills its potential

Aristotle tells us that happiness is the ultimate goal of humankind. His definition of happiness is probably different than ours. True happiness, according to Aristotle, can only come from leading a virtuous life. Moderation is a prime virtue that keeps one free from vice and free to work toward one's potentiality. People are constantly "potentializing," whether they are aware of it or not. Also high on Aristotle's list of the best things in life is friendship. True friendships are to be cultivated and treasured. A good friend is almost like your *doppelgänger*, your spiritual double. Your best friend is more like your "other half" than a romantic partner, according to Aristotle.

Unlike Plato, Aristotle did not believe that art was a weak imitation of reality. Aristotle saw art as a means to enhance and idealize reality, as an opportunity for man to strive in his limited human way to touch the Ideal. Far from being a waste of time, art was ennobling. Aristotle believed that theater helped people see human absurdity and foolishness and tragedy in the classical sense, and allowed the audience to achieve a catharsis; that is, a cleansing emotional response from a safe distance.

God and State

Aristotle called God the primary cause of all things, or the "Unmoved Mover." God was the first thing to exist, separate from all other matter. God is the ultimate Form. Aristotle believed that God is pure mental energy. He called this energy *Nous*. In Artistotle's estimation, Nous was not an especially hands-on God, certainly not the judgmental and often petulant micromanaging God of the three main monotheistic religions. In fact, Nous wasn't terribly interested in the human race, so there wasn't much reason to pay attention to him.

Aristotle viewed the human soul as an integral part of the body, not as a separate entity. He believed in what is now called the *body-mind* concept. That is, we are one human organism comprised of physical and spiritual matter. Hence, the soul did not exist after death. However, each soul is imbued with a piece of the Nous, or universal mind, and that Nous within flies off into the ether at the time of physical death.

Aristotle's political perspective is dated, to say the least. He considered the slavery of other humans as not only acceptable but entirely appropriate. He believed that usury, lending money to be returned with interest, was a terrible thing. He also believed that the three best forms of government are monarchy, aristocracy, and constitutional republic. Only when they are perverted, do they begin to degenerate—into tyranny, oligarchy, and democracy.

CHAPTER 2
The Birth of the Modern Philosophers

René Descartes is considered the father of modern philosophy, and Immanuel Kant is the unofficial founder of German idealism. These two men, in their respective ways, ushered in the modern philosophical era. Another German, Friedrich Wilhelm Nietzsche, was one of the most misunderstood and provocative philosophers of all time. All three men greatly influenced the generations of philosophers who followed.

René Descartes

René Descartes (1596–1650) began his career as a mathematician and is given the distinction of first postulating the notion of analytic geometry. He was also a scientist whose findings tended to support the many concepts proposed by another great thinker, the Italian Renaissance scientist Galileo (see Chapter 6). It was perfectly natural that Descartes had misgivings about going public with theories that would link him to a man who was almost burned at the stake for heresy. Ideas could be dangerous things in those days. If the Inquisition of the Catholic Church targeted you as a suspicious thinker, you could find yourself in something hotter than proverbial hot water.

Descartes eventually buried his controversial theories in a philosophical book called *Meditations*, which he dedicated to the local Church leaders in an effort to get on their good side.

When in Doubt, Doubt Everything

It was Descartes's intention to disassemble philosophy as it had been practiced for centuries and rebuild it in his own paradigm. He decided to start by doubting everything. This is the main precept of the school of philosophy called *skepticism*. Descartes took this doubting task to an extreme degree. He decided that everything he knew and experienced was not to be trusted. He questioned the validity of reality itself!

FACTS

Descartes, a devout Catholic, even began to doubt that there was a loving God. Maybe things were run by a duplicitous evil demon that deluded humans into believing in reality. This *demon hypothesis* clearly influenced other thinkers, including the screenwriters of the hit movie *The Matrix* and its sequels.

Descartes almost went insane in his maniacal doubt-fest. He eventually could not be certain whether things were real or whether he was dreaming, or whether he was a character in someone else's dream. He could no longer find certainty even in the logical realm of mathematics. What he called his *dream hypothesis* was driving him crazy.

Descartes was at his wit's end. His plan to knock down the fortress of philosophy and remake it in his image had blown up in his face. He had to find something that could be absolutely true before he ended up in the madhouse. Then he stumbled upon it, and in doing so changed the face of philosophy forever.

In Latin, the sentence is *Cogito, ergo sum*. In English, it is "I think, therefore I am." What was absolutely true, he thought, was that you cannot be certain of anything in this world except the fact that you are thinking about the fact that you cannot be certain of anything in this world. That is, you can be sure that you exist, because you are a conscious entity who is thinking. "I think, therefore I am" is perhaps the most famous sentence in the history of philosophy. As a skeptic who questioned everything, Descartes had found the one thing that always remained a fact: the thinking of the thinker.

Delighted that he finally had something to hang his philosophical hat on, Descartes used these arguments to "prove" the existence of God:

"I think, therefore I am," proves that I exist, but I am an imperfect, flawed mortal man. If I were my own creator, naturally I would have made myself perfect. This proves that I did not create myself, and if I did not, then who did? God.

I have a conception of what perfection is, even though I am an imperfect being. So where did I get this idea of perfection? Not from me, of course. After all, I'm imperfect, and perfection cannot come from something as so inherently imperfect as I. So there must be a perfect being, and that is God.

What's the Idea?

Having proven that man and God exist, Descartes's next target was the very nature of reality itself. He divided reality into two substances: *thinking* substances and *extended* substances. Thinking substances are the human minds, and extended substances are the physical bodies. But where, he thought, do ideas come from? Are they all electrochemical impulses generated in the human brain or are some divinely inspired? As a religious man, he had to believe that God was more than a mere bystander.

Descartes determined that some ideas come from sensory experiences, but others come preloaded in the mind, like Netscape or Internet Explorer on your new computer. He called them *innate* ideas. Logic, mathematics, the notion of a God, and a sense of morality were all innate ideas, according to Descartes. Still not satisfied, Descartes came up with two other names for types of ideas: *adventitious* ideas are generated by what is experienced through our senses, and *fictitious* ideas are just what their name implies. They are made up.

ESSENTIALS

Descartes was a rationalist. That is, he believed that the human mind can know and comprehend concepts without having to rely on sensory experience. These concepts are called *innate* ideas or *primary* ideas. He called other information that was gleaned from experience *secondary ideas.*

Descartes also proposed the concept of *dualism*, which is a mind-body disconnection. He gave preference and precedence to the mind or spirit. The physical world was merely mechanical, without a soul. Descartes believed that a human body that had no spirit could still walk and talk (although what it would have to say?). Passions had nothing to do with the spirit. They were manifestations of biological impulses and not to be highly regarded or trusted. That the mind can know things without actually experiencing them is called *rationalism*.

Descartes set the stage for the British empiricists, French philosophers, and German idealists who followed him. He overcame his fear of the Inquisition and published his work, which influenced philosophers and thinkers for many generations to follow.

Immanuel Kant

Immanuel Kant (1724–1804) had an interest in metaphysics, which is everything in the world that is beyond the human mind's ability to perceive, and for many even to conceive. The philosopher, however, always has an inquiring mind and a nagging sense that there are, as

Shakespeare said, "more things in Heaven and Earth." Kant called the world that we experience through our senses the *phenomenal* world and the reality beyond that the *noumenal* world. Noumenal translates somewhat awkwardly into English as the "thing-in-itself."

Kant was doubtful whether humans could ever truly understand the true nature of the world. And cosmic questions about the existence of God were really questions of faith and were not in the purview of reason and scientific inquiry. Kant was influenced by the writings of the British philosopher David Hume, who posited that nothing is real and humans could not grasp the nature of reality even if it were real. Kant was also influenced by the work of Sir Isaac Newton, the man who "proved" the laws of gravity and other scientific "realities." Kant sought no less daunting a goal than reconciling these two seemingly mutually exclusive ideologies.

Critique of Pure Reason

As a middle-aged man, Kant read a book by David Hume that woke him from what he called a "dogmatic slumber." Hume's view that were no certainties in life and that we were all merely an electromagnetic chaotic storm of sensory impressions rattled Kant, a fastidious academic of an apparently routine nature. Legend has it that Kant's neighbors could set their clocks by his evening walks. He sought to resolve the conflict between science and faith, which was a philosophical dilemma that was as old as philosophy itself. Kant also sought to build a bridge between the philosophies of rationalism and empiricism. Rationalism said that one can know things without experiencing them through the senses; empiricism maintained that people are all born as *tabula rasas*, or blank slates, and that everything imprinted on the mind comes from sensory experience.

Kant set forth his philosophy, which he called *critical philosophy*, in the book *Critique of Pure Reason*. In it he defined two types of judgments: the *analytic* and the *synthetic*. The analytic judgment is one in which the truth can be determined within itself; that is, the definitions of the words within the statement of truth affirm the truth. For example, "All black houses are houses." Of course a black house is a house. An example of a synthetic truth is simply "The house is black." This truth needs to be determined by the action of looking at the house in question to see if it is indeed black.

FACTS

Two other ways of judgments are what Kant called *a priori* and *a posteriori*, the Latin words for "before" and "after." "All black houses are houses" is an *a priori* judgment; you do not have to see the houses to know this. "The house is black" is an *a posteriori* judgment; you have to see the house to determine its color.

Transcendental and *empirical* are two more terms in this Kantian point/counterpoint. Transcendental knowledge would be *a priori*; it is something that you just know to be true. Empirical knowledge is *a posteriori*; you need to scrutinize it to determine its veracity.

Imagine there is one column made up of analytic, *a priori*, and transcendental knowledge; and another column made up to of synthetic, *a posteriori*, and empirical knowledge. Kant sought to take one from column A and one from column B and see what he came up with. Through this process of matching by trial-and-error, Kant determined that some combinations were illogical. But he liked the notion of the synthetic *a priori*. This concept was nothing less than a Universal Truth that people had been searching for since day one, and it had been arrived at through a scientific method—quite a coup for a philosopher.

Comprehending the Incomprehensible

Kant proposed that reality is not an ordered universe waiting to be perceived by the human mind. Rather, the human mind takes the chaos that is out there and orders it into a reality that the mind can perceive. Time and space as we understand them are not external concepts; they are intrinsic mechanisms that enable us to make sense of reality. Reality, if it could be seen by a means other than our perceptions, would be a surreal, incomprehensible mishmash that would probably prompt a descent into madness.

Kant speculated on the nature of the noumenal, or metaphysical, world and looked at otherworldly realms from an optimistic standpoint. Kant believed we have regular intuitive hints to the nature of the noumenal world. Kant believed that a God, a universal justice, and immortality exist on the "other side."

Kant proposed that the mind has "categories of understanding," which catalogue, codify, and make sense of the physical world. The mind cannot experience anything that it does not filter. Therefore, we can never know the true nature of reality. In this sense, Kant claimed that "perception is reality."

As a result, Kant believed that people do not receive all data from sensory experience alone, as the empiricists claimed. Nor do we get information solely via reason, as the rationalists believed. This was a revolutionary way of thinking in the history of philosophy, and Kant influenced almost every philosopher who followed. Just as we have to accept that there is more out there than we can comprehend, we should accept that Immanuel Kant is a great thinker—even if he leaves us scratching our heads.

Friedrich Wilhelm Nietzsche

One of the most misunderstood (and posthumously maligned) philosophers was Friedrich Wilhelm Nietzsche (1844–1900). His fiery polemics about accessing personal power and achieving the maximum potential, which he called becoming a Superman, were adapted and corrupted by Hitler and the Nazis. This tarnished Nietzsche's reputation and many people labeled him a Nazi, although he died more than thirty years before the Nazis came to power and had no association with them.

When Nietzsche spoke of a becoming a Superman, he did not mean the spandex-clad crime fighter; neither did he endorse an Aryan master race. Another blemish on Nietzsche's reputation was his friendship for a time with celebrated composer Richard Wagner, a brilliant artist who by many accounts was also a nasty little man with definite anti-Semitic views.

Many Nietzsche catch phrases have entered the social consciousness. He was the author of the famous obituary, "God is dead," and spoke of a "will to power" and a theory of "eternal recurrence." Although there is no doubt that Nietzsche took a bleak view of Western civilization and the Judeo-Christian tradition, there was more to his philosophy than common misconceptions.

FACTS

Nietzsche's philosophy is mostly disseminated in the form of aphorisms, which are pithy and poetic short paragraphs that express his viewpoint or commentary on a particular topic. One of Nietzsche's most famous aphorisms is, "That which does not kill us makes us stronger."

High-strung, hypersensitive, lonely, and lovelorn, Nietzsche was a tortured soul whose life was fraught with physical and emotional problems. Unlucky in love, he endured the rejection of several marriage proposals. Nietzsche's breaking point, however, occurred after watching a man beat a horse. He ran to the defense of the animal but was driven to a madness from which he never recovered. He spent the last decade of his life cared for by his mother, and upon her death, by his sister. Many dismiss his later works as symptomatic of increasing mental illness. Others hail him as an original, provocative thinker.

Nietzsche did not originate a specific school of philosophy and did not devise a formal doctrine about logic, ethics, or the nature of reality. He wandered all over the philosophical map, a wild prophet raving against the injustices of his time. For example, your pet peeves may be people who talk during movies or chatter on cell phones in public. Nietzsche's pet peeves were nothing short of Christianity and Western civilization. He took on these formidable opponents and made a career out of explaining, in the language of a poet rather than a traditional philosopher, why he thought they were bad.

Becoming "Superman"

Nietzsche attacked Christianity as a religion that imposed a "slave morality" on its followers. He suggested that, instead of becoming a cowering, craven Christian, we become Supermen. Nietzsche's Superman rejects the traits of humility and passivity, believing they are positioned as Christian virtues, but in truth are really devices used to control us.

The Superman would not be anyone's slave. He would rise above "the herd" and move beyond good and evil to fulfill the ultimate human

Friedrich Wilhelm Nietzsche

potential. The Superman makes his ethical decisions based on his own sense of morality, not the morality imposed by religion and society. The virtues that Christianity encourages are to be eschewed; what we are told are vices are often central to achieving our super goals.

The Superman focuses on this world rather than the next. The next life is not a sure thing; the here and now is all too real. Nietzsche did not believe that any true Supermen had yet burst onto the scene, but he listed Jesus, Socrates, Shakespeare, and Napoleon as role models. Note that he cites Jesus, but attacks Christianity. Jesus rebelled against the established political and religious structure of his day, and Nietzsche, like many people, believed that Jesus would be horrified at many of the things that have gone on in his name.

The Nazis seized upon Nietzsche's Superman principle, but Nietzsche was long gone by then. Nietzsche was not interested in controlling or conquering others. He advocated mastering yourself and achieving your personal potential without allowing a repressive society to inhibit you. He was like an edgier version of motivational speaker Tony Robbins.

A True Visionary or a Disturbed Man?

Nietzsche's first book, *The Birth of Tragedy*, sang the praises of the classical ancient Greek culture and philosophy. The book explains and comments on the differences between what he calls the Dionysian and Apollonian aspects of human nature. Dionysus was the Greek god of sensual delights. Usually in painting and sculpture, he is portrayed as a drunken libertine. Nietzsche steadfastly argued that Dionysus was a far better god to emulate than the stern and sour Apollo. In his opinion, European culture was far too Apollonian and a dose of Dionysian debauchery would be the best medicine for the times.

Nietzsche's preferred form of philosophizing was the aphorism, a short proverb-like observation. Most of his books are collections of varied aphorisms, the first of which is titled *Human, All Too Human*.

Another compilation is *The Gay Science*, which contains Nietzsche's provocative claim, "God is dead." This deliberately volatile remark was devised to annoy and to inspire others to think about their freedom and their human potential. Nietzsche meant it as the philosophical equivalent of, "When the cat's away, the mice will play." Individuals would not live in fear of divine retribution or sacrifice happiness in this life in the hope of being rewarded in the next. Instead, they would shed their psychological shackles and get on with the business of really living.

QUESTIONS?

What is the theory of eternal recurrence?
Eternal recurrence suggests that we may be destined to live our lives over and over again with no variation, and no possibility to make changes or right wrongs.

Nietzsche's most famous book is *Thus Spoke Zarathustra*. It is a flowery, frenetic polemic, a flamboyant attack on the Judeo-Christian tradition. The allegory centers around the spiritual awakening, Zarathustra, the quintessential Nietzschean Superman. The fable proposes eternal recurrence, suggesting that we should strive to create for ourselves the kind of life we would not mind repeating over and over again.

The prologue of *Thus Spoke Zarathustra* distills Nietzsche's views on the objective of the individual in society. In the fable, a camel morphs into a lion, which slays a dragon, and then morphs into a child.

In youth, we are all camels. Born into life as blank slates, we have the weight of the world heaped upon us. We are beasts of burden, carrying all that society and Christianity have imposed on our innocent souls, effectively preventing us from achieving our full potential and finding true bliss. In adulthood, we are lions, venturing into the world. The more the diabolical forces of society and religion try to discourage us, the stronger we become.

The lion is confronted by a dragon with the curious name "Thou shalt." The fire-breathing creature symbolizes all the do's and don'ts that society and religion impose on us. The lion slays the dragon, and becomes a child—an innocent baby bubbling with a positive life force that was cruelly excised from it during the trials and tribulations of life. Paradoxically, becoming this child should be the objective of the mature adult who has survived all that a repressive society has thrown at him and has slain the dragon to emerge as the heroic Superman.

Where There's a Will . . .

In *Beyond Good and Evil*, Nietzsche suggests that the morality imposed on society is invalid; instead, real life occurs in another realm. The "will to power," in a relatively benign interpretation, can simply mean to "go for the gusto" and "be all that you can be." Its darker side disputes the accepted belief that compassion and protection of the weak and disenfranchised is a virtue. There is a Darwinian "survival of the fittest" aspect to this philosophy. You may stomp on someone else and exercise your will to power, but if someone else is exercising his will to power, watch out lest he stomp on you. And this is neither good nor bad. It is in fact "beyond good and evil," as the title suggests.

In *Twilight of the Idols, or How One Philosophizes with a Hammer*, Nietzsche turned his poison pen on just about every major philosopher: He called Socrates, Plato, Kant, and Rousseau decadent, but praised Caesar, Napoleon, and, of all people, the Sophists (see Chapter 1). Was Nietzsche merely functioning as an agent provocateur by infuriating people, or was he was growing less in touch with reality with each passing book?

Nietzsche wrote his own retrospective with *Ecce Homo, How One Becomes What One Is.* Part autobiography and part critical study Nietzsche's book actually included chapters titled, "Why I Am So Wise," "Why I Am So Clever," and "Why I Write Such Good Books." Nietzsche praised himself as an insightful man, a person who lived well and took good care of himself, a bold visionary thinker who would only be understood by an elite corps of fellow great thinkers. In the last chapter, "Why I Am a Destiny," Nietzsche predicted that his legacy would eventually destroy the repressive society that strangles humankind's potential and his polemical philosophy would usher in a new world order in which the libertine pagan god Dionysus would replace Jesus as the influential deity for the next millennium.

FACTS

After Nietzsche's descent into madness, and subsequent death, people manipulated his philosophy for their own ends. The worst offender was his own sister, who allowed the Nazis and Fascists to claim Nietzsche as their spiritual forbear, which he was not.

Nietzsche influenced many generations of philosophers, and fiction writers—and even noted psychiatrist Sigmund Freud. Was Nietzsche a true visionary or simply a deeply disturbed man who had a way with words and a penchant for provocative philosophizing? Perhaps he was both. Love him or hate him, it is difficult to dispute that he was a great thinker of the philosophical world.

Chapter 3

Jesus Christ: Great Spiritual Thinker

Cynics often quip that more evil has been done in the name of religion than anything else. Although there is truth to this, men are responsible for carrying out such deeds. The men whose teachings began great faiths are not responsible for the actions of militant and misguided followers. This caveat certainly applies to Jesus Christ, who would recoil in horror at things done in his name.

Life and Legacy

Jesus' place in history has caused much debate. Although some have tried to deny his existence altogether, Roman writings mention him and confirm that a man named Joshua (or, in Greek, Jesus) lived and died in the area called Judea. The belief that Jesus is the Son of God and rose from the dead is the foundation of the Christian faith. The only "proof" of this is found in the New Testament.

Old and New Testaments

The primary sources for the life of Jesus are the four gospels of Matthew, Mark, Luke, and John that comprise the first part of the New Testament. Before that, many versions of the life of Jesus had been in circulation. Some emphasized his humanity; others stressed his divinity.

ALERT

The four "official" chronicles of the life of Jesus—the gospels of Matthew, Mark, Luke, and John—focus on His divinity. The early Church fathers chose these to describe the life of Christ about 400 years after his death, at which time all other versions were considered blasphemous.

The second part of the New Testament contains the letters of St. Paul and the Acts of the Apostles. Interpretations begin here, as other voices enter into the mix. Saul was a Roman citizen who made a career of persecuting Christians. After a conversion experience (in which he was knocked off his horse by a blinding light), he changed his name to Paul and became a zealous defender and preacher of the Christian faith.

Who Was Jesus?

Tradition maintains that Jesus was the Messiah who was foretold in the prophesy. The Jewish people believed that a savior would appear to restore them to secular and spiritual glory, but they rejected Jesus.

Christians believe that Jesus was the Messiah and that Christianity is a natural extension of Judaism. Islamic tradition gives Jesus credit for being a great prophet, but not the Son of God. According to contemporary Judaism, the messiah is still to come.

Many prophets claimed to be the Son of God before, during, and after Jesus' lifetime. Most of them met a similar fate, and many developed cult followings that lasted long after their death. But their names are long forgotten.

Spreading the Word of God

The tradition is that Jesus was conceived in a divine and chaste union between Mary and God. To avoid scandal, Mary married a carpenter named Joseph. Joseph gets short shrift in the Christian tradition. Little is known about him and he disappears rather quickly from the chronicles.

Jesus was born in Bethlehem circa 4 B.C. We don't know much about Jesus' life from the time he was twelve until he was about thirty. At approximately that time, Jesus assembled twelve disciples and began his ministry, which lasted for about three years. He proclaimed that the kingdom of God was at hand, and sometimes said that it was within one's self. Some scholars have interpreted this as the Apocalypse, but that has obviously yet to happen. Jesus was considered a radical in his day and a threat to the political and religious establishment. The religious authorities of a faith in which rituals were a key component did not take kindly to his teachings.

ESSENTIALS

Jesus taught that what was in one's heart was more important that the rigid, often very public demonstrations of faith.

Jesus often preached in the form of parables, using stories to convey messages in forms that people could understand. An example of a parable is the story of the well-respected man who went to the front of the temple to ostentatiously proclaim his faith. In the back of the synagogue humbly stood a tax collector (considered the lowest of the low in those days—some things never change). The tax collector knew he was a sinner and privately and sincerely sought forgiveness, whereas the respectable man wanted to flaunt his piety. The lesson is, of course, that sincerity of faith counts more than its public manifestation.

The Christian tradition also believes that Jesus performed miracles: from changing water into wine and multiplying a few loaves of bread and fish into a feast to feed 5,000 followers, to curing lepers and the blind, exorcising demons, and raising Lazarus from the dead.

Death and Resurrection

Eventually Jesus' popularity became too threatening to the establishment. The time came to do something about him: Jesus was welcomed into Jerusalem as a hero, and within a week, he was dead.

With some feeling for what was coming, Jesus gathered his disciples for the famous Last Supper. He gave them their mission statement and in essence gave Judas the green light to betray him.

FACTS

The bread and wine consumed during the Last Supper are the origin of the Christian ritual of communion, wherein worshippers consume bread and wine that they believe has been transformed into the body and blood of Christ.

Judas Iscariot got a bad rap. If Christians believe that Jesus came to die for them and to take their sins upon himself, and that his martyrdom was devised in the mind of God eons before it happened, then Judas was merely a player in a predestined drama. Ultimately, Jesus was turned over to his enemies, tortured, and crucified.

According to Christian tradition, Jesus rose from the dead three days after his burial. He is alleged to have appeared to his disciples and continued to instruct them on their mission before ascending to heaven, vowing to return one day.

The Word of Christ

The best way to illustrate the teachings of a great thinker is to let the words speak for themselves. Here is a distillation of the thoughts of Jesus, from the King James Version of the Gospel according to Matthew:

And seeing the multitudes, he went up into a mountain: and
when he was set, his disciples came unto him:
    And he opened his mouth, and taught them, saying,

Blessed are the poor in spirit: for theirs is the kingdom of heaven.
Blessed are they that mourn: for they shall be comforted.
Blessed are the meek: for they shall inherit the earth.
Blessed are they which do hunger and thirst after righteousness:
    for they shall be filled.
Blessed are the merciful: for they shall obtain mercy.
Blessed are the pure in heart: for they shall see God.
Blessed are the peacemakers: for they shall be called the children
    of God.
Blessed are they which are persecuted for righteousness' sake: for
    theirs is the kingdom of heaven.
Blessed are ye, when men shall revile you, and persecute you, and
    shall say all manner of evil against you falsely, for my sake.
Rejoice, and be exceeding glad: for great is your reward in heaven:
    for so persecuted they the prophets which were before you.
Ye are the salt of the earth: but if the salt have lost his savour,
    wherewith shall it be salted? It is thenceforth good for nothing,
    but to be cast out, and to be trodden under foot of men.
Ye are the light of the world. A city that is set on a hill cannot be hid.
Neither do men light a candle, and put it under a bushel, but on
    a candlestick; and it giveth light unto all that are in the house.
Let your light so shine before men, that they may see your good
    works, and glorify your Father which is in heaven.
Think not that I am come to destroy the law, or the prophets:
    I am not come to destroy, but to fulfill.

For verily I say unto you, Till heaven and earth pass, one jot or one tittle shall in no wise pass from the law, till all be fulfilled.

Whosoever therefore shall break one of these least commandments, and shall teach men so, he shall be called the least in the kingdom of heaven: but whosoever shall do and teach them, the same shall be called great in the kingdom of heaven.

For I say unto you, That except your righteousness shall exceed the righteousness of the scribes and Pharisees, ye shall in no case enter into the kingdom of heaven.

Ye have heard that it was said by them of old time, Thou shalt not kill; and whosoever shall kill shall be in danger of the judgment:

But I say unto you, That whosoever is angry with his brother without a cause shall be in danger of the judgment: and whosoever shall say to his brother, Raca, shall be in danger of the council: but whosoever shall say, Thou fool, shall be in danger of hell fire.

Therefore if thou bring thy gift to the altar, and there rememberest that thy brother hath ought against thee;

Leave there thy gift before the altar, and go thy way; first be reconciled to thy brother, and then come and offer thy gift.

Agree with thine adversary quickly, whiles thou art in the way with him; lest at any time the adversary deliver thee to the judge, and the judge deliver thee to the officer, and thou be cast into prison.

Verily I say unto thee, Thou shalt by no means come out thence, till thou hast paid the uttermost farthing.

Ye have heard that it was said by them of old time, Thou shalt not commit adultery:

But I say unto you, That whosoever looketh on a woman to lust after her hath committed adultery with her already in his heart.

And if thy right eye offend thee, pluck it out, and cast it from thee: for it is profitable for thee that one of thy members should perish, and not that thy whole body should be cast into hell.

And if thy right hand offend thee, cut if off, and cast it from thee: for
it is profitable for thee that one of thy members should perish,
and not that thy whole body should be cast into hell.

It hath been said, Whosoever shall put away his wife, let him give her
a writing of divorcement:

But I say unto you, That whosoever shall put away his wife, saving for
the cause of fornication, causeth her to commit adultery: and
whosoever shall marry her that is divorced committeth adultery.

Again, ye have heard that it hath been said by them of old time,
Thou shalt not forswear thyself, but shalt perform unto the Lord
thine oaths:

But I say unto you, Swear not at all; neither by heaven; for it is God's
throne:

Nor by the earth; for it is his footstool: neither by Jerusalem; for it is
the city of the great King.

Neither shalt thou swear by thy head, because thou canst not make
one hair white or black.

But let your communication be, Yea, yea; Nay, nay: for whatsoever is
more than these cometh of evil.

Ye have heard that it hath been said, An eye for an eye, and a tooth
for a tooth:

But I say unto you, That ye resist not evil: but whosoever shall smite
thee on thy right cheek, turn to him the other also.

And if any man will sue thee at the law, and take away thy coat, let
him have thy cloak also.

And whosoever shall compel thee to go a mile, go with him twain.

Give to him that asketh thee, and from him that would borrow of
thee turn not thou away.

Ye have heard that it hath been said, Thou shalt love thy neighbour,
and hate thine enemy.

But I say unto you, Love your enemies, bless them that curse you, do
good to them that hate you, and pray for them which despitefully
use you, and persecute you;

That ye may be the children of your Father which is in heaven: for he maketh his sun to rise on the evil and on the good, and sendeth rain on the just and on the unjust.

For if ye love them which love you, what reward have ye? do not even the publicans the same?

And if ye salute your brethren only, what do ye more than others? do not even the publicans so?

Be ye therefore perfect, even as your Father which is in heaven is perfect.

Jesus Christ is perhaps the most influential figure in the history of the world. Jesus' message is a beautiful and simple one: Love thy neighbor as thyself; do unto others as you would have them do unto you. These are words by which all of us can live.

CHAPTER 4

The Buddha: One with Everything

The Buddha entered his lifetime as an Indian prince named Siddhartha Gautama. He ended that incarnation as the Buddha, the Enlightened One. He added a new spiritual philosophy to the world that continues to be a predominant belief system in the East and also generates interest and attracts practitioners in the West.

A Quest for Enlightenment

Siddhartha was born circa 563 B.C. Although he grew up in luxury, sheltered from the harsh world beyond the palace walls, he eventually wearied of palace life. Deeply affected by the squalor and suffering endured by the majority of the people, Siddhartha took a courageous step into the cruel world. He became a wandering pilgrim in search of enlightenment. He adopted a monastic lifestyle of self-denial.

FACTS

Siddhartha was tempted three times: by lust, fear, and social duty. Overcoming these temptations enabled him to achieve enlightenment. The Buddha spent the rest of his life preaching, teaching, accumulating loyal followers, and establishing a monastery.

The young seeker went from one extreme to the other. Neither opulence nor squalor gave him the answers he sought or assuaged his agitated spirit. He discovered the spiritual principle of balance. He eventually found what he called the "middle way." Siddhartha determined that neither self-indulgence nor self-denial was the key to happiness and enlightenment. The legend is that he sat under a banyan tree and meditated for days, finally achieving enlightenment.

The Four Noble Truths

Like Jesus, the Buddha never wrote anything down. As a result, it was his followers who chronicled his life and philosophy. The Four Noble Truths are the centerpiece of Buddhism.

Noble Truth #1: Life is by its very nature sad and full of suffering. Birth is painful for the mother and a frightening shock to the baby, and what follows is nothing more than a sadness-filled race to the inevitability of your own death. Of course, Buddhists believe in reincarnation, or the transmigration of souls, so we are obliged to do it again and again, learning and growing along the way.

QUESTIONS?

What does the "transmigration of souls" mean?
The transmigration of souls is another name for reincarnation. The Buddha taught that we are reborn into another body after death, learning and growing (we hope) in each subsequent lifetime. The goal is to transcend our humanity and become enlightened spiritual beings.

Noble Truth #2: People are bogged down in the illusory real world, which is why there is so much suffering in the world. The concrete world of the five senses is merely something akin to the holodeck on the *Enterprise* of *Star Trek: The Next Generation*. Reality is only one small part, and not the most significant part, of the cosmic Big Picture. People's obsession with earthly desires and physical sensations inhibits their ability to grasp true enlightenment.

Noble Truth #3: Meditation is an effective path to enlightenment, but in this age of short attention spans, is a very difficult discipline to master. How many of us can sit still and regulate our breathing, waiting to exhale? If people persevere, the results can be extremely rewarding, but it takes time. All good things come to those who wait.

Noble Truth #4: Just as Dorothy followed the Yellow Brick Road to meet the Wizard of Oz, we can follow the Buddhist Eightfold Path of Enlightenment. We will not find a charlatan behind a curtain, either. The Eightfold Path is described as follows:

1. **Right Understanding:** Be aware of the Four Noble Truths. Keep an open mind and heart and reflect on them.
2. **Right Thoughts:** Keep a positive mental attitude. Avoid negative thoughts and hostile emotions. You get back what you put forth, and bad stuff will come back to bite you tenfold.

3. **Right Speech:** If you don't have anything nice to say, then hold your tongue and don't say anything at all.
4. **Right Action:** Be a decent person. Observe the Ten Commandments and exercise restraint of tongue and pen. Do unto others and so forth. You know the drill.
5. **Right Livelihood:** People take classes in Right Livelihood these days. It is quite fashionable among certain circles to eschew the dog-eat-dog ethics that permeate contemporary corporate America. In the Buddha's time, Right Livelihood meant specifically avoiding profiting from these businesses: munitions; livestock slaughterhouses; the slave trade; and the production and sale of wine, spirits, sugar, caffeine, and other mood-altering substances and poisons.
6. **Right Effort:** Avoid exposure to evil in the world, whether as an observer or a participant.
7. **Right Mindfulness:** Be ever-vigilant. "Be still and know" is the Buddhist saying. Be as aware as you can of your body, your emotions, your surroundings, and your thoughts at all times.
8. **Right Meditation:** Learn to meditate and practice this discipline every day in order to achieve enlightenment.

These eight steps really just enumerate the simple process of living well. Although the process is simple, implementing it is a challenge that requires both discipline and dedication.

Instant Karma

Buddhism teaches that karma is a cosmic force that ensures balance and harmony in the universe. We are all bound by the laws of karma. Those who believe in karma believe that we have chosen this life and the events that happen to us are by design. Our experiences in life help us learn and grow and prepare for continued spiritual evolution on the long—but worthwhile—trek toward nirvana.

Nirvana is the highest state of enlightenment. It is almost impossible to achieve nirvana in this lifetime, but you can make a good start by living a life of compassion and kindness. You should also avoid the societal ills of murder, profanity, sexual misbehavior, and drug and alcohol use. Avoiding these pitfalls and not living a life consumed with hatred, lust, greed, and self-delusion will enable you to have a spiritually richer incarnation the next time.

If the Buddha is right, your behavior in this life will affect your karma. Karma is the force of cosmic justice in the universe. If you are an evil person in this life, you can expect payback in the next.

The best way to achieve true enlightenment, according to the Buddha, is to live a life of quietude and contemplation.

CHAPTER 5

Muhammad: Messenger of God

Muhammad, whose name means "commendable," was the prophet and founder of the Islamic religion. His teachings and work emphasized both charitable deeds and equality between men and women.

Muhammad's Vision

Muhammad (circa 570–632) was born in the city of Mecca, located in what is now Saudi Arabia. Orphaned by the age of six, he was raised by an uncle. By all accounts, he was a quiet and decent fellow. He made a living as a traveling trader and married into money at an early age.

Muhammad often retreated to a cave to meditate. On one occasion, Islamic tradition teaches, the Archangel Gabriel visited Muhammad and told him that he was a prophet. In those days, folks of all faiths put more stock in dreams and visions.

Muhammad began to take his message to the people. He spoke of his angelic dialogues in the form of verse. This eventually became the Qur'an (or Quran or Koran), the holy Islamic text. His message, according to Islamic tradition, is the culmination of the prophets who came before him.

Ideally, all Muslims should learn the original dialect in which the Qur'an was written. They believe it is the literal word of Allah, and that the message loses something in translation.

Church and State

Muhammad and Islam linked social and political activism with religious faith. This partnership encouraged—in fact, insisted upon—altruism and care for the downtrodden. It also advocated a *theocracy*, a form of government in which the spiritual leaders are also the lawmakers. Many Muslims see theocracy as the ideal government, although it invariably leads to trouble for those of a different religion.

One extreme and recent example of a theocracy run amok was the Taliban government of Afghanistan. Their barbaric treatment of the populace showed the unremitting dark side of an intolerant theocracy.

A Man Ahead of His Time

Muhammad was contemporary in his belief that all men and women were equal in the eyes of God. Islam makes charitable deeds not only a nice thing to do but also mandatory activity to be a good Muslim. But Muhammad's sense of justice and equality made him the enemy of those in authority. He was forced to leave Mecca, his birthplace, but was welcomed by the city of Medina, which became his adopted home.

ESSENTIALS   Both located in what is now Saudi Arabia, Mecca and Medina are the two holy cities in the Islamic tradition. Devout Muslims are obliged, if financially possible, to make at least one pilgrimage to Mecca in their lifetimes.

Muhammad was a warrior, and in the ensuing battles between the warring cities of Mecca (where his enemies resided) and Medina, he was a ruthless military man who showed no mercy to his enemies. He was magnanimous in victory, however. When he and his followers conquered Mecca, he pardoned the inhabitants of his birthplace.

Muhammad was loyal to his beloved first wife, but after her death, he eventually assembled a harem of nine wives. In line with his religious tolerance, he even took a Christian slave as a concubine.

As the master of the Arabian Peninsula, Muhammad founded an Islamic nation. He allowed freedom of religion for Christians and Jews in his domain. He was forward-thinking in that he saw a world in which barriers of class and race were dissolved. Muhammad died in 632 A.D., but not before he changed the world.

His Spiritual Legacy

As with all great spiritual leaders of antiquity, legends evolved around the life and times of Muhammad. He was posthumously granted the power to perform miracles, given moral infallibility, and accorded ascension into heaven similar to the one that Christians attribute to Jesus.

Muhammad single-handedly transformed the world around him. Much of what he sought to do had both material and spiritual benefits for the common people. The moral and ethical codes of conduct he established still guide much of the Middle East.

FACTS

Filmmakers made a movie about the history of Islam called *Muhammad: Messenger of God*. Their efforts to attract a Muslim audience backfired. Islamic tradition disapproves of images of Muhammad in paintings or movies. The movie was hastily edited to show only Muhammad's hands onscreen, never his face.

The legacy of Muhammad is contradictory. Islam is, in one sense, the most welcoming of religions. You simply have to say you are a Muslim to be one (and abide by its precepts, of course). The Sufi offshoot has produced some of the most mystical and beautiful poetry from its most famous practitioner, Rumi. On the other hand, theocracy, which is a significant part of the Islamic religion, has the potential to be oppressive to people of varying beliefs.

CHAPTER 6

Controversial Scientists of the Renaissance

Renaissance literally means "rebirth" in French, and the period from the late 1400s through the early 1600s was a time of unprecedented scientific, medical, and literary advancement. It was as if a fireworks display had illuminated the long dark night of the Middle Ages. Although progress marched on in spite of religious and political restrictions, many paid an awful price to quench their thirst for knowledge.

Galileo Galilei

Galileo (1564–1642) changed the way we look at the cosmos and our place in it in ways not warmly embraced by those in power. Recall that this was not a time when people simply "agreed to disagree." People were tortured and killed for disputing established doctrine of the Catholic Church. Galileo is to be lauded for his courage, even though, upon threat of a torturous death, he recanted his belief.

A Brave New Voice

Galileo Galilei was a teacher, mathematician, and philosopher. Born in Padua, Italy, Galileo rose in stature and reputation and went to work as a mathematician for Cosimo II of Florence. Galileo believed the heliocentric theory of an earlier scientist and stargazer, Copernicus. Heliocentrism was the proposition that the Sun is the center of the solar system and Earth and other celestial bodies revolve around it. Ancient theories, and even the dogma of the Catholic Church, taught that Earth was the center of not only the solar system but also of the entire universe.

Curb your dogma! Dogma is a rigid authoritarian viewpoint, usually of an organized religion. Church dogma ran contrary to the scientific discoveries of the Renaissance.

Heliocentrism contradicted both church dogma and the speculations of Aristotle, who had over the centuries become the Greek philosopher that the Church for the most part accepted, pagan though he was. The revered Catholic theologian St. Thomas Aquinas had "Christianized" Aristotelian philosophy to put it in accord with church teachings. Many centuries earlier, another great theologian, St. Augustine, had similarly "rehabilitated" Plato.

Galileo put reason above faith in his approach to the natural world. His scientific method was a three-part approach: 1. Observation of a fact; 2. Employing a hypothesis as a possible explanation of the phenomenon; 3. Confirming the hypothesis through new data.

While a professor of math in Pisa, Italy, Galileo challenged the theory of the mighty Aristotle, who maintained that objects of different weights would hit the ground at different times. Galileo dropped two objects off the city's infamous Leaning Tower and they hit the ground at the same time. His reward for proving Aristotle's theory wrong? Galileo lost his job.

Galileo had a weapon in proving some of his theories: the telescope. Although he is credited with its invention, the truth is simply that the improvements he made to his own version were far superior to any telescope used previously.

Doctrine insisted that the stars, moons, and planets were smooth and pristine heavenly orbs. The only topographic and biological diversity was found here on Earth. With his telescope, however, Galileo discovered that the Moon had peaks and valleys, crags and craters, and that the Sun had spots that appeared and disappeared, disproving the party line. He also proved that the celestial bodies were not fixed in place. They moved around, and there were falling stars and comets traversing the heavens. The heavens were abuzz with activity, Galileo maintained; they were not simply a stagnant shell covering Earth.

FACTS

Legend has it Galileo offered to let the pope peer into his amazing invention, the telescope, to see for himself that Galileo was right. The pope declined, citing Jesus' saying, "Blessed are those who have not seen but still believe."

A Buzz of Controversy

Not only did the church disapprove of Galileo's experiment, fellow academics and scientists were also outraged, envious, and out to get him. Galileo published several papers on his findings, and generated quite a controversy. In fact, it was members of the intellectual community who told the ruling Medici family that Galileo was espousing heresy. Not long after that, the church took official action.

In 1616, the church's notorious Inquisition gave Galileo a good talking-to and ordered him to stop espousing the heliocentric theory. It was considered heresy, and heresy was one thing you did not want to be charged with in those days. The Jesuit Cardinal Robert Bellarmine advised him to speak of the heliocentric theory as just that, a theory. He could literally light a fire under himself with such talk. Galileo clammed up for many years, but he continued his research.

Galileo wrote *The Assayer,* in which he reiterated the heliocentric belief and wrote about the newly found moons of Jupiter and comets. He also reaffirmed the theories of Copernicus in a work-in-progress called *Dialogue on the Tides.* The church authorized its printing with a few modifications in 1632; still Galileo was called on to appear before the

Galileo Galilei

Inquisition. Galileo defiantly pursued his research and continued to write about it.

Galileo was threatened again, put on trial, and found guilty. He was sentenced to life imprisonment, but the sentence was reduced to house arrest. Galileo was also required to recant his belief—the alternative would have been a death sentence. And since there was no lethal injection in Renaissance Italy, executions were protracted and painful.

Galileo's scientific method in a time of blind faith and superstition paved the way for modern science. Although he maintained that he was a devout Catholic (not to question his personal belief system, but it would have been imprudent for him to do otherwise), Galileo sought to shed metaphysics from his method and deal only with the concrete and provable.

There is an ironic postscript to Galileo's story. He finally received an apology from the Catholic Church for the way they treated him. The Church eventually acknowledged that Galileo was right and the Earth does, indeed, revolve around the sun. This official apology was made in 1992—better late than never!

Giordano Bruno

Italian philosopher Giordano Bruno (1548?–1600) entered the Dominican Order of the Catholic Church in his teens, but he was eventually kicked out when suspected of heresy. Heresy—espousing theories or beliefs contrary to those established by the Church—was punishable by excruciating torture and a brutal death. Great thinkers took big risks in those less tolerant times. Bruno knew the risks, pushed the envelope, and ultimately paid the price.

Radical Thinking

Bruno wandered through Europe, learning and teaching. He espoused radical, very modern notions for his time, and controversy followed him everywhere he went. He was always one step ahead of the Inquisition, but eventually they caught up with him. Like Galileo, Bruno also believed the heliocentric theory of Copernicus.

Bruno's notion of God differed dramatically from that of the Catholic Church. The doctrine of all monotheistic religions is that God is in heaven, and we must adhere to strict rules and regulations to stay in His good graces or else we will pay the price. The Catholic Church is not alone in this kind of thinking and, in fact, has mellowed considerably in the past few hundred years. But the dark side of repressive dogma continues to rear its intolerant head in various forms (the Taliban in Afghanistan is a contemporary example).

FACTS

According to one theory, the mindshift hypothesis, the government knows all about the existence of extraterrestrials, and they have been preparing us for the eventual disclosure of this breaking news through press, radio, television, and film.

Bruno believed that he (and we) was "one with everything." God was not up there imperiously lording over us. Rather we were all part of a universal god-force that involved not just humanity, but everything. This belief is called pantheism, or monistic immanentism. Bruno also proposed that there were an infinite number of solar systems supporting an infinite number of planets, many of which supported life, both like and unlike life on Earth. The belief that there was life on other planets is a common one today, but during the Renaissance it was radical thinking.

Giordano Bruno believed that the individual soul was like one cell in the giant organism that was God. When we die, we are reabsorbed into the Big Picture but not as the individual entities we were in this lifetime. Such a belief is inherently contradictory to the Church's teachings, which maintain that we stand in judgment before God for our myriad shortcomings and are then consigned either to salvation or to damnation. Although it has a spiritual element, Bruno's philosophy is essentially humanistic.

QUESTIONS?

What is humanism?
Humanism was a popular movement in the Renaissance that placed the human adventure as the ultimate experience. Bruno taught that focusing on the here and now, on this life rather than on the next, was the best way to live.

Nobody Likes an Inquisition

The Inquisition finally caught up with Bruno. He was approached to work as a tutor for an Italian aristocrat named Giovanni Mocenigo. This ignoble nobleman later turned Bruno in to the authorities, charging him with heresy. Bruno was imprisoned and tortured for eight years while being held for "questioning." There was no such thing as innocent until proven guilty when dealing with the Inquisition. In an act of either astounding principle or incredible stupidity, Bruno refused to recant his beliefs and was tortured and burned at the stake in 1600.

Many Catholic saints were martyred for their faith, but the Church martyred this great thinker for his teachings, many of which are common knowledge today. This secular saint is less well known than many of his Renaissance contemporaries, but his life stands as a testament to the pursuit of knowledge, and his death is a reminder of the destructive nature of narrow-minded ignorance.

CHAPTER 7

Great Artists of the Renaissance

The Renaissance produced some of the great art of the Western world. Artists in those days were more than mere painters and sculptors—they studied science and human anatomy, among other disciplines. The two greatest Renaissance artists were Leonardo da Vinci and Michelangelo.

Leonardo da Vinci

Leonardo da Vinci (1452–1519) is the quintessential Renaissance man—literally. He lived during the Renaissance and is the personification of the achievements and accomplishments of the epoch. The Renaissance was the marvelous age of scientific and cultural rebirth (Renaissance is the French word for rebirth) that followed the dog days of the Middle Ages.

QUESTIONS?

Can genius be transferred by osmosis?
Microsoft founder Bill Gates purchased some original da Vinci sketches for a price said to be around $30 million. Perhaps the genius of the digital age hopes some of the genius of the golden age will rub off on him.

The term *Renaissance man* refers to a person who is adept at a variety of disciplines, a jack-of-all-trades and master of each. This term has devolved into a cliché used to describe a well-rounded individual of eclectic interests and abilities, but no one compares to Leonardo da Vinci. Not only was he a painter and sculptor, he was also a scientist whose notes and sketches reveal the schematics for the helicopter, submarine, and other inventions far ahead of his time.

The Pupil Surpasses the Teacher

Born in a town called Vinci in Italy (his name literally means Leonardo of Vinci), baby Leo was born into privilege and received as excellent an education as was possible in that era. He entered the artistic community as an apprentice to Andrea del Verrocchio, the most famous artist and sculptor of the time. Along the way, Leonardo gained the experience that would help him eventually surpass Verrocchio.

Leonardo got his first taste of the big time when he put his stamp on a Verrocchio canvas. The next time you are thumbing through a coffee-table book on Renaissance art, check out the kneeling angel on the left of Verrocchio's painting called *Baptism of Christ*. The angel is da Vinci's contribution to the piece. Da Vinci went solo in 1478, setting up his own studio as an independent master. He sent a letter of introduction to the duke of Milan, in which he unabashedly enumerated his highly-touted talents. The squeaky wheel gets the grease, as they say, and Leonardo

Leonardo da Vinci

got the job. In his entrée, he emphasized his skills as a builder and engineer, particularly of military paraphernalia. He knew that the arts were secondary to a leader of an Italian city-state. During the Renaissance era, the big cities of Italy had their own self contained governments, and they often waged war against one another.

Leonardo served as the engineer for the duke's martial efforts while also finding time for the creative arts. He painted his famous *Last Supper* on and off for two years, in keeping with his idiosyncratic quirk about finishing a work of art. He lingered on it for a long time before applying the final brush strokes. An armchair psychologist might suggest, in the self-help jargon of today, that he had a problem "letting go."

Leonardo later worked for the notorious Cesare Borgia, the son of Pope Alexander VI. Yes, popes had children in those days. Leonardo built fortresses for Borgia and the papacy in addition to pursuing his artistic endeavors.

ALERT

Are you beating yourself up because your supervisor says you don't have good follow-through skills? Tell her that neither did Leonardo da Vinci. Many of his paintings remained unfinished, and although he had numerous sketches of sculptures he planned to carve, he did not complete a single one.

Unfortunately, many of Leonardo's paintings have been destroyed or lost over the centuries. His most famous painting, of course, is the *Mona Lisa*. Paintings were usually commissioned by a wealthy patron and presented to the patron upon completion, but Leonardo was so smitten by the lady with the mystic smile that he kept the *Mona Lisa*. Whether he was enamored of his own creation or of the enigmatic subject is unknown.

Genius of All Trades

Leonardo lived in several Italian city-states and in France during his lifetime. In those days, artists relied on wealthy patrons to sponsor them as they toiled with their oils and marble. His patrons ranged from the city-state potentates to the king of France to the pope. The works created by these artists are vastly superior to anything that we as taxpayers have paid for in these less creative times.

Although Leonardo was not a prolific painter, his style influenced most of the great Renaissance artists who followed him. His attention to detail and the depth perspective given to his backgrounds were innovative, as was his use of color. Rather than simply recreate an event from history or the Bible, Leonardo's paintings transcended reality to create a mood and stir the viewer's emotions.

As an artist, da Vinci studied anatomy in order to paint more realistic looking people. Many artists of the day also examined cadavers to understand and better represent the human form on canvas. Da Vinci's sketches reveal that he had a serious, scientific approach to the study of human and animal anatomy.

FACTS

How different the world would have been if Leonardo's ideas had been implemented in his lifetime and the decades thereafter. Leonardo's underwater diving suit could have enabled an earlier awareness of the fascinating world in the oceans, much of which is still considered the last great frontier today.

His sculptures were never completed, nor were his great architectural designs or his many other inventions, but the sketches that survive clearly reveal genius at work. As a scientist, he was a marvel for the age. He combined the soaring spirit of an artist and the grounded, empirical mind of a scientist. His voluminous notebooks were not widely read and examined until after his death. In fact, they were written in a kind of personal stenography that is difficult to decipher.

Leonardo also proposed the widespread use of canals. He was the first person to make the connection between ocean tides and cycles of the Moon. He examined fossils and had an innate understanding of the true age of the planet (which differs from the age calculated by a literal interpretation of the Bible). He was also an accomplished geologist and meteorologist. His inquiring mind was into everything, and his observations have shown an uncanny and prescient accuracy.

Michelangelo

Michelangelo Buonarotti (1475–1564) and Leonardo da Vinci are considered the two greatest artists of the Renaissance. Michelangelo was less of an all-around genius, but he was a more prolific painter and sculptor. He was also an accomplished architect and, to a lesser degree, a poet.

Early Schooling

Michelangelo was the son of minor nobility, and his father strongly disapproved of his son seeking a career in the arts. Nevertheless, Michelangelo entered into an apprenticeship with the famous artist Domenico Ghirlandajo. Whether in historical relationships or in the banal setting of the contemporary boardroom, the mentor-protégé relationship is often fraught with conflict. It's not surprising, then, that Michelangelo had an acrimonious relationship with Ghirlandajo. Later in life he even tried to rewrite his personal history and claim that he was a self-taught prodigy.

Before the three-year apprenticeship was over, Michelangelo went to a school that was established by a fellow who went by the moniker "Lorenzo the Magnificent." Lorenzo was a member of the Medici family, the most influential and notorious aristocratic clan of the day. The school was a focal point for the great artists, writers, and philosophers of the Renaissance.

While at school, Michelangelo was exposed to the Neoplatonic philosophy that was pervasive among Renaissance intellectuals. Neoplatonism was an amalgam of the philosophy of Plato, Jewish mysticism, and radical early Christian thought that was revived during the Renaissance. God was likened to a universal mind called "the One."

Michelangelo

The One gave all creation something called Nous (divine intelligence) and this animates the universe. Human souls were part of this universal soul just as cells in the body and are created in the image of the One. And humans had an instinctive sense that the body was a temporary shell that they inhabited for a fleeting wisp of time.

The school ended with Lorenzo's death, and afterward Michelangelo studied anatomy in a local hospital. Like Leonardo da Vinci, he was an amateur scientist and forensic examiner. In order to be able to realistically paint or sculpt the human form, they studied its intricacies in clinical detail in primitive autopsy chambers.

FACTS

Michelangelo is reported to have been volatile and contradictory. He derived great pleasure from getting down and dirty with his oils, canvas, and marble, but he enjoyed the finer things in life. He hobnobbed with the social elite and sought to be regarded as their equal.

Michelangelo's earliest acclaim was from a sculpture of the Greek God Bacchus, and his first crack at the religious image called the *Pietá*, which is a representation of the Virgin Mary cradling Jesus. just removed from the cross.

Based on these early triumphs, he was commissioned to sculpt his most famous work, *David*. This is the naked image of the Biblical hero David, in a pose that is presumed to be poised to battle the mighty

Goliath. The statue stands an impressive 14 feet tall, and the head and hands are disproportionately larger than life. Michelangelo had the uncanny ability to suggest movement in an immobile hunk of marble.

High Hopes

While *David* is Michelangelo's most famous sculpture, his best-known paintings are, of course, those that festoon the ceiling of the Sistine Chapel in Vatican City. The undertaking truly was "the agony and the ecstasy" for Michelangelo. Here is a man who literally bent over backwards to create an expansive panorama on an enormous ceiling. Painting flat on his back and in other contortions on a giant scaffold, it took him four years to complete the project. A bit of a control freak, he discharged most of his assistants and essentially did the whole project single-handedly.

ESSENTIALS

For a slightly fictionalized account of the life of Michelangelo, check out the 1965 movie called *The Agony and the Ecstasy*, based on the novel of the same name by Irving Wallace. Charlton Heston plays Michelangelo. The movie chronicles his painting of the Sistine Chapel and his conflicts with Pope Julius II.

The images on the chapel are all scenes from the Bible, including the Creation and Noah's drunken binge. The most famous image is the Creation of Adam, in which God's and Adam's hands reach toward each other and their fingers touch at the tip.

Many people these days make a will and purchase a funeral plot in advance of their own demise. Renaissance popes thought on a grander scale. Michelangelo was commissioned by Pope Julius II to design and create sculptures for the Pope's elaborate tomb. Numerous obstacles delayed its completion, however. One element of the massive project that survives as a testament to Michelangelo's genius is a statue of Moses. Like *David*, it is an incredible example of stationary stone suggesting movement. (The statue also bears a striking resemblance to Charlton

Heston—or more accurately, Charlton Heston bears a striking resemblance to the statue—which led to the actor's casting as Moses in the classic film *The Ten Commandments.*)

In his later years, Michelangelo returned to the Sistine Chapel to work for another pope, the nephew of his former patron Lorenzo the Magnificent. This work was called The Last Judgment. He worked on it for five years, from 1536 to 1541, and it is entirely different in mood and tone than the work he did on the ceiling twenty-nine years earlier.

The Protestant Reformation had rocked the Catholic Church to its very foundations, and it was now attempting its own Counter-Reformation. The Last Judgment is a darker work, depicting the second coming of Jesus who is separating the saints from the sinners. The blessed rising up to salvation are stark-naked heavenly bodies, so it was a controversial fresco, condemned by many and almost destroyed after Michelangelo's death. A compromise was reached, and the more graphic bits were covered up without defacing the masterpiece.

Michelangelo returned to the Pieta theme in his last years with two more versions of note. In one, he placed himself into the painting as the character of Nicodemus. Michelangelo was fond of putting himself into his paintings; in some of his greatest works he gave minor background figures his face. It was just one more way for this Renaissance artist to secure a form of immortality. He lived to the ripe old age of eighty-nine, which was quite a long life in those days. With his larger-than-life statues and the sheer magnitude of his work, Michelangelo is proof that great thinkers also think big.

Chapter 8

Other Notable Thinkers of the Renaissance

The Renaissance was not only an age of great scientists and artists; it was also a time of discovery, exploration, and religious upheaval. What makes certain thinkers great is that they changed the world in ways that still impact us today.

Martin Luther

A gifted young man from the German peasant class, Martin Luther (1483–1546) shocked his family and friends by entering a monastery after getting a master's degree with the intention of becoming a lawyer. He claimed he had a conversion experience after a brush with death. This career change led to a spiritual revolution that shook the world and changed its course in ways that might never have happened if Luther had been a more docile son and followed his father's wishes.

Luther's passionate and volatile temperament, however, made him ill suited for the contemplative life of a monk. He wanted to contribute more to the world than was possible in a monastery, restricted to a confining and rigid lifestyle. Luther's intellect and education earned a promotion from monk to priest in 1506.

Radical Reformer

Institutes of higher learning were springing up like never before during the Renaissance, and Luther was invited to become a theology professor at the University of Wittenberg. In 1510, he visited Rome and saw the

Martin Luther

outrageous excesses of the Roman clerics. Like a pious country parson on a trip to a hedonistic metropolis, he was aghast at the way the ecclesiastical upper crust was carrying on. They were not practicing what they preached, and they were using the monies acquired from the poor of Europe to fund their excesses. Luther seethed with righteous indignation, deeply disheartened by his trip. He returned home plagued by doubts that he was following the right path. While still a Christian, he came to reject several key tenets of the Catholic Church.

Luther created a stir when he published the Ninety-Five Theses. Among other things, the document was critical of the selling of indulgences in order to fund the building of ornate cathedrals in Rome.

This document started the Protestant Reformation in Germany and changed the face of Europe. Legend has it that he nailed the pages to the door of the Church, but others say this is an apocryphal story.

Luther wrote the theses in Latin, the language of the educated classes, but they were quickly translated into the German vernacular and widely disseminated. Pope Leo X condemned and excommunicated Luther, who refused to recant and might have been executed, but he had secular friends in high places. The German ruling class felt that a break with Rome would be economically advantageous. Dissatisfaction with the Church of Rome was reaching critical mass, and the Protestant Reformation was poised to sweep across Europe.

ESSENTIALS

One big pet peeve for Luther was the selling of indulgences, a means of penance that involved contributing money to a worthy cause to receive absolution. Confession was a sacred sacrament of the Catholic faith, and Luther was outraged that some priests were charging money for forgiveness that he felt could only come from God.

Luther contributed to his culture with his translation of the New Testament into German. Most peasants had no direct contact with the Bible; its teachings were always filtered through the clergy. The Catholic Church preferred it that way, as the exclusive conduit of the word of God. Luther's translation and Johannes Gutenberg's invention of the printing press made the Bible and a wealth of other information available to the masses. The printing press was akin to the 1990s Internet explosion. And because educated masses are less docile, the authorities were not thrilled to see this come to pass.

Luther believed that the individual could have a direct experience with God through prayer, meditation, and going back to basics. In other words, everything a Christian needed to know was in the Old and New Testaments. He believed that we were all saints and all sinners, and that all vocations could be in the service of God. The calling to religious life was no nobler than the calling to be a family man. Luther was nothing if not egalitarian.

Luther also had a problem with the hypocrisy he saw concerning celibacy. Catholic priests are obliged to take a vow of celibacy, but he saw little evidence of this in Renaissance Rome. Disillusioned, Luther eventually left his religious order, married a former nun, and had a family.

Winds of Change: The Protestant Reformation

Luther was one of the major players in the Protestant Reformation, a movement that swept across Europe during the Renaissance. Several offshoots of the Catholic Church were established during this time. These Protestant religions include the Church of England, Calvinism, and Lutheranism, the latter based on the teachings of Luther himself. Luther was a major player in effecting religious reform.

FACTS

Luther was influential in more than the spiritual arena. By writing in German, rather than in Latin, he helped Germany develop its native language. He wrote volumes of theological commentary. His slim volume, *Small Catechisms,* offers a distillation of his theology.

The Protestant Reformation changed the face of Europe on every level, not merely the spiritual. It was also inspired by the educational leaps and bounds of the Renaissance and the movement known as humanism. The Catholic Church began a Counter Reformation, and over the centuries Christianity has lost much of the power it had at one time.

Luther's revolutionary words and deeds helped prevent Christianity from becoming an out-of-control theocracy, far removed from the spiritual teachings of Jesus. He proposed a theological alternative and forced the Catholics to take a hard look at themselves, their excesses, and their hypocrisies during that era.

Christopher Columbus

Is a great thinker a man who was heading for India, hit a big continent in his path, and believed until his death that he had indeed found the land described by Marco Polo, an earlier explorer who was one of the first Europeans to venture deep into Asia? Italian navigator Christopher Columbus (1451–1506) represents another aspect of Renaissance achievement. In addition to intellectual and scientific pursuits and religious reform, there was the quest to seek out strange new worlds for trade. Columbus was not the first to discover the New World, but his voyages were as significant as the exploration of space is today. And certainly he was courageous. After all, most people at the time believed the world was flat and that if you sailed far enough you would fall off the planet and into oblivion.

ESSENTIALS During the Crusades, Europeans invaded the Holy Land. Some say their motives were to liberate the holy city of Jerusalem from the clutches of the "infidels." Others see the Crusades as a violent conquest to plunder, and steal riches of all kinds.

The Europeans sought a trade route to Asia that avoided the Indian subcontinent and other Muslim regions. Men like Columbus believed that if you sailed far enough to the west, you would hit Asia from the seaward side. They were right in believing that the world was round; what they did not bargain for was the enormous landmass in their nautical path.

Goodbye Columbus

Columbus went to sea at the age of fourteen, and remained a seaman for the rest of his life. He sailed the known seas, endured hardships and shipwrecks, and was obsessed with finding a sea route to Asia. After one shipwreck, he drifted to Portugal on wreckage and remained there, marrying into an aristocratic family.

Columbus's dream required a considerable amount of money. He first sought patronage from Portugal, but was rebuffed. Next on his list were King Ferdinand and Queen Isabella of Spain. Columbus presented King Ferdinand and Queen Isabella with a lengthy list of demands: one-tenth of the plunder, the rank of admiral at sea, and the title of governor of the discovered land. At first, they king and queen rejected his demands, but later they reconsidered—and Columbus sailed off for his appointment with destiny.

Every schoolchild knows about the three ships under his direction— the *Niña,* the *Pinta,* and the *Santa María*, and their arduous journey. Beyond the mercurial whims of Mother Nature, cramped quarters, hazardous conditions, and the threat of disease plagued the sailors.

Land Ho!

On October 12, 1492, a lookout spotted land. A substantial reward had been offered for the first man to sight land, and in a thoroughly bush-league move, Columbus pulled rank and claimed to have sighted land first. (Even great thinkers have their lesser moments, and this was the least of the many distasteful things Columbus would do in the next few years.)

It is not certain where Columbus and his crew first landed. What *is* certain is that he never landed on the North American continent. He

Christopher
Columbus

landed on an island in the Bahamas. At least ten islands fit the description he entered in his ship's log. Columbus claimed the island in the name of Spain and set up camp. Native people of the area came to greet them, and the first thing the explorers noticed was the gold jewelry the natives wore. Columbus called the natives "Indians," mistakenly believing he had reached "the Indies," which was what the Europeans called Asia.

Columbus explored much of the Caribbean. Still thinking he had reached the Indies, Columbus assumed that Cuba was a peninsula of mainland China. And he stubbornly clung to that belief even as evidence to the contrary mounted.

Columbus sailed home leaving an expeditionary force on one of the islands. After landing in Portugal and being locked up by the Portuguese king, he was later released and received a hero's welcome in Spain.

Columbus brought back exotic plant and animal life and a few natives to show Ferdinand and Isabella—and plenty of gold, of course.

With each trip to the New World, Columbus caused more damage and fell further out of favor with his sponsors. He enslaved the natives to work in the various settlements while he and an expedition went looking for gold. He made one of his brothers the governor and came back to find a civil war raging among the settlers. Columbus was unable to restore order, so King Ferdinand and Queen Isabella sent an envoy to settle troubles. The envoy put Columbus and his brothers in chains and shipped them back to Spain to stand trial. There, Columbus was released by the king and queen, who restored his property but not his titles.

FACTS

Arriving on his second voyage, Columbus found that the sailors he had left behind had been slaughtered and their settlement destroyed. This was the beginning of a long history of violence between the European explorers and indigenous people.

By this time, Columbus was just about the only man in Europe who believed that the New World was in fact China. He made a fourth and final voyage; this time, he was on a quest to find gold and other precious metals and minerals.

A Tainted Hero

Columbus returned home from this last voyage a bitter man and in poor health. He had plenty of money, but he had lost his noble titles. The exploration of the New World was in full swing, and he felt left out. The landmass had not even been named after him. Some Italian map-maker named Amerigo Vespucci had that distinction.

So why all the honors for a man who brought disease and destruction to the native peoples of the New World, thought he was in China when he was half a world away, cheated a lowly lookout sailor out of some money, and in the eyes of many was as an all-around cad? The answer is simple: Columbus changed the world. He had a dream and he made it happen, with beautiful—and tragic—results.

Dante Alighieri

Dante Alighieri (1265–1321) was a Renaissance Italian poet and author of the classic trilogy, *The Divine Comedy*. Dante is proof that seemingly minor events can produce big dividends, and that a romantic devil will go to hell and back for the woman he loves.

An All-Encompassing Love

Little is known about Dante's youth, but we do know that he met and fell in love with a young woman named Beatrice. In typical tearjerker fashion, he loved her from afar—after all, he had seen her only twice in his life—and it was probably unrequited. Beatrice died young, yet she stayed in Dante's heart forever, in essence becoming his muse. Beatrice did much for Dante and the world of arts and letters without ever knowing it. If they had fallen in love and married and had a family, perhaps Dante would have been a happy and fulfilled man, but he may never have penned his soaring verse and a deeply spiritual tale of heaven and hell.

Before he wrote his masterpiece, Dante wrote *La Vita Nuova (The New Life)*, a series of unified poems connected with annotations. The poems described his beloved Beatrice, her death, and his desire to grant her a form of immortality through his writing.

FACTS

Dante wrote in the Italian vernacular, as opposed to Latin, the highbrow language of the educated classes. Dante's use of the vernacular celebrated the language of the people, and eventually those who could read but were not educated enough to understand Latin could appreciate his poetry.

Simply Divine

Midway upon the journey of our life
I found myself within a forest dark,
For the straightforward pathway had been lost.

Thus begins Dante's *Inferno,* as translated by Henry Wadsworth Longfellow. *The Divine Comedy* is divided into three parts: *Inferno* (hell), *Purgatorio* (purgatory), and *Paradiso* (paradise). Dante, the narrator, is given a tour of heaven and hell, which sandwich purgatory. In Catholic tradition, purgatory is a way station where those souls who have died must expiate their sins until they are pure enough to enter Paradise. The ancient Roman poet Virgil guides Dante through hell.

ESSENTIALS

The Divine Comedy is called a comedy (as opposed to a tragedy) not because it is comical, but because it has a happy ending. Actors often wore the famous smiling and frowning theater masks to help the audience better understand what they were watching.

Dante meets many historical figures on his journey. Hell is divided into nine circles, each one more hellish than the one before. The Ninth Circle is reserved for Judas Iscariot, who betrayed Jesus; and Brutus and Cassius, the conspirators who assassinated Julius Caesar. The devil is a grotesque, winged monster that nibbles on them throughout eternity:

At every mouth he with his teeth was crunching
A sinner, in the manner of a brake,
So that he three of them tormented thus.

To him in front the biting was as naught
Unto the clawing, for sometimes the spine
Utterly stripped of all the skin remained.

"That soul up there which has the greatest pain,"
The Master said, "is Judas Iscariot;
With head inside, he plies his legs without.
Of the two others, who head downward are,
The one who hangs from the black jowl is Brutus;
See how he writhes himself, and speaks no word.

And the other, who so stalwart seems, is Cassius.
But night is reascending, and 'tis time
That we depart, for we have seen the whole."

Leading him on the last leg of the journey is his muse in the person of his beloved Beatrice. The reverence for the spiritual depths and reward that can be gained from embracing the feminine mystique are also

Dante Alighieri

expressed in Johann Wolfgang von Goethe's *Faust, Part Two* and in Carl Jung's psychological meditations on the *anima,* which is the feminine energy that resides in all men. For those who decry the chauvinist eons that preceded the twentieth century, it is worth noting that enlightened men of the past have long been advocates of "girl power."

Dante's masterpiece is an allegory—a story in which the characters are symbolic representations of universal themes. It is a tale of the soul's journey on the path to inner peace, and a sweeping and lyrical meditation on the times in which Dante lived. But like all great works, it transcended his time and became ageless.

CHAPTER 9
The Wordsmiths

Homer. Shakespeare. Goethe. The wordsmiths of the past and present create more than an "abstract and brief chronicle of the times," as Shakespeare said. They bring their subjects to life more vividly than any other form. In this chapter, we'll take a look at three of the most renowned.

Homer

Why include Greek epic poet Homer (born eighth century B.C.) in a section on literary great thinkers, when the historical Homer is the subject of much academic controversy and debate? Because Homer survives as one of the first and most famous storytellers, and every active imagination since him—right up to moviemakers Steven Spielberg and George Lucas, and *Harry Potter* creator J. K. Rowling—owes a debt to him.

A Greek Bearing Gifts

Homer is given credit for the two most famous adventures of the classical age, the *Iliad* and the *Odyssey*. These masterpieces were most likely composed in the eighth century B.C. Like Shakespeare long after him, Homer relied heavily on earlier source material, but he eclipsed these historical and mythological documents with his masterful interpretation. Homer's epic tales were based on mythic and quasi-historic events that had been floating around the ancient world for centuries before he added his singular spin to them.

The *Iliad* is the story of a decade-long battle that pitted the ancient Greeks against the Trojans. A Greek beauty named Helen moved to Troy with a man named Paris. Sadly, Helen was already married to someone else, and as the Greeks set out in hot pursuit of the adulterous couple, the story of "the face that launched a thousand ships" begins.

FACTS

Some scholars maintain that Homer was a blind poet who passed everything down via *oral tradition,* and that his works were chiseled into stone at a later date. Others say that his great works were literature "by committee;" meaning that they were written, revised, and adapted by many writers over many years.

Much of the story centers on Achilles, a mighty Greek warrior who apparently never had the benefit of an anger management course. Fellow warrior Agamemnon takes Achilles' favorite concubine and Achilles leaves the battlefield, asking his goddess mother to delay Greek victory until he has regained his sense of honor. What follows has been called the greatest war story ever told, a series of victories and defeats, and clashes of colorful characters.

Most people have some basic knowledge of this tale, if only because *Trojan horse* has stayed in the vernacular of every language. The Greeks laid siege to the walled city of Troy for ten years. Finally, they built a huge wooden horse and placed it outside the walls of the city as a sign of concession. Odysseus and his warriors hid inside the horse, while the rest of the Greek army sailed away.

Against advice from the prophetess Cassandra, the Trojans pulled the horse inside the walls and began to celebrate their victory. Night fell, and Odysseus and his men crept out of the horse and opened the city gates for the rest of the army. They came, they saw, and they conquered. The famous saying "Beware of Greeks bearing gifts" originally comes from Homer's *Iliad*. The heroic but angry Achilles (and his heel), Agamemnon, and the rest were legendary figures before Homer, but his telling of the tale in verse became the last word on the subject.

QUESTIONS?

Looking for a good translation of Homer?
Some well-known and respected translations include those by the eighteenth-century British poet Alexander Pope and by twentieth-century Americans Richard Lattimore, Robert Fitzgerald, and Robert Fagles.

The Odyssey is a sequel of sorts, but it is a rousing adventure rather than a gripping war story. One of the heroes of the *Iliad*, Odysseus (also known as Ulysses), through no fault of his own, takes a roundabout trip getting home after the Trojan War. After ten years of war, he takes another ten years to return to his homeland of Ithaca, off the coast of Greece. En route he encounters a giant cannibalistic Cyclops, the seductive goddess Calypso, the alluring yet deadly song of the sirens, and numerous other treacherous obstacles.

While he was away fighting the Trojan War and struggling to return home, Odysseus' wife, Penelope, was being badgered to find a new husband to run Ithaca. Her pesky, lethargic "suitors" overran her household, eating and drinking everything in sight. Odysseus eventually returned, exacted vengeance on the suitors, and restored his house to order.

Lesser known are the "Homeric Hymns," shorter poems that have survived the ravages of time and are also attributed to the elusive Homer. The technical term for the type of verse used by the author or authors who fall under the Homer umbrella is called *dactylic hexameter*.

Authentic or Not?

Homer's works are all stylistically similar, yet the controversy over their origin has continued through the ages. One problem in authenticating the tales is that the translations that survive are all copies of copies of copies. Another problem is that centuries passed before the works of Homer were carved on stone tablets, let alone scribbled on papyrus. For ages, the stories were transmitted orally by bards, roving poets or performers who enacted the tales in one-man shows. The logical assumption is that the epics were embellished by each performer. This does not diminish Homer, rather it makes him the literary poster boy for "collective consciousness" (see Chapter 18).

Homer's work has endured because his heroic tales of gods and monsters taps into something deep in the recesses of our psyche, That connection is something every great thinker accomplishes, either intentionally or inadvertently. Thus Homer, and his probable collaborators, influenced all the literature and drama that followed.

William Shakespeare

England's William Shakespeare (1564–1616) is almost uniformly regarded as the English language's greatest poet and playwright. Even those who have never read his work are familiar with some of his verse. Misquoted or incomplete paraphrases such as "a method to his madness," "something rotten in Denmark," and "a rose by any other name" have entered the vernacular and remain there. Most recently, he's been seen as a hunk in tights who romanced Gwyneth Paltrow in the movie *Shakespeare in Love*, but there is much more to the immortal Bard.

Shakespeare wrote thirty-seven plays, 154 sonnets, and a few other poems that established him as the greatest English-speaking writer of all time. Of course, controversy surrounds all great men and women, and Shakespeare is no different. There has been some speculation over the authorship of Shakespeare's plays. Some critics have even suggested that he did not write this body of work at all. One theory posits that Shakespeare was an actor who, for whatever reason, fronted for a nobleman named Edmund De Vere. These revisionists often use as evidence limited facts from that era that indicate that Shakespeare was something of a cipher. How could someone so seemingly pedestrian produce the greatest works of all time?

ESSENTIALS

Many fine Shakespeare movie adaptations are available for those who want to get a palatable introduction to the Bard. A variety of actors, from Laurence Olivier to Mel Gibson and Ethan Hawke, have played Hamlet on screen. For a traditional experience, try Olivier's adaptation of *Richard III*.

Whoever wrote the plays—and they were clearly written by one person—he was a genius, and for our purposes we will assume it was William Shakespeare, the Bard of Stratford-on-Avon.

The Early Bard

Little is known about Shakespeare's life and times, hence the challenges to his authorship over the centuries. We know that he lived and wrote in Elizabethan England. Queen Elizabeth was on the throne; the Renaissance was in full swing; and there were quantum leaps in every arena.

When Shakespeare was eighteen, he married twenty-six-year-old Anne Hathaway and they had three children. He was an actor as well as an author, but rarely did he have starring roles. He played the ghost of Hamlet's father in *Hamlet* and other supporting parts. Shakespeare was financially successful and popular in his lifetime and was able to retire in comfort.

We can divide Shakespeare's playwriting into stages. After an experimental start, he found his voice and wrote the major comedies and historical plays. His "dark" phase includes the major tragedies and the more complex comedies that provided more than mere laughter. This period probably coincided with reaching midlife and the death of his eleven-year-old son Hamnet. This tragedy seems to have infused Shakespeare with despair and a keen awareness of the fleeting nature of life that he turned into high art. *Hamlet, Macbeth, Othello,* and *King Lear* were all written during this period. The final period saw Shakespeare's style become more fanciful and romantic, culminating with *The Tempest,* generally regarded as his swan song.

The Play's the Thing

Some of Shakespeare's contemporaries, particularly Ben Johnson and Christopher Marlowe, are regarded as great playwrights, but most others have fallen by the wayside. And the plays composed in Europe prior to Shakespeare were generally *morality plays,* clear-cut tales with cardboard representations of good and evil, or bawdy comedies with stupid husbands, shrewish wives, and flatulent buffoons. This sounds like something you might see on the WB or UPN networks, or among the crop of current teenage movie comedies.

FACTS

In Shakespeare's time, women were forbidden from performing. As a result, young men and boys played all women's parts. Women were not allowed to express themselves in the theatrical profession until many decades later.

Shakespeare added a subtlety and depth previously unseen. The characters were complex and unique. Each character (even the minor ones) was imbued with a distinct personality and voice. Revisionist critics who consign him to the "dead white male" category are oblivious to the fact that he also wrote great female characters. They seize upon the apparent sexism of *The Taming of the Shrew* and forget about the rich characterizations of Lady Macbeth and Cleopatra.

He broke the stodgy Aristotelian rule that comedy was a lower form of art and should never be included in a tragedy. The comic relief segments in the tragedies are often funnier than the comedies, and the comedies often include a poignancy not seen in the typical farce of the day.

Like another great poet of the age, Dante (see Chapter 8), Shakespeare wrote in the vernacular. The upper crust spoke and read Latin and Greek, the languages of the classical age. The native language of the people was considered coarse and common. Shakespeare and Dante took the language of the people and elevated it to new heights.

Listen to Shakespeare speak to us through the ages. What follows are some of the most famous passages. Even those not very familiar with Shakespeare are probably familiar with these from their school days.

From *Hamlet*:

To be, or not to be: that is the question.
Whether 'tis nobler in the mind to suffer
The slings and arrows of outrageous fortune,
Or to take arms against a sea of troubles,
And by opposing end them. To die; to sleep;
No more; and by a sleep to say we end
The heartache and the thousand natural shocks
That flesh is heir to. 'Tis a consummation
Devoutly to be wish'd. To die; to sleep;
To sleep? Perchance to dream! Ay, there's the rub;
For in that sleep of death what dreams may come,
When we have shuffl'd off this mortal coil,
Must give us pause. There's the respect
That makes calamity of so long life.
For who would bear the whips and scorns of time,
The oppressor's wrong, the proud man's contumely,
The pangs of dispriz'd love, the law's delay,
The insolence of office and the spurns

That patient merit of the unworthy takes,
When he himself might his quietus make
With a bare bodkin? Who would fardels bear,
To grunt and sweat under a weary life,
But that the dread of something after death,
The undiscovered country from whose bourn
No traveller returns, puzzles the will
And makes us rather bear those ills we have
Than fly to others that we know not of?
Thus conscience does make cowards of us all;
And thus the native hue of resolution
Is sicklied o'er with the pale cast of thought,
And enterprises of great pith and moment
With this regard their currents turn awry,
And lose the name of action.

From *Romeo and Juliet*:
Two households, both alike in dignity,
In fair Verona, where we lay our scene,
From ancient grudge break to new mutiny,
Where civil blood makes civil hands unclean.
From forth the fatal loins of these two foes
A pair of star-cross'd lovers take their life;
Whose misadventur'd piteous overthrows
Do with their death bury their parents' strife.
The fearful passage of their death-mark'd love,
And the continuance of their parents' rage,
Which, but their children's end, nought could remove,
Is now the two hours' traffick of our stage;
The which if you with patient ears attend,
What here shall miss, our toil shall strive to mend.

From *Macbeth*:
To-morrow, and to-morrow, and to-morrow,
Creeps in this petty pace from day to day

To the last syllable of recorded time;
And all our yesterdays have lighted fools
The way to dusty death. Out, out, brief candle!
Life's but a walking shadow, a poor player
That struts and frets his hour upon the stage
And then is heard no more. It is a tale
Told by an idiot, full of sound and fury,
Signifying nothing.

From *The Tempest* *(this is believed to be Shakespeare's farewell to the theater; it was one of his last plays and he retired soon after):*
Our revels now are ended. These our actors,
As I foretold you, were all spirits and
Are melted into air, into thin air:
And, like the baseless fabric of this vision,
The cloud-capp'd towers, the gorgeous palaces,
The solemn temples, the great globe itself,
Ye all which it inherit, shall dissolve
And, like this insubstantial pageant faded,
Leave not a rack behind. We are such stuff
As dreams are made on, and our little life
Is rounded with a sleep.

The Sonnets

Shakespeare wrote 154 sonnets. The sonnet is a fourteen-line poem that can have several rhyme schemes. Shakespeare's sonnets may give us insight into his character or his complex love life—or they may just be poems.

SSENTIALS

Shakespeare's poetic style is called *blank verse*, which does not rhyme, but you may see the occasional rhyming couplet at the end of a soliloquy. Often, Shakespeare had comedic or lowbrow characters speak in prose, while the heroes and heroines spoke in verse.

The order in which the sonnets are traditionally published tells a story of a love triangle between the poet, a young aristocrat, and the infamous "dark lady." The gender-bending in the sonnets often makes it

Shakespeare

difficult to ascertain the sex of the poet. Some of the poems are clearly love poems to a man, others to the "dark lady," leading some scholars to conclude that Shakespeare was bisexual.

The collection is dedicated to a certain Mr. W. H. There is fraternal advice to the young man, and discussions of a rival poet who is also interested in the young man. The "dark lady" sonnets are about a dysfunctional relationship. The poet is obsessed with the lady even though he is painfully aware that she is bad news. The young man and the "dark lady" both betray the poet, presumably with each other. Here is one of the sonnets, one of the most famous verses ever written:

> Shall I compare thee to a summer's day?
> Thou art more lovely and more temperate:
> Rough winds do shake the darling buds of May,
> And summer's lease hath all too short a date:
> Sometime too hot the eye of heaven shines,
> And often is his gold complexion dimm'd;
> And every fair from fair sometime declines,
> By chance, or nature's changing course untrimm'd;
> But thy eternal summer shall not fade,
> Nor lose possession of that fair thou ow'st,
> Nor shall death brag thou wander'st in his shade,
> When in eternal lines to time thou grow'st;
> So long as men can breathe, or eyes can see,
> So long lives this, and this gives life to thee.

Shakespeare did nothing less than change the way we look at the world and ourselves, the way we think and behave. The world would be a dramatically different, and spiritually poorer, place had the Bard never put quill to paper and enriched our lives and inflamed our souls.

Johann Wolfgang von Goethe

Johann Wolfgang von Goethe (1749–1832) has been called the "German Shakespeare." He was a titanic literary personality during the romantic period. He was also a political figure and a scientist. This section will concentrate on two works that are still widely read today: a teen soap opera that might have starred Leonardo DiCaprio, and a mature work (in two parts) about nothing less than Satan himself.

Werther-Mania

The great flowering of youthful rebellion did not begin in the 1960s. There has always been a "youth versus the establishment" tradition in human affairs, and in many periods of history it became a genuine movement. Such was the case in late eighteenth century Germany when the movement became a political, philosophical, and literary rebellion against traditional mores. The literary wing of this rebellion was called *Sturm and Drang*. Although this sounds like a law firm, it is actually a German phrase that is roughly translated "Storm and Stress."

Literature was a highly structured, stylized art form in Goethe's day. The younger generation of authors sought to celebrate the passion of youth and a nonconformist approach, writing from the heart and ignoring traditional morality. Of course they hailed themselves as geniuses for whom the bourgeois rules did not apply—such is the case among many *artistes*. And such souls tend to die young and leave good-looking corpses, making their tales self-indulgent tragedies of misunderstood youth. From *Romeo and Juliet* to television's *Dawson's Creek*, this is a time-honored tradition in drama and literature.

Goethe jumped on the *Sturm und Drang* bandwagon with a novel that made a long-lasting impression, called *The Sorrows of Young Werther*. At the tender age of twenty-three, Goethe penned the novel from the heart in just about a month, and information suggests it was a highly autobiographical piece of fiction. The novel's style is called *epistolary,* meaning that it is told though a series of letters between the main characters. Bram Stoker's *Dracula* is the most famous epistolary novel.

Werther is a disaffected youth, a mooning, lovesick lad who becomes obsessed with a woman who is engaged to another man. The novel is a one-sided correspondence of Werther's letters to his friend Wilhelm. Werther recounts the sad story of meeting the betrothed Lotte. Young Werther spends every day with Lotte, who likes him but is not enchanted with grand notions of absolute and unconditional love. He leaves for a while but then returns to bask in the aura of his beloved. By this time she has married. He creates an embarrassing scene, and she runs out of the room. He becomes despondent and commits suicide by shooting himself. The end.

Think that angst-laden teen soap operas started with *The Breakfast Club* and continued through *Dawson's Creek*? Think again. Goethe's *The Sorrows of Young Werther* was a runaway bestseller that had young people dressing like the lovelorn hero, and alas, committing suicide like him as well. Young men were found dead with copies of the book nearby.

This *Monarch Notes* version does not do justice to the cult craze that followed the publication of the novel. Even in the days before mass media, the novel swept across Germany and then, when translated, gripped the dreamy adolescents of Europe. It was the *Titanic* of its day, as popular, but not as uplifting in the least, as *Harry Potter*.

Hundreds began to dress as Werther. The Werther uniform included a blue coat, brown boots, and a felt hat. Werther wannabes appeared all over Europe. The craze spawned something very modern—a merchandising campaign. People gobbled up Werther figurines, fragrances, and tea sets festooned with memorable moments from the novel.

Goethe was contemptuous of his hysterical fawning fans and horrified that people took his book as a romantic endorsement of suicide as a solution for a broken heart. He became the eighteenth-century equivalent of a teen idol and remained a celebrity for the rest of his very long life.

The Devil Made Him Do It

Goethe's crowning achievement is *Faust*, parts one and two. The first part was released to great acclaim, a far more mature work than the lugubrious tale of lovelorn Werther. Goethe spent the rest of his life writing the next part, between other works, scientific study, and political and social activism. *Faust, Part Two* was published posthumously.

Johann
Wolfgang
von Goethe

There was a historic Faust. He lived from approximately 1480 until 1540. He was a *magus,* another word for magician, and a teacher in German universities. Although Faust was regarded as a charlatan by other intellectuals of the day, he was alleged to have supernatural powers. Even Martin Luther, leader of the Protestant Reformation in Germany (see Chapter 8), believed that Faust had the magic touch.

After Faust's death, the legend really took off and he became a figure of mythic proportions. The legend involved a deal with the devil, called Mephistopheles, who granted Faust twenty-four years of knowledge, power, and license, after which he would be carted off to the infernal regions. Christopher Marlowe's *The Tragical History of Dr. Faustus* written circa 1588 was an instant classic and long considered the last word on the subject.

FACTS

Everyone knows the Faust legend even if they have never read Goethe's version. Its most recent incarnation is the movie comedy *Bedazzled,* starring Brendan Fraser and Elizabeth Hurley, a remake of a far superior 1967 comedy.

Goethe changed the Faust legend to suit his literary purpose. The drama, written in rhyming verse, portrays Faust as less malevolent than his earlier literary incarnations. He makes the deal with the devil in a misguided, yet noble goal to gain knowledge and wisdom, not for money or power or lust.

Faust is an allegory for the human condition, and the second part of the story ends with a message that things are not always the clear-cut good and evil of a medieval morality play. Mephistopheles is humanized by his encounter with Faust, and Faust manages to escape damnation.

Ironically, Goethe thought he would be remembered more for his scientific studies than his literary endeavors. He studied and wrote about medical matters including anatomy, biology, and optics. Of course, he is remembered as a man of letters, not as an ophthalmologist. Goethe saw a bigger picture with his literary vision than he would have grinding lenses.

The Brontë Sisters

Literary talent sometimes runs in families, and the Brontë sisters are perhaps the most famous literary sisters. Their lives were as Gothic and tragic as anything they concocted for Heathcliff and Mr. Rochester.

Charlotte Brontë (1816–1855), Emily Brontë (1818–1848), and Anne Brontë (1820–1849) were the daughters of a clergyman of Irish descent. As little girls, they used their toys to create romantic adventures in fanciful kingdoms, and as young adults they turned their creativity to the art of the novel, enriching the world of literature.

QUESTIONS?

How did these women get their works published?
During the time when the Brontës were writing, books written by men were better sellers. Charlotte, Emily, and Anne used the pen names Currer Bell, Ellis Bell, and Acton Bell, respectively.

Charlotte is famous for *Jane Eyre*, the story of the naïve and innocent governess and her experiences in the employ of the brooding, secretive

Rochester. The story set the standard for all Gothic novels to follow: the lovers who take forever to get together, only after numerous trials, tribulations, and tragedies. It is a classic of English literature.

Rarely do we get more than one classic of English literature per family, but younger sister Emily soon followed with *Wuthering Heights*. This story of the passionate and preternatural love between Cathy and another brooding Brit, the Byronic Heathcliff, was another instant classic. Not to be outdone, Anne wrote the lesser-known *Agnes Grey* in the same year her sisters' works were completed.

The year 1847 was a good one for the Brontë girls, but things went downhill after that. Emily died in 1848 and Anne in 1849. Charlotte lived a little longer and wrote other books, but none were as well remembered as *Jane Eyre*. She married in 1854, but died of complications from pregnancy the following year.

Though their lives were tragically brief, the legacy of these three young women lives on in their work. *Jane Eyre* is still widely read and there have been many movie adaptations, and even a Broadway musical. *Wuthering Heights* remains equally popular. Its heartbreaking love story continues to prompt lonely hearts to get out their handkerchiefs.

Ayn Rand

Ayn Rand (1905–1982) was an American novelist and philosopher famous for the novels *The Fountainhead* and *Atlas Shrugged* and the philosophy called Objectivism. She came to the United States from Russia in 1926 to enjoy the freedoms and opportunities that America offered.

The four pillars of Objectivism are the belief in Objective Reality, Reason, Self-Interest, and Capitalism. Objective Reality simply means that reality is reality and it exists whether you are there or not. Objectivists do not bother themselves with philosophical speculations on the nature of the universe. Objectivism teaches that we can perceive the world through reason alone. Objectivism does not have a spiritual bone in its philosophical body. It teaches that your own self-interest should be your primary goal—so don't waste your time and money with altruism. The ideal political expression of Objectivism is capitalism. Individual rights and property rights are what it's all about. Government interference is an anathema to the Objectivist.

Rand's novel *The Fountainhead* is the story of Howard Roark, an uncompromising architect who will not budge one iota in his artistic vision. He does not sacrifice his integrity or make any accommodations for anyone or anything. He suffers much for his art, but does so stoically, with the endurance of Prometheus. He blows up a building he designed because other people have meddled with it and corrupted his vision. He goes to trial, defends himself, and delivers a summation speech to the jury that, a little too melodramatically, acquits him. *Atlas Shrugged* is Ayn Rand's other major work of fiction. Its female protagonist struggles to run a railroad in a man's world. She encounters all manner of mealy-mouthed politically correct types who are out to thwart her capitalist ambitions. Throughout the novel many characters ask the cryptic question, "Who is John Galt?" It is used the way a singsong "whatever" is today. Without dropping any spoilers, the protagonist eventually meets the mysterious John Galt, the Uber-Objectivist incarnate.

QUESTIONS?

What is Objectivism?
Objectivism maintains that the primary purpose of mankind is to achieve great success, and optimize its human potential. Self-interest eclipses all other objectives, and charity is counter-productive and foolish.

Fans of the free market economy, capitalism, libertarianism, individualism, self-responsibility, laissez-faire government, and the American dream will continue to read and discuss Ayn Rand. She never wrote another novel after *Atlas Shrugged*, but she continued to philosophize, publishing a newsletter and writing the nonfiction books *The Virtue of Selfishness: A Concept of New Egoism* and *Introduction to Objectivist Epistemology*.

CHAPTER 10

Scoundrel, Storyteller, Adventurer, Poet

Like most great thinkers, literary giants usually stand apart from the herd. Consider four literary rebels: a sadistic Frenchman, a British social critic and gifted storyteller, an English adventurer whose escapades surpassed those of Indiana Jones, and an American who revolutionized the world of poetry.

THE EVERYTHING GREAT THINKERS BOOK

The Marquis de Sade

The Marquis de Sade (1740–1814) is one of the most misunderstood literary figures of his or any age. Born Donatien Alphonse François, he became *Comte de Sade* after his father's death in 1767. De Sade was a product of eighteenth-century France, and to this day is perceived by many as nothing more than a pervert in pantaloons and a powdered wig. An informal survey conducted among college-educated Americans revealed that those under thirty, as is too often the case these days, have never even heard of him. Many who have heard of him believe that de Sade was a serial killer, pedophile, or child murderer who wrote dirty books as a sideline.

A Bad Rep

The fact is the Marquis de Sade never killed anyone. He had the misfortune to live in an age when rattling society's cage through controversial words and deeds meant being locked up, or worse. De Sade spent over half his adult life charged with scandalous conduct or sexual offenses and locked up in various prisons and mental institutions, including the notorious Bastille. While he was imprisoned, he wrote many of his books. De Sade's best-known works include *Juliette, Justine, 120 Days of Sodom*, and *The Bedroom Philosophers*. Although the authorities locked up de Sade's body, they couldn't imprison his active imagination. Even if you find him and his ideology to be bizarre and repugnant, he was an original and provocative thinker who, like so many other provocative thinkers, suffered for his art.

ALERT

It's always a sign of notoriety when a person's name becomes a word in the dictionary. *Sadism* means to derive sexual pleasure from inflicting pain or humiliation on someone else. De Sade was actually more of a sadomasochist, meaning that he enjoyed both giving and receiving pain.

De Sade was an aristocrat who outraged the genteel French upper crust with his salacious writings and scurrilous antics. He married, but he was a neglectful husband. He also had the misfortune of having a mother-in-law who was personally responsible for much of the time he spent behind bars.

True, his books are quite an ordeal—ribald tales of libertine men and scarlet women engaging in all manner of debauchery. There are lengthy ravings between the naughty bits, and even they are oddly clinical and not particularly titillating. But he also wrote many essays, antireligious pamphlets, and plays (some of which were later produced by the Comédie Française). To some he is a philosopher, to others a social satirist. And to many, he remains nothing more than a pornographer. So what's all the fuss about? Why did this man spend half his life in the slammer, turning a chicken bone into a quill pen and writing on toilet paper?

Heart of Darkness

In Thomas Moore's fascinating book, *Dark Eros: The Imagination of Sadism* (1995), he makes the case that de Sade was an amateur psychologist, kinkily going where no one had gone before. There is a psychological and spiritual principle that maintains that to reach the exalted heights you have to descend to the lowest depths. You have to wallow in the muck for a while and embrace your shadow, which is Jungian parlance for your nastier impulses. Freud called it the id, as you'll see in Chapter 18.

The marquis had quite a shadow; his id was rich with activity. His world was an upside-down realm where virtue was punished and vice was rewarded. His libertines and virginal maidens and the dance of indignity they perform were like the gods and goddesses of ancient mythology. Most of us have not had the benefit of a classical education and are not aware that the denizens of Mount Olympus, when viewed from a psychological perspective, are aspects of the complex human mind and spirit. So too are the rather one-dimensional *dramatis personae* of de Sade's fiction. They are like the ethereal archetypes that Jung speaks of in his theory of the collective unconscious. Collectively they comprise our dark side.

De Sade's strange worldview is repellent to most of us in this politically correct age. The world is awash in violence, corruption, and evil. The dark side of the soul rampages freely in society. Perhaps a better awareness and acknowledgement of our own less-than-noble impulses could help us keep them in check.

ESSENTIALS

The recent movie *Quills* tells a largely fictionalized account of the life of the Marquis de Sade. It plays fast and loose with some of the facts—for example, his tongue was not cut out for his crimes in real life—but it presents a vivid portrait of a gifted but disturbed man.

De Sade died in the Charenton insane asylum, and there is no doubt that he was a troubled man. He was more than just a guy who wrote dirty books, however. His vision, even though distasteful to most, cries out for exploration. For, like it or not, we all have, in the recesses of our soul, a heart of darkness. It may manifest itself in minor outbursts of antisocial behavior; in more extreme cases it can manifest itself more intensely.

De Sade believed that sexual deviation exists in nature; therefore, it is natural. Of course, this view was in violent opposition to the times he lived in, but it made him a precursor of modern psychological thought. The mention of the Marquis de Sade induces reactions ranging from profound disgust to intrigue in polite society, but he is one of us, and his distant cries from his dank dungeon demand to be heard.

Charles Dickens

English novelist Charles Dickens (1812–1870) produced an enormous body of work, collectively, and most of his books are of enormous length individually. Some may quip that this was because he was paid by the word, but most of Dickens books were serialized in the periodicals of the day, and the citizens of the English-speaking world hung on his every word, eagerly awaiting the next installment in the adventures of David Copperfield, Oliver Twist, Pip, and his many other colorful waifs. There is no better way to study nineteenth-century London than to read Dickens.

Humble Beginnings

Dickensian has entered the language to describe a story of epic scope, usually about someone from humble beginnings who makes their way in an uncaring world, eventually finding happiness after a series of melodramatic situations and interactions with unusual characters. The world of Dickens is filled with much humor and great suffering, resourceful orphans, and mean old misers. He effectively combined comedy, drama, stinging satire, and the angry righteousness of a social reformer in works that have entertained readers for over a century.

QUESTIONS?

What's in a name?
The names of Dickens's characters (Scrooge, Pecksniff, Sweedle-pipe, Honeythunder, Bumble, Pumblechook, Podsnap, Muddle-branes, and many more) presage Carl Jung's observation that "nomenclature is destiny." How could someone named Ebenezer Scrooge be anything other than a greedy, unrepentant old sinner?

Dickens's father ended up in debtor's prison, a common fate in nineteenth-century London. People, locked up until they paid their debts, could leave during the day to find work, but they had to be back at the prison by nightfall. As a result, Dickens had to leave school at a young age and go to work. There were no child labor laws, and very young children worked extremely long hours in inhumane conditions. Young children were treated cruelly and many died from accidents and maltreatment. The indignities Dickens suffered as a child laborer became the basis for his novel *David Copperfield*.

Dickens's first published works were a series of literary sketches, accompanied by actual drawings written under the alias Boz. *Sketches by Boz* became an instant hit. His sketches were short pieces about life in London. His next project was the picaresque novel *The Pickwick Papers*. The novel is an ambling affair, in which the protagonist wanders through life meeting interesting characters and having a series of adventures and misadventures. Dickens scored with his first novel, and it became an instant bestseller.

Henceforth, Dickens was the Stephen King and John Grisham of his day, only better. He wrote a string of serialized bestsellers, including

Charles Dickens

Nicholas Nickelby, *Our Mutual Friend*, *Bleak House*, *Oliver Twist*, *Tale of Two Cities*, *The Old Curiosity Shop*, and *Great Expectations*. Dickens also wrote the nonfiction pieces *American Notes* and *Pictures from Italy*.

Dickens was an accomplished showman. He performed one-man shows of his novels, which often had hundreds of speaking parts. He took his act on the road, touring America to great acclaim.

According to classic TV legend, he even ended up on the Ponderosa. Ben Cartwright and his sons made him welcome on an episode of *Bonanza*, and inspired his muse when he was reluctant to write the final installment of *Oliver Twist*.

Like many celebrities, Dickens's personal life suffered. After bringing ten children into the world, he and his wife apparently fell out of love and he took up with a young actress. Dickens died of a stroke in 1870 after a whirlwind theatrical tour.

A Christmas Classic

His contribution of *A Christmas Carol* into the Western canon is by itself enough to rate Charles Dickens a place in the pantheon of great literary thinkers. The holiday tale has been adapted literally hundreds of times. George C. Scott, Patrick Stewart, Michael Caine, and Albert Finney have all played Scrooge on the screen, and there have been female versions of the Scrooge character as well. The Muppets, the Jetsons, the Flintstones, Mr. Magoo, and other cartoon characters have also presented their version of the story. It has been animated and it has been set to music. In short, it is one of the most durable stories ever told. What a better world it would be if we could all experience the miraculous transformation of Ebenezer Scrooge after his visitation by three spirits on Christmas Eve. Dickens describes the new Scrooge:

> Scrooge was better than his word. He did it all, and infinitely more; and to Tiny Tim, who did not die, he was a second father. He became as good a friend, as good a master, and as good a man, as the good old city knew, or any other good old city, town, or borough, in the good old world. Some people laughed to see the alteration in him, but he let them laugh, and little heeded them; for he was wise enough to know that nothing ever happened on this globe, for good, at which some people did not have their fill of laughter in the outset; and knowing that such as these would be blind anyway, he thought it quite as well that they should wrinkle up their eyes in grins, as have the malady in less attractive forms. His own heart laughed: and that was quite enough for him.

Sir Richard Francis Burton

Sir Richard Francis Burton (1821–1890) was a Renaissance man of a decidedly macho variety. In addition to being an author, linguist, translator, and historian, he was an explorer and adventurer who braved many dangers in the quest for knowledge—and perhaps a little fortune and glory as well.

World-Class Adventurer

Expelled from Oxford, Burton joined the fabled East India Company and served in its private army for seven years. He lived in a part of India that is now Pakistan and learned as much as he could about the native culture. A natural linguist, he became adept at many languages and dialects and could pass himself off as a native in many areas of central Asia and the Muslim world. This skill enabled him to perform thorough field research on the local color and perhaps even alert Her Majesty's government about potential unrest.

Burton eventually became confident enough to make a pilgrimage to Mecca and Medina. He would not have been well received if worshipers had known he was a non-Muslim Westerner taking in the sights and sounds of the holiest Islamic cities. Burton became a celebrity by writing of his adventures in the book *Personal Narrative of a Pilgrimage to El-Medinah and Meccah.*

ESSENTIALS For a highly entertaining exploration of Richard Francis Burton's life and adventures, check out a 1990 movie called *Mountains on the Moon*. It chronicles Burton's eventful journey and should be available at your local video and DVD rental store.

Buoyed by his brazen success, he pulled off the same stunt in the Islamic city of Harer, located in what is now the African country of Ethiopia. This town was definitely off-limits to all non-Muslims, who would suffer a most painful demise if discovered. Burton got out of Harer alive and again told the tale to a voracious readership.

A Real-Life Indiana Jones

Burton teamed with another British adventurer, John Hanning Speke, and together they set out to explore darkest Africa. Their first foray was cut short when their group was attacked in Somalia. Burton caught a spear in the face, yet he survived to tell the tale. A few years later, Speke and Burton returned to Africa determined to discover the source of the Nile. The source was thought to be deep in the interior of Africa.

The journey was a difficult one. Speke and Burton were the first Europeans to venture that deeply into the African continent. They were the first Westerners to see Lake Tanganyika, which Burton believed to be the source of the Nile. His later explorations proved that it was not, however. Burton could not continue the journey due to illness, and Speke continued on to Lake Victoria, proclaiming *it* to be the source of the Nile. Burton disagreed, but Speke returned to England and announced his discovery, receiving the acclaim and the credit. That was the end of a beautiful friendship.

Burton's later travels took him to South America, the United States, and much of the world. He worked for the British Foreign Office as an ambassador. He was assigned to Brazil, Damascus (Syria), and finally Trieste (Italy). He was eventually knighted and continued writing and translating until his death.

Burton immersed himself in the cultures he wrote about, but his thoroughness and attention to detail drew criticism and suspicion. His vivid descriptions of both the heterosexual and homosexual practices in far-off lands led many to believe that he had personally sampled all the myriad delights there. Burton claimed his interest in the erotic escapades of other cultures was strictly academic and maintained that his curiosity was purely of an anthropological nature. He also introduced the West to *Arabian Nights*, which has been adapted and filmed many times, even by Walt Disney (see Chapter 21) as the animated movie *Aladdin*.

FACTS

Burton's most famous translation was a controversial one. He translated the *Kama Sutra*, a Hindu collection of ancient erotic tales that was the *Joy of Sex* of its day. It ruffled the righteous feathers of Victorian England and made Burton as notorious as he was acclaimed.

Richard Francis Burton had an unorthodox and maverick personality, and the ability to translate thinking into action. Scholarly research in dusty laboratories—or in today's age, safely ensconced at home surfing the Web—certainly has value. But there is nothing like fieldwork, and Burton took to the field with swashbuckling abandon. He also educated the Europeans and Americans in the ways of Islam and the Arab world, something with which Westerners should reacquaint themselves.

Walt Whitman

Walt Whitman (1819–1892) changed the face of poetry as it had been written since Homer's time, and in doing so became one of the quintessential American literary figures of his age. He was also something of a perfectionist, and only wrote one book—but what a book! He compiled one collection of verse and then spent the rest of his life editing and revising it.

An American Original

Whitman was born on Long Island, New York, and his large family later moved to Brooklyn. He was, at various times, a printer, a school-teacher, a newspaper editor, and a journalist. At the age of thirty-six, after years of struggle and a nonexistent reputation, Whitman burst onto the literary scene with a collection of poems called *Leaves of Grass*.

ESSENTIALS

Whitman's poetry was written in what is called *free verse;* his verse was not restricted by the forms of meter and rhyme used by most great poets. Whitman's poetry also had an earthy quality and a candid celebration of sexuality that shocked many who read the privately printed collection.

Whitman subsequently influenced generations of writers, as well as philosophers. Whitman's verse was written for the common man. He hoped to be a truly American original, a poet for the masses. Unfortunately, in those days, as is the case today, the "common man" does not read much poetry. And so, Whitman achieved recognition but among the mostly European *literati*. The celebrated fop Oscar Wilde (the antithesis of the common man) made a pilgrimage to the aged Whitman's Camden, New Jersey, home with the same devotion a true believer would visit a shrine.

Song of Himself

In addition to being a poet of mystical insight, Whitman was a skilled self-promoter rivaling P. T. Barnum and Ron Popeil. Whitman did not wait for the reviewers and the reading public to hail him as the most exciting thing since the cotton gin; he announced it himself in the preface of his book.

After the first edition of *Leaves of Grass* was released, Whitman received a rave review from the foremost literary and philosophical figure of the American landscape, Ralph Waldo Emerson. Emerson wrote a letter to Whitman hailing him as a genius. The letter was meant to be a private correspondence, but Whitman used it in the nineteenth-century equivalent of press kits that he sent to the major media of the day.

He was also inspired by Emerson to produce a revised edition of the collection. One of the most well known poems is "Song of Myself." It opens with the famous lines:

> I celebrate myself,
> And what I assume you shall assume,
> For every atom belonging to me as good belongs to you.
> I loafe and invite my soul,
> I lean and loafe at my ease observing a spear of summer grass.
> My tongue, every atom of my blood, formed from this soil, this air,
> Born here of parents born here from parents the same, and their
>   parents the same,
> I, now thirty seven years old in perfect health begin,
> Hoping to cease not till death.

This poem and others in the Whitman canon are very Zen in nature, in that they speak of the universal nature of humankind and its place in

Walt Whitman

the cosmos. They speak of a pantheism that was popular among Emerson, Thoreau, and the other American transcendentalists. *Pantheism* is the belief that God is in all things and all things are God.

Whitman served as a male nurse during the Civil War and attended to wounded Union soldiers. He was also deeply affected by the assassination of Abraham Lincoln in 1865. The poem "When Lilacs Last in the Dooryard Bloom'd" is a moving elegy to the fallen president. Whitman writes of the funeral procession when Lincoln's coffin was taken by train from Washington, D.C. to his home state of Illinois, and a crowd of thousands lined the railroad tracks to pay their respects and hear the poem.

Over the breast of the spring, the land, amid cities,
Amid lanes and through old woods, where lately the violets peep'd
    from the ground, spotting the gray debris,
Amid the grass in the fields each side of the lanes, passing the
    endless grass,
Passing the yellow-spear'd wheat, every grain from its shroud in the
    dark-brown fields uprisen,
Passing the apple-tree blows of white and pink in the orchards,
Carrying a corpse to where it shall rest in the grave,
Night and day journeys a coffin.
Coffin that passes through lanes and streets,
Through day and night with the great cloud darkening the land,
With the pomp of the inloop'd flags with the cities draped in black,
With the show of the States themselves as of crape-veil'd women
    standing,
With processions long and winding and the flambeaus of the night,
With the countless torches lit, with the silent sea of faces and the
    unbared heads,
With the waiting depot, the arriving coffin, and the sombre faces,
With dirges through the night, with the thousand voices rising strong
    and solemn,
With all the mournful voices of the dirges pour'd around the coffin,
The dim-lit churches and the shuddering organs—where amid these
    you journey,
With the tolling tolling bells' perpetual clang,
Here, coffin that slowly passes,
I give you my sprig of lilac.

Whitman stayed in Washington, D.C. after the war and continued to revise his magnum opus while working as a federal employee. He was partially paralyzed by a stroke in 1873 and moved in with a brother in Camden, New Jersey, where he remained until his death. By the end of his life, Whitman was world famous, but he preferred to live humbly, enjoying the fame but not the wealth of his celebrity.

CHAPTER 11

The Founding Fathers

Prior to 1776, American resources were exploited, and the native people were abused, ill used, and conquered. The Founding Fathers should not be dismissed as merely self-aggrandizing, well-to-do white men, however. The principles on which the United States of America was founded are noble, and the accomplishments of the men who forged this nation are among the most impressive achievements in the history of the world.

Benjamin Franklin

Benjamin Franklin (1706–1790) was one of the most amazing men of his or any age. An author, inventor, scientist, and revolutionary, Franklin invented the bifocals and the stove. He was the first postmaster general, established the first lending library, founded the first volunteer fire brigade, and bravely experimented with lightning. And, he was a prominent voice in the American Revolution and the birth of a new nation.

American Renaissance Man

Franklin was born in Boston, the fifteenth of seventeen children. He went to work at the tender age of ten and apprenticed in various trades until a little nepotism landed him a position as printer's apprentice to his

Benjamin Franklin

older brother James. The job gave him exposure to an eclectic assortment of literature that he voraciously consumed. James Franklin founded a newspaper, the *New England Courant*, and the teenage Benjamin wrote numerous articles. They were published anonymously and developed an enthusiastic following.

After a feud with his brother, Franklin went to Philadelphia and later to England to pursue a career as a printer. Returning to Philadelphia, he purchased the *Pennsylvania Gazette* and made the foundering tabloid popular and successful.

In 1732 he published the first edition of *Poor Richard's Almanack*, written under the pseudonym of Richard Saunders. He published annual editions of the *Almanack*, which became enormously popular, for more than twenty years. The *Almanack* contained much of the wit and wisdom for which Benjamin is remembered. He is often portrayed in drama as a man who speaks exclusively in homespun bromides. Enjoy this brief sample of the wit and wisdom of Benjamin Franklin, also known as Poor Richard.

Silence is not always a Sign of Wisdom, but Babbling is ever a Mark
of Folly.

Great Modesty often hides great Merit.

Virtue may not always make a Face handsome, but Vice will certainly
make it ugly.

You may delay, but Time will not.

He that's content, hath enough; He that complains, has too much.

Half the Truth is often a great Lie.

The Honey is sweet, but the Bee has a Sting.

He that would rise at Court, must begin by Creeping.

One To-day is worth two To-morrows.

Dally not with other Folks' Women or Money.

Work as if you were to live 100 Years, Pray as if you were to die To-morrow.

A Change of Fortune hurts a wise Man no more than a Change of
the Moon.

Speak little, do much.

When the Wine enters, out goes the Truth.

If you would be loved, love and be loveable.

The Wolf sheds his Coat once a Year, his Disposition never.

ESSENTIALS

Who is wise? He that learns from every One.
Who is powerful? He that governs his Passions.
Who is rich? He that is content.
Who is that? Nobody.

Diligence overcomes Difficulties, Sloth makes them.

Neglect mending a small Fault, and 'twill soon be a great One.

Bad Gains are truly Losses.

A long Life may not be good enough, but a good Life is long enough.

Love your Neighbour; yet don't pull down your Hedge.

Praise little, dispraise less.

The learned Fool writes his Nonsense in better Language than the
unlearned; but still 'tis Nonsense.

You may give a Man an Office, but you cannot give him Discretion.

To be intimate with a foolish Friend, is like going to bed to a Razor.
   Little Rogues easily become great Ones.
Paintings and Fightings are best seen at a distance.
Haste makes Waste.
He that best understands the World, least likes it.
He that is of Opinion Money will do every Thing, may well be
   suspected of doing every Thing for Money.

Entry into Politics

Franklin was elected to the Pennsylvania Assembly and served there
from 1750 until 1764, selling his printing business and devoting himself to
political life. Presaging his role in the American Revolution, he devised
what was called the Albany Plan in 1754, named for Albany, New York,
the meeting place of the congress. (Franklin was the Pennsylvania
representative.) The plan was similar in structure to the United States
Constitution, which Franklin would help craft more than thirty years later.

Remember to keep your sense of humor in a crisis. Always ready
with a quip, Franklin told the other Founders who were poised to
sign the Declaration of Independence and commit treason against
Great Britain, "We must all hang together, or assuredly we shall all
hang separately."

Franklin spent much of his middle age in England, representing the
interests of the American colonies. He was there from 1757 to 1762 and
from 1764 to 1775. He was an intimate of such celebrated thinkers as
David Hume (Scottish philosopher and historian) and Adam Smith
(Scottish economist). Franklin spent much of this time negotiating for
peaceful relations between the colonies and Britain, but war was
becoming increasingly inevitable. Franklin returned to America in 1775
and joined the movement for independence.

During the Revolution, Franklin served as an ambassador to France.
He was a very popular character with the French, especially the French
ladies, despite the fact that he was an old codger. The sheer force of his

personality, in flamboyant opposition to some of his more dour fellow Yanks, prompted the French to offer much aid and comfort to the struggling colonies. The fact that the English and the French had been warring for centuries was also a factor in France's willingness to help America.

Franklin's detractors considered him an overbearing egotist. He addressed this issue in his *Autobiography*. He wrote eloquently of his struggle with pride:

> In reality, there is, perhaps, no one of our natural passions so hard to subdue as pride. Disguise it, struggle with it, beat it down, stifle it, mortify it as much as one pleases, it is still alive, and will every now and then peep out and show itself; you will see it, perhaps, often in this history; for, even if I could conceive that I had completely overcome it, I should probably be proud of my humility.

Perhaps Franklin had more of a right to pat himself on the back than most men. His accomplishments and gifts were legion.

In his last years, Franklin did not retire into the background. In his eighties, he returned from France, where he had remained as an ambassador after America won its independence, and became a member of the Constitutional Convention, the men who hammered out the document that is the linchpin of our body politic that begins with these secular yet strangely holy words:

> We the People of the United States, in Order to form a more perfect Union, establish Justice, insure domestic Tranquility, provide for the common defence, promote the general Welfare, and secure the Blessings of Liberty to ourselves and our Posterity, do ordain and establish this Constitution for the United States of America.

One of Franklin's last acts was to sign a petition to end slavery. In fact, he was the president of the Pennsylvania Abolition Society. It is fashionable these days to call the Founding Fathers hypocritical in their approach to slavery, but it was a hotly debated topic in the Continental Congress, and compromises were made in order to ensure the cooperation of the southern colonies. They hoped that once the new nation was firmly established, they could then take on the slavery issue. Of course, we know the issue was not resolved until after the carnage of the Civil War almost a hundred years later.

Wit and Wisdom

One hilarious anecdote is like something straight out of a sitcom involving Franklin and another Founding Father, John Adams. They were traveling together as part of their diplomatic efforts and were obliged to share a room, and a bed, at a roadside inn. They got into an Odd Couple argument about whether the window should be opened or closed. The ever-voluble Franklin put the cantankerous Adams to sleep as he expounded on his theory of the benefits of the brisk night air.

ESSENTIALS Franklin was quite a character. He enjoyed what he called "air baths." He would open up all the windows and stand stark naked basking in the cross ventilation. He was a proponent of fresh air in an age when people kept their doors and windows closed to avoid contagions.

Franklin was also a contradictory character, as are many great men. The man who said "Early to bed, early to rise, makes a man healthy, wealthy and wise" rarely rose before 11 A.M. and loved the nightlife. The fellow who said "A penny saved is a penny earned" was often extravagant and in debt as a result.

He wrestled with this side of himself, seeking to improve himself by making lists. He wrote in his *Autobiography*:

> . . . I included under thirteen names of virtues all that at that time occurr'd to me as necessary or desirable, and annexed to each a short precept, which fully express'd the extent I gave to its meaning. These names of virtues, with their precepts, were:

> Temperance. Eat not to dullness; drink not to elevation.
> Silence. Speak not but what may benefit others or yourself; avoid trifling conversation.

Order. Let all your things have their places; let each part of your
business have its time.

Resolution. Resolve to perform what you ought; perform without fail
what you resolve.

Frugality. Make no expense but to do good to others or yourself; i.e.,
waste nothing.

Industry. Lose no time; be always employ'd in something useful; cut
off all unnecessary actions.

Sincerity. Use no hurtful deceit; think innocently and justly, and, if you
speak, speak accordingly.

Justice. Wrong none by doing injuries, or omitting the benefits that
are your duty.

Moderation. Avoid extreams; forbear resenting injuries so much as you
think they deserve.

Cleanliness. Tolerate no uncleanliness in body, cloaths, or habitation.

Tranquillity. Be not disturbed at trifles, or at accidents common or
unavoidable.

Chastity. Rarely use venery but for health or offspring, never to
dullness, weakness, or the injury of your own or another's peace
or reputation.

Humility. Imitate Jesus and Socrates.

Even if he did not always follow his own advice, it is good advice
nevertheless. Benjamin Franklin was a steady stream of wit and wisdom
for his eighty-four years of life, and is one of the great American
immortals whose life and wisdom can still inspire us.

George Washington

Some believe that George Washington (1732–1799) was not necessarily a
great thinker. Rather, it was the force of his dynamic personality and his
convictions that inspired men to follow him as a soldier, and the nation
to follow him as its leader. However, an episode of Martha Stewart's
television show, during which she tours Washington's Virginia plantation,
Mount Vernon, corrects this misconception. George Washington's
innovative thought processes become quite evident.

An Ingenious Thinker

We have all heard the phrase "separate the wheat from the chaff." But how many of us have personally attempted that chore? It is an arduous process of laying out the stalks (chaff) and beating them to dislodge the grains of wheat, which are then swept up.

Washington designed a barn with an upwardly spiraling track for his horses to trot up and down to their equine heart's content. He placed the chaff on the wooden planks of the track and the horses did the work of separating the wheat from the chaff. The wheat fell through the cracks in the wood and was collected below. This saved someone, probably a slave, the backache of whacking the wheat. On a related note, Washington freed all his slaves upon his death, lest the detractors of the Founding Fathers leap to dismiss all their other accomplishments because of this unsightly national stain.

FACTS

We all know George Washington as the little fellow who chopped down a cherry tree and then owned up to it, saying, "I cannot tell a lie." He's also known for his wooden teeth. In fact, there is no concrete evidence of the cherry tree legend, and the teeth were a dental hodgepodge of other people's teeth and animal teeth.

Another sign of Washington's ingenuity, also revealed on Stewart's television show, was a unique chair from his study. He designed and built a chair with pedals that operated an overhead fan. Remember, there was no air conditioning in colonial times. Of course, some might suggest that one could work up a sweat pedaling away, so perhaps it was also the first home exercise device. Now *that's* a great thinker.

Military Man

Washington was the scion of a wealthy Virginia family. As a member of the elite class, he could have been a self-absorbed dilettante, but he devoted his life to public service in a variety of venues. As a member of the colonial army, he served with distinction during the French and Indian Wars. He served the British Crown in that conflict, but his greatest distinction would be as commander of the Continental Army.

Washington braved hostile and horrible conditions, as did all the troops, not only from the British soldiers, but from the elements as well.

George Washington

A bout with smallpox as a younger man had left his face and body pockmarked and scarred, but having weathered the ravages of the insidious disease before, he was immune as it swept through his troops.

Washington's military career was not without blunders—he barely escaped from New York with his army, which may have spelled the end of the Revolution. His triumphs, however, were inspirational. Take, for example, his celebrated crossing of the Delaware River during a dangerous storm in order to launch a sneak attack on a garrison of Hessians the day after Christmas. Washington calculated that the Hessians, German mercenaries hired by the British, would be hung over after a Christmas party and hence quite vulnerable. Indeed they were, and the victory rallied the troops and the colonies.

Washington and his troops endured the hellish freeze of Valley Forge and scored the decisive victory at Yorktown, where General Cornwallis's surrender ended the war and thus the United States of America gained independence from Great Britain, a famous first in history.

Washington's military achievements were glorious, to be sure, but his greatest triumphs came after the war, when his keen insight and foresight saved America from descending into a monarchy. Had America become the very thing it had fought against for so long, world history would be very different indeed.

Washington wanted to retire to his farm and live a humble life, but he never shirked from responsibility. He bade farewell to his troops at Fraunces Tavern in New York City (which still stands in lower Manhattan) and went home after a job well done.

But he was not allowed to rest on his laurels for long. The new nation was in its birth-throes and a central government had yet to be firmly ensconced. The British loomed in Canada and on the high seas, and Washington was concerned that if America did not get its collective act together, the British might try to retake their colony. The British did try again, in the oft-forgotten War of 1812, when British troops actually burned Washington, D.C. to the ground.

ESSENTIALS
Many in America wanted to declare George Washington king. He nipped such rumblings in the bud with firmness and finality. Had he been a more vainglorious man and seized the opportunity for personal power, it is doubtful that America would have survived and thrived to this day.

The country again needed a steady hand, and Washington was chosen to lead the Virginia delegation to the Constitutional Convention. His presence was enough to help get the proceedings on track. In 1787 the final draft of the United States Constitution was signed, but not ratified until the next year.

Father of Our Country

Of course there was an important office to fill—that of president of the United States. Washington was naturally the popular choice, much to his chagrin and reluctance.

Only the Electoral College voted in the first presidential election. The voters in the states picked these men to represent them. Washington won easily, with John Adams coming in second. In the early presidential elections, the man with the second largest number of votes became the vice president. And so the "father of our country" became the first president of the United States. In his inaugural address, Washington spoke with deep humility and spirituality about the undertaking before him:

In tendering this homage to the Great Author of every public and private good, I assure myself that it expresses your sentiments not less than my own, nor those of my fellow-citizens at large less than either. No people can be bound to acknowledge and adore the Invisible Hand which conducts the affairs of men more than those of the United States. Every step by which they have advanced to the character of an independent nation seems to have been distinguished by some token of providential agency; and in the important revolution just accomplished in the system of their united government the tranquil deliberations and voluntary consent of so many distinct communities from which the event has resulted can not be compared with the means by which most governments have been established without some return of pious gratitude, along with an humble anticipation of the future blessings which the past seem to presage.

Washington was very wary of fiddling with the Constitution. He did not see it as a "work in progress," as some contemporary politicians have called it. There was a movement to insert a very specific Bill of Rights, which ultimately happened. The Bill of Rights are the first ten amendments to the Constitution, and we should be very glad that they are there.

Amendment I

Congress shall make no law respecting an establishment of religion, or prohibiting the free exercise thereof; or abridging the freedom of speech, or of the press; or the right of the people peaceably to assemble, and to petition the Government for a redress of grievances.

Amendment II

A well regulated Militia, being necessary to the security of a free State, the right of the people to keep and bear Arms, shall not be infringed.

Amendment III

No Soldier shall, in time of peace be quartered in any house, without the consent of the Owner, nor in time of war, but in a manner to be prescribed by law.

Amendment IV

The right of the people to be secure in their persons, houses, papers, and effects, against unreasonable searches and seizures, shall not be violated, and no Warrants shall issue, but upon probable cause, supported by Oath or affirmation, and particularly describing the place to be searched, and the persons or things to be seized.

Amendment V

No person shall be held to answer for a capital, or otherwise infamous crime, unless on a presentment or indictment of a Grand Jury, except in cases arising in the land or naval forces, or in the Militia, when in actual service in time of War or public danger; nor shall any person be subject for the same offence to be twice put in jeopardy of life or limb; nor shall be compelled in any criminal case to be a witness against himself, nor be deprived of life, liberty, or property, without due process of law; nor shall private property be taken for public use, without just compensation.

Amendment VI

In all criminal prosecutions, the accused shall enjoy the right to a speedy and public trial, by an impartial jury of the State and district wherein the crime shall have been committed, which district shall have been previously ascertained by law, and to be informed of the nature and cause of the accusation; to be confronted with the witnesses against him; to have compulsory process for obtaining witnesses in his favor, and to have the Assistance of Counsel for his defence.

Amendment VII

In suits at common law, where the value in controversy shall exceed twenty dollars, the right of trial by jury shall be preserved, and no fact tried by a jury, shall be otherwise reexamined in any

Court of the United States, than according to the rules of the common law.

Amendment VIII

Excessive bail shall not be required, nor excessive fines imposed, nor cruel and unusual punishments inflicted.

Amendment IX

The enumeration in the Constitution, of certain rights, shall not be construed to deny or disparage others retained by the people.

Amendment X

The powers not delegated to the United States by the Constitution, nor prohibited by it to the States, are reserved to the States.

The early years of America were a rocky road of rivalries and growing pains. Even then there was a competition and hostility between North and South, which would explode sixty-plus years later in the Civil War. Washington saw the rivalry and clashing ideologies of Thomas Jefferson and Alexander Hamilton as dangerous and divisive. This was actually the beginning of the two-party system (with some short-lived third and fourth parties).

FACTS

Washington, unlike most of his successors, genuinely wanted to be a one-term president, but he realized that his calming presence was needed to maintain stability during this national infancy. His even temper and sound judgment helped America through its growing pains.

Washington served a second term, and the rough spots and kinks continued to be worked out of the government. He finally got to deliver what he felt was a long overdue farewell address. The address is famous for its admonition to "avoid foreign entanglements," but that phrase is not used. What he actually said was:

> Observe good faith and justice toward all nations. Cultivate peace and harmony with all. Religion and morality enjoin this conduct, and can it be that good policy does not equally enjoin it? It will be worthy of a free, enlightened, and at no distant period a great nation to give to mankind the magnanimous and too novel example of a people always guided by an exalted justice and benevolence.
>
> Why forego the advantages of so peculiar a situation? Why quit our own to stand upon foreign ground? Why, by interweaving our destiny with that of any part of Europe, entangle our peace and prosperity in the toils of European ambition, rivalship, interest, humor, or caprice? It is our true policy to steer clear of permanent alliances with any portion of the foreign world, so far, I mean, as we are now at liberty to do it; for let me not be understood as capable of patronizing infidelity to existing engagements. I hold the maxim no less applicable to public than to private affairs that honesty is always the best policy. I repeat, therefore, let those engagements be observed in their genuine sense, but in my opinion it is unnecessary and would be unwise to extend them.

Sadly, George Washington lived only two years after leaving office. He became ill and was treated by the then common practice of "blood-letting," which involved large withdrawals of blood in the hope of regulating the body's "humours." This loss of blood may have led to his death. Needless to say, he was mourned and eulogized as the first American hero. During his first inaugural address, John Adams—Washington's vice president and successor—praised him in life:

> Such is the amiable and interesting system of government (and such are some of the abuses to which it may be exposed) which the people of America have exhibited to the admiration and

anxiety of the wise and virtuous of all nations for eight years under the administration of a citizen who, by a long course of great actions, regulated by prudence, justice, temperance, and fortitude, conducting a people inspired with the same virtues and animated with the same ardent patriotism and love of liberty to independence and peace, to increasing wealth and unexampled prosperity, has merited the gratitude of his fellow-citizens, commanded the highest praises of foreign nations, and secured immortal glory with posterity.

In that retirement which is his voluntary choice may he long live to enjoy the delicious recollection of his services, the gratitude of mankind, the happy fruits of them to himself and the world, which are daily increasing, and that splendid prospect of the future fortunes of this country which is opening from year to year. His name may be still a rampart, and the knowledge that he lives a bulwark, against all open or secret enemies of his country's peace.

John Adams

John Adams (1735–1826) often does not receive his due as one of the great Americans of his time. George Washington is the stalwart "father of our country." Ben Franklin was the flamboyant genius. Thomas Jefferson was the agrarian egalitarian. Adams is often thought of as a cantankerous fusspot who had a failed presidency, in which he employed some very undemocratic practices. There is much more to the man than this narrow view.

Another Call for Independence

Adams was a New England Yankee who considered entering the religious life before going to Harvard and studying law. His marriage to Abigail Smith, his "dearest friend," as they called each other, lasted fifty-four years. Of their five children, their son John Quincy Adams also went on to become president.

Adams was opposed to the unfair practices the British government imposed on the colonies, but he stopped short of armed insurrection in his earlier years. In fact, one of his earlier claims to fame was as the defense attorney for the British soldiers involved in the Boston Massacre of 1770. Adams supported the action taken by the men who initiated the Boston Tea Party in 1773, and from then on, he was one of the loudest voices calling for independence. He went to Philadelphia as one of the Massachusetts delegates to the Continental Congress in 1774.

Adams was a member of the Declaration Committee, which also included Thomas Jefferson, Benjamin Franklin, Roger Sherman, and Robert R. Livingston. Jefferson was the man selected to write the document, and after heated debate and some tweaking, the Declaration of Independence was ratified and signed.

FACTS

During much of the Revolutionary War, Adams, like Franklin, was on diplomatic missions in France. There had always been animosity between England and France, and America needed all the help it could get to defeat the mighty British Empire.

Adams, Ben Franklin, and John Jay were the representatives who brokered the Treaty of Paris, which officially ended the war. America was a new nation. Adams was the first vice president of the United States, serving under George Washington for eight years.

The Adams Presidency

Adams was elected president and Thomas Jefferson was his vice president. Political parties did not yet exist, but there were certainly differences of political opinion. Adams and Jefferson were of opposing ideologies and did not function well as a team. The two Founding Fathers were not as chummy as president and vice president as they were in the days when they had a common enemy.

Adams expressed his vision of an ideal America in this section from his inaugural address. Not only is it a distillation of his philosophy, it is also one of the longest sentences ever written (just try reading it aloud!). One assumes he paused for applause or to catch his breath from time to time.

> On this subject it might become me better to be silent or to speak with diffidence; but as something may be expected, the occasion, I hope, will be admitted as an apology if I venture to say that if a preference, upon principle, of a free republican government, formed upon long and serious reflection, after a diligent and impartial inquiry after truth; if an attachment to the Constitution of the United States, and a conscientious determination to support it until it shall be altered by the judgments and wishes of the people, expressed in the mode prescribed in it; if a respectful attention to the constitutions of the individual States and a constant caution and delicacy toward the State governments; if an equal and impartial regard to the rights, interest, honor, and happiness of all the States in the Union, without preference or regard to a northern or southern, an eastern or western, position, their various political opinions on unessential points or their personal attachments; if a love of virtuous men of all parties and denominations; if a love of science and letters and a wish to patronize every rational effort to encourage schools, colleges, universities, academies, and every institution for propagating knowledge, virtue, and religion among all classes of the people, not only for their benign influence on the happiness of life in all its stages and classes, and of society in all its forms, but as the only means of preserving our Constitution from its natural enemies, the spirit of sophistry, the spirit of party, the spirit of intrigue, the profligacy of corruption, and the pestilence of foreign influence, which is the angel of destruction to elective governments; if a love of equal laws, of justice, and humanity in the interior administration; if an inclination to improve agriculture, commerce, and manufacturers for necessity, convenience, and defense; if a spirit of equity and humanity toward the aboriginal nations of America, and a disposition to meliorate their condition by inclining them to be more friendly to us, and our citizens to be more friendly to them; if an inflexible

determination to maintain peace and inviolable faith with all nations, and that system of neutrality and impartiality among the belligerent powers of Europe which has been adopted by this Government and so solemnly sanctioned by both Houses of Congress and applauded by the legislatures of the States and the public opinion, until it shall be otherwise ordained by Congress; if a personal esteem for the French nation, formed in a residence of seven years chiefly among them, and a sincere desire to preserve the friendship which has been so much for the honor and interest of both nations; if, while the conscious honor and integrity of the people of America and the internal sentiment of their own power and energies must be preserved, an earnest endeavor to investigate every just cause and remove every colorable pretense of complaint; if an intention to pursue by amicable negotiation a reparation for the injuries that have been committed on the commerce of our fellow-citizens by whatever nation, and if success can not be obtained, to lay the facts before the Legislature, that they may consider what further measures the honor and interest of the Government and its constituents demand; if a resolution to do justice as far as may depend upon me, at all times and to all nations, and maintain peace, friendship, and benevolence with all the world; if an unshaken confidence in the honor, spirit, and resources of the American people, on which I have so often hazarded my all and never been deceived; if elevated ideas of the high destinies of this country and of my own duties toward it, founded on a knowledge of the moral principles and intellectual improvements of the people deeply engraven on my mind in early life, and not obscured but exalted by experience and age; and, with humble reverence, I feel it to be my duty to add, if a veneration for the religion of a people who profess and call themselves Christians, and a fixed resolution to consider a decent respect for Christianity among the best recommendations for the public service, can enable me in any degree to comply with your wishes, it shall be my strenuous endeavor that this sagacious injunction of the two Houses shall not be without effect.

A Tarnished Reputation

The presidency of John Adams cannot be called a successful one. A number of scandals and some controversial actions stained his legacy, including The United States' undeclared naval war with France, prompted by the XYZ Affair.

The French were, in essence, trying to extort money from the United States though a bribe to the French foreign minister, Charles Talleyrand. Adams got the news but elected to keep it a secret. Adams was sour on the French after seeing the bloody mess they made of their revolution. Mob rule run amok was as horrific as any atrocities committed by the monarchy. Jefferson, however, was a Francophile who turned a blind eye to the carnage of the French revolution. Jefferson's followers accused Adams of not releasing information that would have cast France in a positive light. Actually, he was doing France a favor by not releasing any information.

When Adams finally released the information to the public, the only thing he censored was the names of the participants, calling them X, Y, and Z. Ambitious Alexander Hamilton, who despised Jefferson, called for war. The army and navy were strengthened. Adams took matters into his own hands and, without consulting his cabinet, sent an ambassador to France. As a result, his own party, the Federalists, turned against him. Although John Adams had stopped a full-blown war with France, his actions satisfied neither his opponents nor his own team.

Signing the Alien and Sedition Acts was the biggest blow to Adams's reputation. The acts struck at the heart of the American tradition—albeit a new tradition at that time—of freedom of speech. The Federalists faced bitter criticism because of their opposition to France. Although most of the criticism came from Americans, some of the critics were French. The Alien and Sedition Acts were designed to limit this criticism. These acts granted the president the power to banish foreigners with a simple order and also made the act of criticizing the government, the president, or Congress a crime. Naturally, this created quite an uproar and helped make John Adams a one-term president.

The Federalists did not stand by Adams and he lost the election. His problematic presidency had also soured popular opinion toward him. Adams left the public square a bitter man. In the last twenty-five years of his life, though, his reputation was rehabilitated. In 1812 his rift with Jefferson was healed, and they became pen pals. Adams was able to live to see his son become the sixth president.

ESSENTIALS

Believe it or not, John Adams and Thomas Jefferson died on the same day: July 4, 1826, fifty years to the day after they signed the Declaration of Independence. John Adams's last words were "Thomas Jefferson still survives," but Jefferson had died a few hours earlier. This was a fitting closure to two amazing and influential lives.

John Adams, the forgotten and misunderstood Founding Father, was a wise man and his philosophy of government helped make America a great nation. His essay, "On Government," does not have the literary punch of the Declaration of Independence, but it still expresses a philosophy of government that celebrates life, liberty, and the pursuit of happiness—a philosophy that the citizens who enjoy the benefits of the legacy of the Founding Fathers should never take for granted:

> We ought to consider what is the end of government, before we determine which is the best form. Upon this point all speculative politicians will agree, that the happiness of society is the end of government, as all divines and moral philosophers will agree that the happiness of the individual is the end of man. From this principle it will follow, that the form of government which communicates ease, comfort, security, or, in one word, happiness, to the greatest number of persons, and in the greatest degree, is the best.
>
> All sober inquirers after truth, ancient and modern, pagan and Christian, have declared that the happiness of man, as well as his dignity, consists in virtue. Confucius, Zoroaster, Socrates, Mahomet, not to mention authorities really sacred, have agreed in this.
>
> If there is a form of government, then, whose principle and foundation is virtue, will not every sober man acknowledge it better calculated to promote the general happiness than any other form?

Fear is the foundation of most governments; but it is so sordid and brutal a passion, and renders men in whose breasts it predominates so stupid and miserable, that Americans will not be likely to approve of any political institution which is founded on it.

Honor is truly sacred, but holds a lower rank in the scale of moral excellence than virtue. Indeed, the former is but a part of the latter, and consequently has not equal pretensions to support a frame of government productive of human happiness.

The foundation of every government is some principle or passion in the minds of the people. The noblest principles and most generous affections in our nature, then, have the fairest chance to support the noblest and most generous models of government.

Thomas Jefferson

Like most of the Founding Fathers, Thomas Jefferson (1743–1826) was more than simply a politician. He was a true Renaissance man whose interests included science, philosophy, farming, and music; he even played the violin. He was an architect and also considered the best writer of the founders, if not of the time. Jefferson became the third president, and the nation saw great expansion during his two terms as chief executive.

The Declaration of Independence

Jefferson was a wealthy Virginian and, as a member of the Continental Congress, was chosen to write the Declaration of Independence. He based the document on the principles espoused by British philosopher John Locke. Locke rejected the tried and true European belief in the divine right of kings. Kings were to be obeyed without question because God had deemed it so. Locke believed that freedom, not blind fealty to a monarch, was the inalienable right of all humankind. Freedom comes from God and therefore cannot be arbitrarily taken and given by mere mortals. Jefferson was greatly influenced by these views, and the United States of America is the first and most successful example of Locke's principles put into practice.

Here is an abridged version of the document:

The Declaration of Independence
IN CONGRESS, July 4, 1776.

The unanimous Declaration of the thirteen united States of America,

When in the Course of human events, it becomes necessary for one people to dissolve the political bands which have connected them with another, and to assume among the powers of the earth, the separate and equal station to which the Laws of Nature and of Nature's God entitle them, a decent respect to the opinions of mankind requires that they should declare the causes which impel them to the separation.

We hold these truths to be self-evident, that all men are created equal, that they are endowed by their Creator with certain unalienable Rights, that among these are Life, Liberty and the pursuit of Happiness.—That to secure these rights, Governments are instituted among Men, deriving their just powers from the consent of the governed,—That whenever any Form of Government becomes destructive of these ends, it is the Right of the People to alter or to abolish it, and to institute new Government, laying its foundation on such principles and organizing its powers in such form, as to them shall seem most likely to effect their Safety and Happiness. Prudence, indeed, will dictate that Governments long established should not be changed for light and transient causes; and accordingly all experience hath shewn, that mankind are more disposed to suffer, while evils are sufferable, than to right themselves by abolishing the forms to which they are accustomed. But when a long train of abuses and usurpations, pursuing invariably the same Object evinces a design to reduce them under absolute Despotism, it is their right, it is their duty, to throw off such Government, and to provide new Guards for their future security.—Such has been the patient sufferance of these Colonies;

and such is now the necessity which constrains them to alter their former Systems of Government. The history of the present King of Great Britain is a history of repeated injuries and usurpations, all having in direct object the establishment of an absolute Tyranny over these States. . . .

In every stage of these Oppressions We have Petitioned for Redress in the most humble terms: Our repeated Petitions have been answered only by repeated injury. A Prince whose character is thus marked by every act which may define a Tyrant, is unfit to be the ruler of a free people.

Nor have We been wanting in attentions to our British brethren. We have warned them from time to time of attempts by their legislature to extend an unwarrantable jurisdiction over us. We have reminded them of the circumstances of our emigration and settlement here. We have appealed to their native justice and magnanimity, and we have conjured them by the ties of our common kindred to disavow these usurpations, which, would inevitably interrupt our connections and correspondence. They too have been deaf to the voice of justice and of consanguinity. We must, therefore, acquiesce in the necessity, which denounces our Separation, and hold them, as we hold the rest of mankind, Enemies in War, in Peace Friends.

We, therefore, the Representatives of the united States of America, in General Congress, Assembled, appealing to the Supreme Judge of the world for the rectitude of our intentions, do, in the Name, and by Authority of the good People of these Colonies, solemnly publish and declare, That these United Colonies are, and of Right ought to be Free and Independent States; that they are Absolved from all Allegiance to the British Crown, and that all political connection between them and the State of Great Britain, is and ought to be totally dissolved; and that as Free and Independent States, they have full Power to levy War, conclude Peace, contract Alliances, establish Commerce, and to do all other Acts and Things which Independent States may of right do. And for the support of this Declaration, with a firm reliance on the protection of divine Providence, we mutually pledge to each other our Lives, our Fortunes and our sacred Honor.

The version of the Declaration of Independence that was signed on July 4, 1776, was not the first draft of the document as written by Jefferson. John Adams, Ben Franklin, and other members of the Declaration Committee added their two cents' worth, and it was debated in Congress. A passage denouncing slavery was removed to gain the cooperation of the South. Jefferson spoke eloquently about the evils of slavery. Yet he owned many slaves, and it is generally accepted that he fathered children with at least one, Sally Hemmings, who was his mistress after the death of his wife.

ALERT

Hypocrisy alert! Jefferson compiled his musings into a collection called *Notes on the State of Virginia.* It was part natural history, part sociocultural study, and part political tract. The book was a popular read in America and Europe. In it he reiterated his disdain for slavery, denouncing it as evil, but he still did not free his own slaves.

Jefferson briefly left public life after the war started. He retreated to his plantation, called Monticello, and worked the land and invented the swivel chair and the dumbwaiter. Like Benjamin Franklin, Jefferson was a multifaceted individual who was as good with his hands as he was with his mind. He tried to introduce new crops to his fields, including orange trees. He was a stargazer and a voracious reader of philosophy. He was also a very private person. After the death of his first wife, he burned their entire correspondence.

Farmer, Inventor, Writer, Politician

Fellow Virginian George Washington exhorted Jefferson and other prominent Americans not to retire into the background during those revolutionary times. Jefferson took Washington's words to heart. He re-entered the public arena and was elected governor of Virginia.

After the War of Independence ended and America was a sovereign nation, Jefferson served as a diplomat in France, working with colleagues

Thomas
Jefferson

Adams and Franklin. France had given invaluable support to America during the war, and now the new nation sought to make nice with all the powers of Europe, in peace and in mutually beneficial capitalist endeavors.

Jefferson came to a strong sense of "there's no place like home" during his European stay. He did laud the efforts of the French in their own revolution, which was a bloody affair. A democracy did not emerge from the rubble and the terrors and the awful shadow of the guillotine. Jefferson was abroad during the Constitutional Convention. He returned to the United States and was offered the position of secretary of state in George Washington's presidency.

FACTS

Jefferson become vice president in 1796, serving under his friend and now, more importantly, political rival John Adams. Despite their years of friendship, Adams and Jefferson were at political odds during those years.

Embroiled in the volatile politics of a fledgling government, Jefferson found an enemy in Alexander Hamilton. (There's a picture of Hamilton on every ten-dollar bill.) Jefferson's ideal was an agrarian utopia, a farming culture with minimal government interference. Hamilton had an urban mentality and favored a powerful federal government.

These two rivals embodied the first American political parties. Hamilton's camp became known as the Federalists; Jefferson's followers became known as the Republicans, later known as the Democratic-Republican Party. Hamilton's Federalists resemble the Republicans of today; Jefferson's group was more like the Democrats. This is not a precise analogy, though the rancor and name-calling between the two is very similar. The Federalists were accused of being the party of the rich and secretly plotting to create a royal monarchy of the American ruling class. And Jefferson was accused of being an atheistic rabble-rouser.

Conflicts and Accomplishments

Thomas Jefferson was elected president in the hotly contested election of 1800. Jefferson and Aaron Burr tied with seventy-three electoral votes, while Adams came in third. Although Burr was his party's vice-presidential choice, his tie with Jefferson created a crisis, because the members of the Electoral College did not specify whether their votes were for president or vice president.

The election went to the House of Representatives, where it was deadlocked. Like the election 200 years later, both Jefferson and Burr claimed that they should be the president. Alexander Hamilton threw his support to Jefferson. Though Hamilton hated Jefferson, he hated Burr even more. Ironically, these two men would have a duel a couple of years later and Burr would kill Hamilton. Eventually the deadlock was broken. After thirty-six ballots, in which neither candidate could achieve a majority, Jefferson won and Burr became the vice president.

In Jefferson's inaugural address, he tried to smooth ruffled feathers. He called for unity while expressing his philosophy. Here are a few paragraphs frm his address.

> Called upon to undertake the duties of the first executive office of our country, I avail myself of the presence of that portion of my fellow-citizens which is here assembled to express my grateful thanks for the favor with which they have been pleased to look toward me, to declare a sincere consciousness that the task is above my talents, and that I approach it with those anxious and awful presentiments which the greatness of the charge and the weakness of my powers so justly inspire.
>
> Utterly, indeed, should I despair did not the presence of many whom I here see remind me that in the other high authorities provided by our Constitution I shall find resources of wisdom, of virtue, and of zeal on which to rely under all difficulties. To you,

then, gentlemen, who are charged with the sovereign functions of legislation, and to those associated with you, I look with encouragement for that guidance and support which may enable us to steer with safety the vessel in which we are all embarked amidst the conflicting elements of a troubled world . . .

All, too, will bear in mind this sacred principle, that though the will of the majority is in all cases to prevail, that will to be rightful must be reasonable; that the minority possess their equal rights, which equal law must protect, and to violate would be oppression. Let us, then, fellow-citizens, unite with one heart and one mind. Let us restore to social intercourse that harmony and affection without which liberty and even life itself are but dreary things. And let us reflect that, having banished from our land that religious intolerance under which mankind so long bled and suffered, we have yet gained little if we countenance a political intolerance as despotic, as wicked, and capable of as bitter and bloody persecutions. During the throes and convulsions of the ancient world, during the agonizing spasms of infuriated man, seeking through blood and slaughter his long-lost liberty, it was not wonderful that the agitation of the billows should reach even this distant and peaceful shore; that this should be more felt and feared by some and less by others, and should divide opinions as to measures of safety. But every difference of opinion is not a difference of principle. We have called by different names brethren of the same principle. We are all Republicans, we are all Federalists.

ESSENTIALS

The more things change, the more they remain the same, as the saying goes. Just as there was a disputed election in 1800 and 2000, so too there was a war against terrorism in Jefferson's first term. In those days it took the form of piracy on the high seas.

If there be any among us who would wish to dissolve this Union or to change its republican form, let them stand undisturbed as monuments of the safety with which error of opinion may be tolerated where reason is left free to combat it.

I know, indeed, that some honest men fear that a republican government can not be strong, that this Government is not strong enough; but would the honest patriot, in the full tide of successful experiment, abandon a government which has so far kept us free and firm on the theoretic and visionary fear that this Government, the world's best hope, may by possibility want energy to preserve itself? I trust not. I believe this, on the contrary, the strongest Government on earth . . .

Equal and exact justice to all men, of whatever state or persuasion, religious or political; peace, commerce, and honest friendship with all nations . . .

I shall often go wrong through defect of judgment. When right, I shall often be thought wrong by those whose positions will not command a view of the whole ground. I ask your indulgence for my own errors, which will never be intentional, and your support against the errors of others, who may condemn what they would not if seen in all its parts . . .

John Adams did not attend the inauguration.

FACTS

Prior to the Louisiana Purchase, Jefferson authorized the Lewis and Clark expedition. Everyone knew there was a great unknown part of the continent they called home and they wanted to get a grasp of its grandeur. The intrepid explorers embarked under the guise of a nature trip, but of course national expansion was the aim.

The Barbary pirates were Muslims from North Africa's Barbary Coast. The potentate of Tripoli, in what is now Libya, demanded tribute from European and American ships to sail unmolested in their waters. When Jefferson was ambassador to France, he tried to build a European and American coalition to smoke out the Barbary pirates, get them on the run, and bring them to justice. After many seafaring skirmishes, the pasha of Tripoli sued for peace. The line from the Marine Corps anthem, "to the shores of Tripoli," refers to this conflict.

One of the greatest accomplishments of the Jefferson presidency was the Louisiana Purchase. America at that time was just the Northeast, with fledgling forays into the undiscovered country. The territory owned by France was a massive chunk of the North American continent: from the Gulf of Mexico to the Canadian border and from the Mississippi River to the Rocky Mountains. Napoleon Bonaparte was strapped for cash and needed to fund his efforts to conquer the world. Jefferson seized the opportunity and the United States gained an enormous chunk of land for a mere $15 million.

ESSENTIALS

Jefferson was most proud of founding the University of Virginia in 1825. He designed the buildings and insisted that it make itself welcome to the scions of the aristocracy. Scholarships were also offered to the academically gifted poor folks.

Jefferson was elected to a second term in 1804, without the notorious Aaron Burr, who was replaced by Governor George Clinton of New York. There was little acrimony this time around, and Jefferson won by a landslide. Like his Washington, he elected not to run for a third term. He, too, wanted to return to his Virginia farm and enjoy a pleasant and productive retirement.

Both Jefferson and Adams died on the same day: July 4, 1826, fifty years to the day after they signed the Declaration of Independence. Jefferson wrote his own epitaph. It was short and sweet, singling out the things that he was most proud of in his long and eventful life:

Here was buried
Thomas Jefferson
Author of the Declaration of American Independence
Of the Statute of Virginia for Religious Freedom
And Father of the University of Virginia

Chapter 12
Political Thinkers

Consider the notable leaders, politicians, and strategists who came to power during perilous times, and through political skill and the sheer force of their dynamic personalities, served their country admirably. And in the case of Winston Churchill, it can be argued that he literally saved the planet.

Elizabeth I

Elizabeth I (1533–1603) was the queen of England from 1558 until 1603. She was the daughter of Henry VIII and his second wife, Anne Boleyn, who got the ax (quite literally) for alleged infidelity. Elizabeth was the first woman to have any staying power on the throne, the others dying young of both natural and unnatural causes. She triumphed in a man's world in the days when the glass ceiling was built of a sturdier, far more impenetrable substance.

Young Elizabeth

Elizabeth began life as an unwanted child. Those were the days when a male heir was the preferred choice, particularly among royalty. A king wanted a son to continue the monarchy, and the king's wife wanted a son to stay in His Majesty's good graces, and often to save her head. Anne Boleyn lost her head when Elizabeth was only two years old, and the bombastic King Henry was an absentee dad thereafter. The young princess was sent off to be raised by relatives, unwelcome in King Henry's court.

ESSENTIALS

England broke from the Vatican in Rome when the pope refused to grant Henry VIII a divorce from his first wife, Catherine of Aragon. Thus a Protestant sect, the Church of England, was formed so a rich guy could marry a trophy wife. Religions have been founded for stranger reasons.

She was raised a Protestant in the tumultuous age of the Protestant Reformation. The Catholic Church was under the gun by clerical rebels such as Martin Luther (see Chapter 8) and John Calvin. Elizabeth received a better education than most women of her day who scarcely received any at all. She got the same schooling that a young nobleman would have received, and she proved to be gifted student. She was, however, given little hope of ever ascending to the throne. She had a half brother and half sister ahead of her in the line of succession.

When Henry VIII died, his nine-year-old son Edward assumed the throne, but he died young. He was from a later marriage; Henry ultimately had six wives before he shuffled off this mortal coil. Elizabeth's half-sister

Elizabeth I

Mary came to power after that, and the political machinations ensued. Mary was a Catholic in an increasingly Protestant land. She was married to the king of Spain, a Catholic country. "Bloody Mary," as she came to be known, persecuted Protestants while they conspired against her.

Elizabeth was imprisoned for a time in the notorious Tower of London; she was charged with conspiring against the queen in an attempted coup. Elizabeth was later released, yet remained under the watchful eye of the queen's operatives. Queen Mary could not bring herself to execute her half-sister, as she was urged to do by many in her court. Mary's untimely death brought Elizabeth to the throne in 1558; most people did not think she would last. Not only did she survive, by the time she died, England had become the premier power in the known world.

Reforms and Conspiracies

Elizabeth's policies may seem draconian by today's sensitive standards, but hers was a world in transition, on a slow, consistent course from barbarism toward civility. Laws like establishing workhouses and making begging a crime punishable by a tad more than a slap on the wrist would be roundly condemned today.

This was an age when life was nasty, brutish, and short for the overwhelming majority of the populace. Diseases still wiped out thousands at a clip. Elizabeth enacted numerous economic reforms that were neither warm nor fuzzy by any stretch of the imagination, but they did improve the status quo. Something akin to the gold standard was enacted, which made the British currency more stable. Trade with other nations was expanded. The New World of the Americas was colonized and its natural resources were aggressively exploited.

Elizabeth sought to achieve religious harmony in England. The Catholics lost the battle and the Protestant Church of England became the official religion. Constant conspiring by Catholics, usually with the backing of France, Spain, and the Vatican itself, did not inspire in Elizabeth a "can't we all just get along" philosophy. Mary, Queen of Scots, Elizabeth's cousin, was often at the center of these conspiracies, and was eventually executed. Elizabeth has been considered harsh in her lack of religious tolerance, but if you are aware that a group of people is constantly plotting your death, it is not easy to turn the other cheek.

FACTS

For a tiny island nation, the British Empire once had tentacles that spread across the globe. "The sun never sets on the British Empire" was the rather cocky boast for many centuries, and Elizabeth I was largely responsible.

The Puritans, radical Protestants, also came into conflict with the queen, but most of them left the country and landed at Plymouth Rock. A little later, they had the first Thanksgiving, and as a result we have a four-day weekend in November. Such are the vicissitudes of history.

The Catholic conspiracies came to an end with a "Protestant wind." After years of political and military conflicts, Spain launched its formidable Armada against England. The Spanish fleet was considered unbeatable, yet a combination of weather and British intrepidity sent many to the bottom of the English Channel. From that moment forward, supremacy over the seven seas belonged to the British.

The Virgin Queen

Throughout her forty-five-year reign, one of the biggest problems Elizabeth faced was something over which she had no control—her gender. This was not a woman's world and she encountered prejudice and problems as a result. She was constantly being exhorted to marry and produce an heir. To do so would have diminished her power because for the most part royalty only married royalty in those days. Thus her personal freedom and the sovereignty of her nation would have been dramatically diminished. She surrounded herself with politically astute, influential men in what was called her Privy Council, but as the queen, hers was the last word on the subject. And she proved she could play with the big boys.

The downside of her independence was that she never produced an heir and was the last Tudor to sit upon the throne of England. Her nickname, the "Virgin Queen," was given to her because she never married. Anyone who has seen the Cate Blanchett movie *Elizabeth* knows that she decided to "become" a virgin again after a torrid affair with a pantalooned pretty boy. (She apparently concurred with sex therapist Dr. Ruth Westheimer, who says the most important sexual organ is the brain.) When Elizabeth died, her Scottish cousin became James I. The Queen was dead; long live the King.

Winston Churchill

Sir Winston Leonard Spencer Churchill (1874–1965) was a personification of his age. He was born into Victorian England, the period of the late nineteenth century when the British Empire was at the top of its game in power and influence. But beneath every golden age lies a sleazy underbelly. Much of England's wealth was derived from exploiting the natural resources of other people's lands, while native people had to deal with strange invaders. In London, then the unofficial capital of the Western world, squalor and disease, along with Jack the Ripper, prowled the foggy streets.

With Churchill's death, the sun set on the British Empire. Former colonies were gaining independence, and Britain was eclipsed by the new Western superpower, the United States. Churchill was born into an empire and many of his actions contributed to the end of an empire, but in the process, he helped save the world from total, irreversible disaster.

Coming of Age

Winston Churchill came from a world of privilege. He was raised in a palace called Blenheim, named for a battle in which an ancestor had scored a big victory. His father was Lord Randolph Henry Spencer

Churchill, an aristocrat and politician. His mother was an American named Jennie Jerome, the daughter of a member of a group that saw themselves as the American aristocracy—the Wall Street crowd.

Churchill's parents were both absentee. He was sent to boarding schools and his letters home poignantly chronicle a lonely little boy pleading in vain for his parents' attention. He was also a weak, sickly child with a speech impediment. Children are cruel in every corner of the world, but notoriously so in all-male British boarding schools. Feeling ignored, unloved, and bullied, Churchill's character was forged.

QUESTIONS?

Can that which does not kill you really make you stronger? In Winston Churchill's case, it can. Unbowed by life's slings and arrows, the pudgy little fellow with a lisp became a tenacious bulldog. Many years later, when the time came that the world needed a bulldog to stand between civilization and the abyss of barbarism, Churchill was there.

Churchill went into the army after school, and worked as a journalist when on leave. His military and journalistic travels took him to Cuba, India, Egypt, and South Africa. He saw action many times and got a macho thrill from combat. In South Africa, during the Boer War (which pitted the Dutch against the British, two European nations fighting over somebody else's property), Churchill the journalist was captured by the enemy and made a prisoner of war. He escaped and rode a bicycle through enemy territory, a capital offense had he been caught. This adventure made him a hero back home and he was elected to the House of Commons in the British Parliament.

Lord of the Admiralty

Churchill was a controversial MP (member of Parliament), and during his long career switched political parties more than once. He married Clementine Ogilvy Hozier in 1908. During World War I, Churchill was a lord of the admiralty, responsible for keeping the British navy shipshape. He modernized the fleet in preparation for the modern age of warfare that the twentieth century would bring. Churchill was also largely responsible for helping to make the tank a mainstay of modern armies.

World War I is famous for its trench warfare. Opposing sides dug ditches in the muddy European landscape, from which they could shoot and gas each other. The armies often remained stagnant for interminable periods or advanced literally inch-by-inch and yard-by-yard. Churchill tried a daring back-door move, but it backfired with disastrous results to the soldiers involved and Churchill's reputation.

Churchill had proposed a naval operation to clear the Dardanelles Strait that was controlled by the Turkish Ottoman Empire. Access to this water route to Russia would enable the British to supply their Russian allies and defeat the Turks. The naval campaign failed and Churchill agreed to a land assault on the Gallipoli Peninsula. It was an unmitigated disaster, and Churchill bore the brunt of the blame. Many of the troops slaughtered were Australian. In fact, an early Mel Gibson movie called *Gallipoli* chronicles this military blunder.

ESSENTIALS

Churchill had a creative life outside politics. The legendary Picasso once took a look at some of Churchill's paintings and deemed them quite good. Churchill was awarded the Nobel Prize for Literature in 1953 for his prolific body of nonfiction and history.

Churchill's political career went into a tailspin after the Dardanelles disaster. He had periodic, severe bouts of depression. He referred to his melancholia as "the black dog." Churchill spent the 1930s in semi-retirement, living in his country home and generating income through writing efforts and painting as a hobby.

Despite the fact that he could live in comfort and indulge his creative avocations, Churchill continued to feel bitter and depressed. He wanted to be in the political arena. On a more ominous note, his warnings about a second world war were ignored, and he was derided as an alarmist and an extremist. In the 1920s, Churchill read a book by a disgruntled and disturbed political revolutionary who, with shocking candor, laid out his abhorrent philosophy and his diabolical plans. The book was *Mein Kampf;* the man was Adolf Hitler.

His Finest Hour

In the 1930s, Hitler came to power in Germany and began to snatch pieces of other nations as the great powers of Europe stood by and watched. The policy was called *appeasement,* and as any kid in a schoolyard knows, a bully will escalate his abuse until you finally stand up to him. Neville Chamberlain, the prime minister of England who bent

Winston Churchhill

over backward to appease the ranting tyrant in Berlin, apparently never learned this lesson.

When Chamberlain returned from Berlin waving a piece of paper from Herr Hitler, Churchill was unimpressed. He knew the document was worthless. Churchill was concerned by the buildup of the German air force, called the *Luftwaffe.* He was convinced that it could wage devastating destruction upon England.

Hitler finally crossed the line when he invaded Poland in September 1939, and World War II officially began. Churchill was called back into public service. After more than twenty years, he was again in charge of building up the British navy as a member of his rival Chamberlain's government. The public was less and less enthused by the passive Chamberlain and he finally resigned. At age sixty-five, Winston Churchill's time had come. He was the right man in the right place at the right time. He became prime minister and gave powerful and passionate speeches that rallied the British people. For example:

> You cannot tell from appearances how things will go. Sometimes imagination makes things out far worse than they are; yet without imagination not much can be done. Those people who are imaginative see many more dangers than perhaps exist; certainly many more than will happen; but then they must also pray to be given that extra courage to carry this far-reaching imagination. But for everyone, surely, what we have gone through in this period—I am addressing myself to the School—surely from this period of ten

months this is the lesson: never give in, never give in, never, never, never, never—in nothing, great or small, large or petty— never give in except to convictions of honour and good sense. Never yield to force; never yield to the apparently overwhelming might of the enemy. We stood all alone a year ago, and to many countries it seemed that our account was closed, we were finished. All this tradition of ours, our songs, our School history, this part of the history of this country, were gone and finished and liquidated.

I have nothing to offer but blood, toil, tears and sweat.

We have before us an ordeal of the most grievous kind. We have before us many, many long months of struggle and of suffering. You ask, what is our policy? I can say: It is to wage war, by sea, land and air, with all our might and with all the strength that God can give us; to wage war against a monstrous tyranny, never surpassed in the dark, lamentable catalogue of human crime. That is our policy. You ask, what is our aim? I can answer in one word: It is victory, victory at all costs, victory in spite of all terror, victory, however long and hard the road may be; for without victory, there is no survival. Let that be realised; no survival for the British Empire, no survival for all that the British Empire has stood for, no survival for the urge and impulse of the ages, that mankind will move forward towards its goal. But I take up my task with buoyancy and hope. I feel sure that our cause will not be suffered to fail among men. At this time I feel entitled to claim the aid of all, and I say, "come then, let us go forward together with our united strength."

And this famous speech:

What General Weygand called the Battle of France is over. I expect that the Battle of Britain is about to begin. Upon this battle depends the survival of Christian civilization. Upon it depends our own British life, and the long continuity of our institutions and our Empire. The whole fury and might of the enemy must very soon be turned on us. Hitler knows that he will have to break us in this Island or lose the war. If we can stand up to him, all Europe may be free and the life of the world may move forward into broad, sunlit uplands. But if we fail, then the whole world, including the United States, including all that we have known and cared for, will sink into the abyss of a new Dark Age made more sinister, and perhaps more protracted, by the lights of perverted science. Let us therefore brace ourselves to our duties, and so bear ourselves that, if the British Empire and its Commonwealth last for a thousand years, men will still say, "This was their finest hour."

Churchill and Britain stood alone against the Nazi menace. France fell to the Germans. Churchill could not send the RAF (Royal Air Force), because he knew they would be needed in the inevitable German air war. When France fell, Churchill urged the French to send their navy across the English Channel to Britain to avoid having them fall into German possession. The French refused, so Churchill was obliged to sink the French fleet. Not a politically correct thing to do, but the alternative would have been a dangerous and deadlier German naval threat.

The next phase of the war was the Battle of Britain. Britain was pummeled by the German air force in almost nightly raids that came to be known as the Blitz. Forty thousand civilians lost their lives, half of them in the city of London alone. Britain bravely fought on. What was America doing while all this was going on?

ALERT

Even during World War II, freedom of speech reigned in America. A Catholic priest and popular talk radio host of the day, Father Coughlin, preached fascist sentiments, and a Nazi rally held in New York's Madison Square Garden filled the arena.

America remained neutral during this period of the war. President Franklin Roosevelt sympathized with Churchill and his plight. He did his best to help through legal and other means. But there was a large isolationist movement in America, and some subtle and not-so-subtle Nazi sympathizers.

Roosevelt finagled for the United States to supply Britain with some old ships and planes and financial aid. American's neutrality ended at Pearl Harbor on December 7, 1941, "a date which will live in infamy."

During the war, the balance of power shifted between Churchill and Roosevelt. By the war's end, Great Britain was no longer the pre-eminent world power. The United States and the former Soviet Union emerged from the war as the big boys on the block. It was Churchill, however, who stood alone for a long time against a marauding madman and thwarted his ambitions until the cavalry, in the form of the United States, came onto the scene and helped save the day.

QUESTIONS?

Where did the term Iron Curtain originate?
Churchill the wordsmith coined the phrase *iron curtain* in reference to the wall, both literal and figurative that divided East and West.

Churchill and Roosevelt were at odds over their approach to the Soviet Union. Russia under the tyrant Josef Stalin, who killed more people than Hitler, was originally Germany's ally until Hitler violated a nonaggression treaty and attacked Russia in 1941. Russia then became a member of the Allies (Germany and Italy, and later, Japan, were called the Axis). Churchill did not trust the Russians and warned FDR about them. He believed that they intended to seize much of Eastern Europe after the war, and that their ambition might extend further. Roosevelt ignored Churchill's entreaties, and the postwar world became a forty-year Cold War between the United States and the Soviet Union.

Churchill, the man who saved the world, was actually defeated at the polls in the very last days of the war, between the surrenders of Germany and Japan. The British citizenry had always had a love/hate relationship with him. In the British system, if the prime minister's party is defeated yet he is reelected, he stays in the House of Commons as the head of the opposition party.

In 1951, Churchill was once again prime minister for a less successful tenure. He was knighted by Queen Elizabeth II and became Sir Winston. After resigning in 1955, he continued to be celebrated as a living legend, and became an honorary American citizen. Winston Churchill died in 1965, at the ripe old age of ninety.

Golda Meir

Golda Meir (1898–1978) made a nomadic trek through the twentieth century. Born in Russia, she came of age in America, and later left to help establish a new nation, eventually becoming its first female leader.

In the years before the World War II, many Jewish people, called Zionists, returned to the land of their ancestors with the hope of establishing a homeland. The Jews had been scattered across the globe over the millennia, and they sought to return to the Promised Land and create a nation. In 1948, the nation of Israel was created, and it was immediately attacked by all its neighbors the next day. Contemporary headlines remind us that the region is still a hotbed of violence.

Golda Meir left the United States for Palestine in 1921 and worked to establish the state of Israel. Upon its foundation she held various offices, including ambassador to the Soviet Union, member of parliament (called the Knesset), minister of labor, and minister of foreign affairs. From 1969–1974, she was the prime minister of Israel. It was on her watch that Israel was attacked in 1973. Though she resigned under controversial circumstances (she was criticized for the lack of readiness to handle the surprise attack), she remains a great stateswoman and inspiration for women of all races and faith. Egyptian leader Anwar Sadat, himself a victim of an assassination because of his pursuit of peace, once called Golda Meir, "a mean old lady." But even he, an enemy, came to respect her. Golda Meir died in 1978.

Margaret Thatcher

Margaret Thatcher (b. 1925) was the first woman to be elected prime minister of Great Britain. Educated at Oxford, she entered politics in 1959, when she was elected to the House of Commons as a member of the Conservative party. She served a minister of education under Prime Minister Edward Heath. When the Conservative party fell out of power in 1974, she challenged and defeated Heath, becoming head of the party.

The British parliamentary system is different than the American system in that the entire party of the Prime Minister is in power if he or she is elected. The other party is called the "loyal opposition." The Labour Party is akin in philosophy to the Democratic Party and the Conservatives are ideologically similar to the Republicans. Thatcher brought the Conservatives into power when she became prime minister, serving from 1979–1990.

ESSENTIALS

Thatcher was a fervent anticommunist leader during the same period as her American counterpart, Ronald Reagan. In fact, the Russians nicknamed her "The Iron Lady." They did not mean it as a compliment, but she liked it.

In her first term, she led the Britons to victory in the 1982 war with Argentina over the Falkland Islands, located in the Atlantic close to Argentina, which both claimed as their own. The formerly formidable United Kingdom, on whose empire the sun once never set, tenaciously hung on to this minor possession. Nothing rallies a nation like a war, however minor, and the Falklands affair helped Thatcher gain a second term. In that term, she survived an attack by the Irish Republican Army, who bombed a conference she was attending.

In 1987, Thatcher was elected to an unprecedented third time, making her the first prime minister in the twentieth century to do so. Margaret Thatcher, like Ronald Reagan, had a conservative vision that reshaped her nation. She was an extremely influential figure in twentieth-century British history. In 1990, she was challenged within her own party in large part due to her resistance to embrace what has become the "European Union," the integration of all the Western European nations as essentially one meganation. In her heart, Thatcher probably adhered to the old nationalist adage that "God is an Englishman" and her resistance to the New World Order brought about her resignation.

Her impact and influence remained, however. She was made a member of the House of Lords and became "Dame Thatcher."

Condoleeza Rice

Condoleeza Rice (b. 1954) is the first African-American woman to hold a cabinet post in a presidential administration. She is the Chief Foreign Policy Adviser to George W. Bush. Along with Secretary of State Colin Powell, she is one of two African-Americans in the same administration, and it's worth noting that it's a Republican administration.

Born in Alabama to parents who were teachers, she was a gifted student who followed her parents into academia. Her impressive credentials and expertise in global political science (with particular emphasis on Russia) caught the attention of the Bush family, and she went to work in the administration of George H. W. Bush from 1989–91. She served as the director of Soviet and East European affairs on the National Security Council. She played a pivotal role in policy making during the days when the Soviet Union collapsed and was Bush's go-to gal regarding Russia and Eastern Europe.

When "W." was assembling his team while still running for President in 2000, Condoleezza Rice was a prominent figure in his inner sanctum. Having a woman like Rice on his team may have allayed some of the fears that Bush was a lightweight, and there is no denying the fact that her race was politically beneficial for a Republican president.

Rice has achieved enormous success. She continues to play an active role coaching the president in foreign policy issues. Many Americans are very pleased to know that Bush has such an accomplished and savvy counselor during the difficult days the nation currently faces.

CHAPTER 13
Military Thinkers

Politics and military force have been intimate bedfellows through the centuries. Although it is not fashionable to call a military man a great thinker in this day and age, it is an undeniable fact that great military leaders have, depending on their leanings, helped preserve all that is good in the world or have done their best to destroy it.

Sun-tzu

Even though little is known about the ancient military and political tactician Sun-tzu (544–496 B.C.), he ranks as one of the greatest strategists in his field because he has staying power. People are still reading and studying him thousands of years later. Always popular in political and military circles, he has recently become fashionable in the business world.

The Art of War

Sun-tzu, whose name means "master sun" in Chinese, wrote *The Art of War*, during an age of violent civil war in China. The book is a primer for politicians and military men on the best ways to defeat the enemy. Some say that Napoleon studied the strategies in the book before conquering Europe.

The Art of War starts from the premise that if you are on the battlefield facing your enemy, you have not gotten the point at all. The best way to win a battle is not to have to fight one. Sounds like a paradox? It is. Ancient Chinese secrets are replete with paradoxes. They may seem contradictory but upon closer examination they make sense.

ESSENTIALS

According to Sun-tzu, armed conflict should be the last resort. Many other avenues to victory should be explored before a warrior takes up arms. The true warrior should be able to best his adversary without firing a shot.

The Art of War is structured in a series of question-and-answer sessions covering a variety of topics. Here is a sampling of his shrewd advice, which can be applied to situations other than military matters:

All warfare is based on deception.
Hence, when able to attack, we must seem unable; when using our
forces, we must seem inactive; when we are near, we must make

the enemy believe we are far away; when far away, we must make him believe we are near.

Hold out baits to entice the enemy. Feign disorder, and crush him.

If he is secure at all points, be prepared for him.

If he is in superior strength, evade him.

If your opponent is of choleric temper, seek to irritate him.

Pretend to be weak, that he may grow arrogant.

If he is taking his ease, give him no rest.

If his forces are united, separate them.

Attack him where he is unprepared, appear where you are not expected.

These military devices, leading to victory, must not be divulged beforehand.

The principle on which to manage an army is to set up one standard of courage which all must reach.

How to make the best of both strong and weak—that is a question involving the proper use of ground.

Thus the skillful general conducts his army just as though he were leading a single man, willy-nilly, by the hand.

It is the business of a general to be quiet and thus ensure secrecy; upright and just, and thus maintain order.

He must be able to mystify his officers and men by false reports and appearances, and thus keep them in total ignorance.

By altering his arrangements and changing his plans, he keeps the enemy without definite knowledge.

By shifting his camp and taking circuitous routes, he prevents the enemy from anticipating his purpose.

Regard your soldiers as your children, and they will follow you into the deepest valleys; look upon them as your own beloved sons, and they will stand by you even unto death.

If, however, you are indulgent, but unable to make your authority felt; kind-hearted, but unable to enforce your commands; and incapable, moreover, of quelling disorder: then your soldiers must be likened to spoilt children; they are useless for any practical purpose.

> At first, then, exhibit the coyness of a maiden, until the enemy gives
>> you an opening; afterwards emulate the rapidity of a running hare,
>> and it will be too late for the enemy to oppose you.
> If you know the enemy and know yourself, your victory will not stand
>> in doubt; if you know heaven and know Earth, you may make
>> your victory complete.

His Wisdom Endures

Despite the many management and business books on the market, the wisdom of *The Art of War* endures. Much of the wisdom can be translated into business-speak. For example, these are all philosophies expressed by Sun-tzu, but you will also find them in the glut of coaching and mentoring books flooding the market: Win through intimidation, be proactive, be prepared, know thyself, think outside the box, be adaptable, learn everything you can about the competition (including industrial espionage for the unethical).

Sun-tzu has influenced more people than motivational speaker Tony Robbins or any of the coaches whose lectures you may have been forced to endure during conventions and sales conferences. It is a sign of genius that his principles can be applied to almost any situation, and that they have endured for thousands of years.

Alexander the Great

Studying under another great thinker certainly has its advantages. For a man who had Aristotle as a tutor, young Alexander took a very different career path than his celebrated mentor. He eventually had the suffix "the Great" tagged on to his name and he went off to conquer the world—literally.

Alexander the Great (336–323 B.C.) was the son of a king, Philip of Macedonia. Macedonia was in what is now northern Greece. The Greek city-states regarded the Macedonians as the ancient equivalent of bumpkins and hillbillies, but they were a powerful force. Such a wealthy father could afford the best education for a monarch-in-training. Why not get the best that the Greek city-states had to offer? The best just happened to be Aristotle, (see Chapter 1). Aristotle trained Alexander in rhetoric to make him a gifted orator, a necessary requirement for a future head of state. Alexander also learned the sciences, medicine, literature, and, of course, philosophy.

Young King and Conquerer

When Alexander was twenty, his father was assassinated and he became king. Uneasy is the head that wears the crown, as Shakespeare shrewdly remarked. Enemies, both domestic and foreign, in his own court and in neighboring nations, surrounded Alexander. Perhaps these conspirators underestimated the abilities and the will of the young king. More fools they, for Alexander promptly identified the conspirators at home and abroad and had them all executed in short order. He was nothing if not decisive.

Then Alexander invaded the neighboring land called Thessaly and squashed a rebellion. A congress of Greek city-states elected him ruler of what is now modern Greece. Alexander next set his sights on the Persian Empire, an area that is now Iran but extended much farther in Alexander's time. His 35,000 troops defeated a Persian army of greater strength and lost only 110 men.

FACTS

Before William Shatner played Captain Kirk and Adam West played Batman, the two starred in a TV movie about the life of Alexander the Great. Shatner played the Great One, while West played his "friend." No homoerotic inferences were made, but with those two guys, you can bet it was camp.

One of Alexander's skills as a military tactician was the lightning speed with which he acted. In no time at all, he stopped a revolt among the Thracians, the Illyrians, and the Thebans. He showed no mercy, sparing only temples and the home of a poet whom he admired; then he sold the survivors into slavery. All the other city-states that were considering rebellion immediately ceased and desisted.

His antagonist in the continued campaign was the king of Persia, Darius III. At the Battle of Issus, the defeated Darius fled for his life, neglecting to take his wife and children. Alexander spared their lives and treated them with the civility befitting their station.

Alexander swept through Asia and arrived in Egypt. There he built the city of Alexandria, which became a cultural capital of the ancient world for many centuries after Alexander's death. Its library contained the wisdom of the time, much of which was lost to subsequent generations when it was destroyed by fire in the time of Cleopatra.

Still not satisfied, Alexander conquered the nation of Carthage. He made a pilgrimage to the temple of the Egyptian god Amon-ra. There he spoke with the oracle of the temple. The oracle, an ancient psychic, apparently confirmed what Alexander wanted to hear: that he was the son of Amon-ra, who Alexander would have interpreted to be the Egyptian equivalent of his hometown god, Zeus.

Buoyed by this news, Alexander set off to conquer Babylonia. He met his old enemy Darius and a formidable army en route. Alexander handily defeated them and Darius fled yet again, hoping to live to fight another day. No such luck. He was killed by his own troops for talking the talk, but not walking the walk.

QUESTIONS?

What is the connection between Alexander the Great and actor Bruce Willis?
Alan Rickman, playing the villain in the first *Die Hard* movie, says this quotation about Alexander: "When Alexander saw the breadth of his domain, he wept for there were no more worlds to conquer."

Having conquered Babylon, Alexander made his way to the Persian capital city of Persepolis. He sacked the city, stole the booty, then got drunk, and in a rage, torched the place. In three years, Alexander the Great had conquered most of the known world.

His last campaign was his least successful, but he still got the job done. To finish off the Persian Empire, he crossed the Indus River and invaded what is now modern India. Many of his once loyal Macedonian troops would go no farther. With the troops who were willing to follow, he built a fleet of ships and achieved his lofty goal of world domination.

What Price Glory?

How can you top conquering the world while still in your early thirties? Alexander was spared that decision. He caught a fever and died soon after his triumph. With no heirs, he willed his empire to "the strongest." All this did was initiate a protracted bloodbath among his ruthless, ambitious followers. Alexander lived the life described in the rock-and-roll credo: Die young and leave a good-looking corpse. He was one of the greatest generals and military minds in history. And, like many great men, he was awash in contradictions. The very model of an overachiever, he was also an alcoholic.

Alexander the Great

He was also most likely gay, or at least enjoyed the company of both men and women. There was no conception of gay or straight in ancient Greece. People were sexual beings and partnered with whomever they chose. Homosexuality was actually encouraged in the Greek armies. The phrase *buddy system* comes from this ancient tradition of pairing up men who became "more than friends," the theory being that you would fight longer and harder to stay alive and keep your buddies alive.

Some discreet chronicles call Alexander's buddy Clitus his "friend," but he was probably more than that. Alexander made a fine point of the phrase "You always hurt the one you love." In a drunken rage, he impaled Clitus with a spear. While it was of no consolation to Clitus, Alexander did feel terrible about it afterward.

Since he died before he could put most of his ideas into action, as a political thinker, Alexander was an unknown quantity. He had plans for a sort of world order that he hoped would be a "world brotherhood of all men." He married the daughter of his deceased archenemy Darius and sought to merge Macedonia and Persian cultures.

On the hubris scale, Alexander was off the charts. He established many cities on his trail of world domination. He encouraged his soldiers to settle in these cultural centers and even intermarry with women from the conquered territories. No shrinking violet, he also named every city Alexandria, after himself! He also ordered these new metropolises to worship him as a god. His premature death from something as mundane as a fever made this practice seem a little silly, and eventually moot. Such fates do not befall the divine.

Niccolò Machiavelli

Italian Niccolò Machiavelli (1469–1527) is the major political strategist to come out of the Renaissance. While Galileo was stargazing and da Vinci was sketching blueprints for the helicopter and the submarine, Machiavelli was influencing people. Unlike the other Renaissance giants who brought beauty into the world and devised mechanical marvels, Machiavelli has become the poster boy for another historical constant: the crooked politician and the sleazy businessperson.

How to Succeed à la Machiavelli

Machiavelli was a secretary in the Florentine Republic. Renaissance Italy was comprised of city-states, similar to the structure of the classical Greek world. Each city was like a small country, with an independent government and army. One of Machiavelli's jobs was to reorganize the Florentine military. In those days, most armies were composed of mercenaries. Machiavelli realized that these "guns for hire" had little or no loyalty to their employers; switching sides to a higher bidder was a common occurrence. Machiavelli shrewdly instigated a draft among the local men. These soldiers would be fighting for their homes, so they would be highly motivated. He later discussed this practice in a book, *On the Art of War*.

When the notorious Medici family came to power, Machiavelli fell out of favor, was discharged from his post as secretary, and was imprisoned for a time. Upon his release, he spent the rest of his life trying to get back into the good graces of the tyrannical Medici clan. One of his attempts was to write his seminal primer on how to succeed in politics without really caring how you treat others, called *The Prince*. The book is a basic guidebook for the Renaissance ruler and has been studied by everyone from the robber barons to Wall Street yuppies to the dot.com set (although the latter took a major fall through a combination of hubris and bad management).

So significant (or one might say, notorious) was Machiavelli's thinking that his name has been given to an individual who strives to succeed by any means necessary without letting obstacles like ethics and morality get in the way. This kind of person is said to be Machiavellian.

The Catholic Church was the most powerful political force of the time, and the tenets of Christianity preached love and forgiveness and other good lessons that the Renaissance papacy did not always practice. Machiavelli believed that these spiritual principles were mutually exclusive from those required to manage and expand a successful government. The noble ideals were all well and good, he said, but they were impractical for the prince and politician. In fact, they were pretty hard to find in the real world, so they should not be factored into the political equation.

The End Justifies the Means

Machiavelli saw the history of the world as one of conflict and conflagration. Violence and ruthlessness were the rules of order. The prince must eschew Christian morality in order to triumph over his adversaries and expand his city-state. The ideal prince, he said, was a man who would conquer the lesser city-states and created a unified Italy. Rather than rise above the fray of hardhearted brutality, cunning, and guile, the perfect prince should be better at it (or worse, depending on how you look at it) than all the others around him.

Machiavelli's political philosophy can be reduced to the credo: The end justifies the means. Plato and Aristotle (see Chapter 1) had ideas about the ideal state that Machiavelli denounced as unattainable. Even if that state were attainable, he said, it would be a bad system.

According to Machiavelli, power and control, not compassion and justice, were the objectives of a prince. Lying was an accepted method of achieving goals. The name of the game was to do what thou wilt and not get caught. Engendering respect was secondary to inspiring fear. Of course, the argument is that all this is done for the greater good of the citizenry.

FACTS

Machiavelli did not renounce ethics altogether. He espoused a humanist form of morality. Renaissance humanism was the popular philosophy of the day. It emphasized the greatness of man, the boundlessness of the human potential, which could enable mankind to boldly go without divine intervention.

Shakespeare's Richard III boasts that he can "set the murderous Machiavel [sic] to school." There is no evidence that Machiavelli ever killed anyone, but this homage from the venerable Bard of Avon a few short decades after Machiavelli's death indicates how fast the political philosopher's reputation had grown and how quickly his name had become synonymous with all things unsavory. Not all great thinkers are necessarily noble people.

George Patton

General George S. Patton (1885–1945) is nowadays synonymous with George C. Scott, the actor who played him in the 1970 epic film biography, *Patton*. Unlike many Hollywood biopics, *Patton* is an accurate depiction of this fascinating and complex man. Although you may wonder at the inclusion of a man whose sole claim to fame is warfare in a book about great thinkers, but in times of crisis these are the men we rely on. Complacent, indulged, and indolent yuppies who tout the merits of "coaching and mentoring" and apply the martial writings of Sun-tzu and Carl von Clausewitz (Prussian army officer known for his writings on the science of war) to the business world would sniff and liken career military men to Neanderthals. Despite fashionable ambivalence for such military thinkers, these are the guys who have saved the world from an eternal dark night of barbarism and must do so yet again.

Patton was a man who, like many driven professionals, sought to be the best at his calling. Like the ambitious whippersnapper in a claustrophobic cubicle who has Walter Mitty–esque dreams of usurping the CEO, Patton had wanted to lead men into battle since his earliest days.

A Family Tradition of Service

Patton was born in California to a wealthy family. His grandfather had served with distinction in the Civil War. So it was a family tradition—in Patton's view a cosmic tradition—that he take up arms against a sea of troubles and find fame and glory. He was trained at Virginia Military Institute and the U.S. Military Academy at West Point, New York.

It is possible that Patton may have had a learning disability as a child. He did not learn to read until he was twelve years old, and he was a terrible speller well into his adulthood. But with typical Patton panache, he did not let this handicap interfere with achieving his lofty goals.

ESSENTIALS

A natural athlete, Patton represented the United States in the 1912 Olympics held in Stockholm, Sweden. He participated in an event called the modern pentathlon, which consisted of running, riding, swimming, fencing, and marksmanship. Patton came in fifth.

He first saw combat as an assistant, or aide-de-camp, to the flamboyant General John Joseph "Black Jack" Pershing in his 1917 foray into Mexico to catch the notorious bandito Pancho Villa. Villa was a Mexican revolutionary who turned terrorist when the U.S. government officially recognized the government established by his rival. Villa crossed the border and attacked the town of Columbus, New Mexico. He killed many civilians and destroyed much of the town.

The Pershing force went into Mexico to essentially smoke out Villa and bring him to justice. Pershing took 10,000 men, including young Second Lieutenant Patton, in what was called the Mexican Punitive Expedition. They never caught Villa, who was assassinated by his own people in 1923. Though the mission was a failure, Patton personally killed two of Villa's lieutenants in a gunfight. He carried the same weapon on his hip, two notches on the handle, during World War II.

Shortly after the expedition, when America entered World War I, Patton was sent to Europe. He commanded a tank brigade and also established a training school for tank warfare. Like Winston Churchill (see Chapter 12), Patton believed in the profound combat capabilities of those early tanks. He would take tank warfare to the next level during World War II.

The Right Man for the Times

Patton saw action in the war. He was wounded by machine gun fire and received the Purple Heart. He entered World War I a lieutenant and emerged a colonel.

Between the two wars, Patton designed innovations for the tank and continued to advocate it as an important part of the military arsenal for any future conflicts. Patton knew, and probably hoped, that another war was inevitable. While serving in Hawaii in the 1930s, he warned of the strong possibility of spies among the civilian Japanese residents. And, of course, then December 7, 1941, dawned.

Patton had his opportunity for greatness during World War II, and he almost blew it due to his independent streak and his big mouth. Now a general, his expertise in armored warfare was put to the test in Operation Torch, the invasion of North Africa.

The first exchange between the American and German forces ended in a disastrous defeat for the U.S. forces at the Kasserine Pass in Morocco. Supreme Commander of the Allied Forces Dwight D. Eisenhower knew that a hard-nosed dynamo was needed to whip the American troops into shape so that they could whip the Germans. The right man for the times was Patton.

Patton was a strict disciplinarian and he enforced every military rule, no matter how petty. Dress codes and personal hygiene rules were strictly enforced. Spit and polish, Patton reasoned, would make men think and act like soldiers. Unshaven GIs in unkempt uniforms would behave as lackadaisically as they appeared.

Patton's macho approach worked. The troops rallied and took the Germans. Patton faced and defeated his rival, the brilliant German tank commander Erwin Rommel. Rommel was not such a bad guy. In the last years of the war, he was part of a conspiracy to assassinate the out-of-control Adolf Hitler. Unfortunately the plan was foiled.

FACTS

Patton was a firm believer in reincarnation. He was quite convinced that he had lived in many guises and fought in many battles as a bombastic caveman, a Roman soldier, and an officer who accompanied Napoleon Bonaparte on his fateful attempt to conquer Russia. One wonders in what army Patton is serving now.

After beating the Germans in North Africa, Patton was put in charge of the invasion of Sicily. Patton let his ambition affect his decision-making during this campaign. He had a bitter rivalry with the British general Bernard Montgomery. The two men disliked each other intensely and both were intent on getting to the Sicilian city of Medina first. Reaching this city, while cleaning house along the way, would liberate the island country from the Germans and place it firmly under Allied control. Patton made it to Medina first and imperiously greeted the seething Montgomery.

Political correctness existed even during World War II. Patton got in big trouble and was almost sent stateside when, in a fit of rage, he slapped a soldier that he accused of cowardice. Patton was disciplined for this act and forced to make what was no doubt a series of humiliating public apologies. He took it like a man and was not relieved of duty. One can speculate that in this day and age he would have been sent packing despite his obvious and necessary skills needed in the war effort. The outcome of the war might have been tragically different if Patton had gotten the boot.

Patton's Decline

The Germans respected and feared Patton more than any other Allied general, yet he was not given a command after the slapping incident. He thought he was being ostracized as he was bounced around to Corsica, then Cairo, then England giving public relations speeches. Patton did not realize that the Germans were following his moves his closely. The Germans assumed that everywhere he turned up would be the site of the next big military push. As a result, they were shifting troop movements according to Patton's schedule and were wasting time and personnel in the process.

Patton felt slighted that he had no major role in D-day, the invasion of the Normandy beaches of France on June 6, 1944. This command went to his former subordinate, now his superior officer, General Omar Bradley. Bradley was a skilled general who also possessed a modest and even temper, something Patton lacked.

FACTS

Patton and his troops liberated the concentration camp of Buchenwald and saw firsthand the unimaginable atrocities that the Nazis had committed upon the Jewish prisoners. Patton took the controversial step of physically assembling the local civilian population and forcing them to tour the camp and look upon the horror for themselves.

Eisenhower knew a good thing in Patton and put him in command of the Third Army. He swept though France like an inexorable juggernaut. With speed and ruthlessness, he covered an enormous amount of ground in a few short weeks. Patton was a hands-on commander during this campaign, exhibiting personal heroism just as he demanded it from his officers and men. He barreled through France and into Germany and on to victory.

Patton the military man was without equal. Patton the politician, however, lacked diplomacy. He was forever mouthing off to his superiors and the press, getting himself in hot water as a result. After V-E (Victory in Europe) Day, Patton initially wanted to go to the Pacific and fight the Japanese. But General Douglas MacArthur was as gifted a soldier and as titanic an egotist as Patton, and there was a very real possibility that they would be fighting each other more than the enemy.

Patton's postwar downfall was twofold. He kept Nazi officials in their jobs in order to keep the infrastructure functioning, and he was quite vocal in his disdain for and suspicion of the Russians. He believed that the United States would inevitably have to fight them and he suggested that the Allies arm the Germans and together take on the Russians. That was the last straw. Patton was relieved of command. History proved that Patton was right in his estimation of the Soviet Union. The United States and the Soviet Union were engaged in the Cold War for over forty years, until the former Soviet Union collapsed in 1991.

FACTS

Patton believed that the only way for a professional solder to die was from the last bullet fired during the last battle of the last war. It is therefore a historical irony that Patton, the mighty warrior who often put himself in harm's way during combat, died as a result of injuries suffered in a traffic accident.

The opening speech from the movie *Patton* is not the work of a Hollywood screenwriter. These were the words that Patton delivered to his troops on May 31, 1944, a week before the Allied forces stormed the beaches of Normandy on D-day. Flamboyant, tough, uncompromising, and blunt, the speech distills the philosophy of a great military mind:

> Now I want you to remember that no bastard ever won a war by dying for his country. You won it by making the other poor dumb bastard die for his country. Men, all this stuff you've heard about America not wanting to fight, wanting to stay out of the war, is a lot of horse dung. Americans traditionally love to fight. All real Americans love the sting of battle. When you were kids, you all admired the champion marble shooter, the fastest runner, the big league ball players, the toughest boxers . . . Americans love a winner and will not tolerate a loser. Americans play to win all the time.

CHAPTER 14

Social Thinkers of the Nineteenth Century

The nineteenth century saw major social reform. Prominent reformers effected huge changes, and as with many great thinkers, the full impact of their actions was not appreciated until after their deaths.

Frederick Douglass

Frederick Douglass (1817–1895) is a true American success story. He was born a slave, escaped, and fought to eradicate this evil from the national landscape. His autobiography is considered a classic chronicle of the times, an insider's view of the most tumultuous era in American history since the Revolutionary War.

Alone in a Cruel World

Born Frederick Augustus Bailey, Douglass was separated from his slave mother at a young age and never knew the white man who had fathered him. A kindly white woman taught him how to read, and the door to a brave new world opened a crack. Douglass was determined to open it wide, stride through, and slam the door on the old world behind him.

An influential book in his life was called *The Columbian Orator*, which taught Douglass techniques that he would refine to become one of the greatest public speakers of his age. With greater knowledge of the life that was denied him and his people, Douglass became rebellious and drastic measures were taken to break his spirit. They did not work.

FACTS

Once Frederick Douglass was exposed to the written word, he realized exactly what a wonderful world was being denied him, and he became more determined than ever to be part of it. To paraphrase a saying originated after World War I, "You can't keep a slave on the plantation after he has seen Par-ee."

While working in the Baltimore shipyards, he was helped by a free black sailor. Using his papers and wearing a maritime uniform, Douglass took a train from Baltimore to New York City. That's a short distance as train rides go, but it was a giant leap to freedom. Douglass made connections with the abolitionist movement in the North, which was composed of both free blacks and white sympathizers who were fighting to end slavery. He changed his last name to Johnson and his fiancée came up from Baltimore to join him. They married and moved to New Bedford, Massachusetts.

Although there was no slavery in the North, discrimination was everywhere. Douglass was obliged to take work as a low-level laborer, even though he had learned a marketable skill while in the Baltimore shipyards. In New Bedford, he changed his last name to Douglass, deeming Johnson to be too commonplace. He took the last name from a character in an epic by Sir Walter Scott, of *Ivanhoe* fame.

Antislavery Crusader

Douglass began to attend antislavery meetings in New England held by famous abolitionist William Lloyd Garrison. As a man who had lived in the slave system for his childhood and young adulthood, Douglass's views naturally interested the abolitionists. He began to give speeches about his experiences, and his public speaking skills found expression. Douglass was hired by the abolitionist organization, and traveled the North giving speeches and recruiting new members. He still encountered violence from white racists, but he did not give up the fight. Douglass became a national figure and published the first edition of his autobiography, *Narrative of the Life of Frederick Douglass,* in 1845. In this work, he educated people as to the harsh realities of slavery, and sought to dispel the many stereotypes about slaves and their culture:

> I have often been utterly astonished, since I came to the north, to find persons who could speak of the singing, among slaves, as evidence of their contentment and happiness. It is impossible to conceive of a greater mistake. Slaves sing most when they are most unhappy. The songs of the slave represent the sorrows of his heart; and he is relieved by them, only as an aching heart is relieved by its tears. At least, such is my experience. I have often sung to drown my sorrow, but seldom to express my happiness. Crying for joy, and singing for joy, were alike uncommon to me while in the jaws of slavery. The singing of a man cast away upon a desolate island might be as appropriately considered as evidence of contentment and happiness, as the singing of a slave; the songs of the one and of the other are prompted by the same emotion.

I may be deemed superstitious, and even egotistical, in regarding this event as a special interposition of divine Providence in my favor. But I should be false to the earliest sentiments of my soul, if I suppressed the opinion. I prefer to be true to myself, even at the hazard of incurring the ridicule of others, rather than to be false, and incur my own abhorrence. From my earliest recollection, I date the entertainment of a deep conviction that slavery would not always be able to hold me within its foul embrace; and in the darkest hours of my career in slavery, this living word of faith and spirit of hope departed not from me, but remained like ministering angels to cheer me through the gloom. This good spirit was from God, and to him I offer thanksgiving and praise.

I had not long been a reader of the "Liberator," before I got a pretty correct idea of the principles, measures and spirit of the anti-slavery reform. I took right hold of the cause. I could do but little; but what I could, I did with a joyful heart, and never felt happier than when in an anti-slavery meeting. I seldom had much to say at the meetings, because what I wanted to say was said so much better by others. But, while attending an anti-slavery convention at Nantucket, on the 11th of August, 1841, I felt strongly moved to speak, and was at the same time much urged to do so by Mr. William C. Coffin, a gentleman who had heard me speak in the colored people's meeting at New Bedford. It was a severe cross, and I took it up reluctantly. The truth was, I felt myself a slave, and the idea of speaking to white people weighed me down. I spoke but a few moments, when I felt a degree of freedom, and said what I desired with considerable ease. From that time until now, I have been engaged in pleading the cause of my brethren—with what success, and with what devotion, I leave those acquainted with my labors to decide.

In later years, Douglass published two additional volumes of memoirs, *My Bondage and My Freedom* and *Life and Times of Frederick Douglass.*

The Quest for Freedom

Being a celebrity had its disadvantages. By going public, Douglass faced the possibility of capture and return to bondage. Unbelievable as the whole situation is to contemporary Americans, it would have been

Frederick Douglass

perfectly acceptable for his former masters to kidnap him and return him to the South, and the authorities would have done nothing to intercede. He left the country for two years, lecturing on his experiences in England and Ireland. Benefactors in Britain ultimately bought off Douglass's former owners, and he was, in the eyes of the law, a free man.

Douglass founded the first American newspaper written by and for African-Americans. Others felt he should be out on the stump making speeches, since his public speaking skills always stirred the assembled throngs. In addition to his antislavery efforts, Douglass championed the growing cause of women's rights.

ESSENTIALS

The Emancipation Proclamation did little to free any slaves in the South during the Civil War. It was important as a public relations device and an official declaration that the North opposed slavery, but the South was a separate and sovereign nation at the time and was not about to pay attention to Honest Abe Lincoln's edict.

In the years before the Civil War, Douglass was a civil rights activist and a crusading reformer. He was active in the Underground Railroad—a network of sympathizers with resources to help escaped slaves reach the Northern United States and Canada. Both free black men and women and white sympathizers were involved in this noble effort. He ultimately came to reject William Lloyd Garrison's belief in passive resistance and became friends with the blood-and-thunder white abolitionist John Brown.

He declined to attend Brown's violent raid on the military armory at Harper's Ferry and had to leave the country for a while to avoid being charged with treason.

Douglass was a supporter of Abraham Lincoln and saw the Civil War as the way to end slavery once and for all. Historians debate the true causes and aims of the Civil War. Some say its roots were economic, and statements from Lincoln, certainly early in the conflict, indicate that his goal was to preserve the Union. He even said that if it meant maintaining slavery to do so, then so be it. The famous Emancipation Proclamation did not free a single slave, despite its strong language:

> . . . I do order and declare that all persons held as slaves within said designated States, and parts of States, are, and henceforward shall be free; and that the Executive government of the United States, including the military and naval authorities thereof, will recognize and maintain the freedom of said persons.
>
> And I hereby enjoin upon the people so declared to be free to abstain from all violence, unless in necessary self-defence; and I recommend to them that, in all cases when allowed, they labor faithfully for reasonable wages.
>
> And I further declare and make known, that such persons of suitable condition, will be received into the armed service of the United States to garrison forts, positions, stations, and other places, and to man vessels of all sorts in said service.
>
> And upon this act, sincerely believed to be an act of justice, warranted by the Constitution, upon military necessity, I invoke the considerate judgment of mankind, and the gracious favor of Almighty God.

The South, having declared itself a separate nation, saw no reason to obey the edict of the commander-in-chief of the enemy. Slavery, technically, ended when the North won the war, but true equality was a long way off. Douglass dedicated the postwar years, as he had the prewar years, to the never-ending struggle for civil rights. He fought for the passage of the Thirteenth, Fourteenth, and Fifteenth Amendments to the Constitution, which officially ended slavery. Douglas also held several government posts during those years, including ambassador to Haiti. Douglass was a great thinker and a man of action who helped a nation shake off the last vestiges of barbarism and advance toward a more civilized and egalitarian era.

Karl Marx

Karl Marx (1818–1883) was the architect of what became modern communism, an ideology embraced by millions and opposed by just as many. It is a political system that went on to change the world in ways that Marx himself may never have imagined. A student of philosophy (in fact, he called himself a scientific philosopher and sometimes a scientific socialist), he, along with Friedrich Engels, wrote *The Communist Manifesto*. He sought social reform to combat the injustices of the Industrial Revolution. Needless to say this made him an unpopular figure with the European powers-that-were, and he was exiled from numerous nations, eventually settling in London. There he wrote another equally influential polemic, *Das Kapital*.

The Haves and the Have-Nots

Certainly Karl Marx is one of the most controversial thinkers in history. Although Marx never lived to see it, his writings influenced the Bolsheviks to launch the Russian Revolution of 1917. In fact, Marx thought that the world revolution would begin in England. The subsequent rise of the Soviet Union launched a seventy-year reign of terror and an unprecedented suppression of freedom and personal liberty for all those under the tyrannical banner of hammer and sickle, the symbols on the Soviet flag.

Marx believed that economic relationships were the primary force in human affairs, and that tension between the social classes was inevitable because of the inequity between the haves and have-nots. He called this the *social conflict* theory.

In Marx's world view, the majority of people toiled with little reward while the upper classes reaped the rewards. He believed that the history of mankind was an inevitable juggernaut racing toward a revolution of the masses that would result in what he called a "dictatorship of the proletariat" (proletariat meaning the working classes).

Karl Marx

Marx saw the world as divided not by borders and nationalities but by socioeconomic classes. He believed that the major force in world affairs is production: the production and accumulation of things. Workers hired to produce the goods that make the world go around feel no great pride in their labors. This only leads to alienation, unrest, and, ultimately, revolution.

A famous quotation from Chairman Marx is that religion is the "opiate of the masses." In other words, you would not have found him seeking salvation at a revival meeting. Marx maintained that religion's emphasis on people being good in this life in order to be rewarded in the next created a populace of lemmings. In turn, the ruling class exploited this passivity to further their capitalist goals and keep the masses docile, yet of service.

ALERT

File this away in the "be careful what you wish for" folder: The Russian Revolution, ostensibly intended to liberate the masses from the oppression of the monarchy, actually elicited an even more repressive society, in which dissidents were routinely imprisoned and executed. Remember that next May Day.

While living in Paris, Marx was paid a call by another intellectual, his soon-to-be-collaborator Friedrich Engels. They had come to the same conclusions about communism and the dream of a worker's paradise. They combined forces to write *The Communist Manifesto*. Engles gets short shrift in the legacy department, but he worked with Marx until Marx's death. People still refer to themselves as Marxists, but how many Engles-ists do you run across in your travels?

Planting the Seeds of Communism

The Communist Manifesto is one of the most influential pamphlets ever produced. Although it was written as a rallying cry for the working man, working men and women today, as then, are not likely to spend their precious leisure time reading a political polemic. Thus the pamphlet was voraciously consumed by the educated upper classes, Marx's putative enemies. Ironically, student radicals—the wastrel, indulged rebellious sons of the *bourgeoisie*, as Marx contemptuously called the upper classes— ultimately brought Marxism to violent fruition. *The Communist Manifesto* ends with the clarion call "Workers of the world unite!" This never happened, in Marx's lifetime or afterward, but communism did become, along with fascism, the scourge of the twentieth century.

FACTS

Marx believed that England was the logical place for the "revolution of the proletariat" to happen. The Industrial Revolution was in full swing and the working class, for the most part, worked in dangerous conditions and lived in squalor. Little did he know that revolution would happen long after his death in Russia.

Marx was more than a theorist. He was a social activist and often found himself in jail or on the run. He was thrown out of Belgium, France (twice), and later Germany for his radical writing and penchant for fomenting discord and rousing the rabble. He organized groups such as the Communist Correspondence Committees, which later became the Communist League. Marx eventually settled in England and lived there for the remainder of his life. He made a living as a journalist and even wrote for an American newspaper, the *New York Daily Tribune*, edited by Horace ("Go west, young man") Greeley.

Marx did not have a big impact on world affairs in his lifetime, but the seed he planted sprouted into a strangling vine a few decades later. Marx could not have foreseen that the communist governments that emerged in the twentieth century became the cruelest dictatorships and most wanton human rights violators the world has ever known. The injustices of his age were real and reformation was needed, but the legacy he bequeathed the twentieth century brought only more terror and totalitarianism into the world. Not all the thoughts of great thinkers make the world a better place.

Harriet Tubman

Harriet Tubman (circa 1820–1913) was a slave who escaped the South and then functioned as one of the more successful "conductors" on the "Underground Railroad," the network of abolitionists, both black and white, who risked their lives to help thousands of slaves flee to the North and Canada.

Born Araminta Ross, she was a slave whose master permitted her to marry a free black man, John Tubman, putting her in the unusual position of being a slave who worked in the fields by day yet could go home to her free husband at night. She eventually fled to the North and obtained her freedom, but her husband chose not to join her and later remarried.

FACTS

While working on the Underground Railroad, the first people Harriet Tubman helped escape were her sister and her two children. She later helped a brother and both her parents.

Tubman was innovative in her methods and never lost one of her charges along the way. She was a mistress of disguise, often masquerading as a mentally challenged man. There was a price on her head and she lived for a time in Canada, the last stop for many on the Underground Railroad. She was nicknamed Moses, and the volatile abolitionist John Brown gave her a promotion to "General Tubman."

During the Civil War, she worked as a spy for the Union Army. After the war she continued to work for equal rights for both blacks and women. Though illiterate, friends helped her with her memoir *Scenes from the Life of Harriet Tubman*. She continues to serve posthumously as a role model, not only for African-Americans and women, but as an inspiration to all those who feel driven to fight injustice.

CHAPTER 15

Social Thinkers of the Twentieth Century

The twentieth century witnessed more great reformers, each of whom employed a unique method to achieve his goals. How can one bend the will of a mighty empire, and another change an entrenched and unfair centuries-old system of inequality? These people did just that, and their triumphs made the world a better place for all concerned, not just the people they championed.

Mahatma Gandhi

Mohandas Karamchand Gandhi (1869–1948) faced down the mighty British Empire and defeated it without firing a shot. His practice of passive resistance, the philosophy of nonviolent activism, makes him without a doubt one of the greatest thinkers of any era.

More commonly known as Mahatma Gandhi (Mahatma is a title meaning "great soul"), he was born in India but educated in England. The British Empire once ruled much of what is now known as the Third World, and although their primary motivation was the exploitation of natural resources of these far-flung lands, they did introduce Western culture to these people. Contrary to popular opinion in certain academic circles, Western culture has much to recommend it.

Extreme prejudice was nevertheless a blemish on the relations between the Britons and the locals, and Gandhi had a hard time establishing a law practice when he returned to Bombay, India. Eventually business picked up and he was sent to be the legal counsel for the South African branch of an Indian company. South Africa was notorious for its institutionalized racism, called *apartheid*. This "rude awakening" to what it meant to get the short end of the societal stick ignited the activist streak in Gandhi.

The Path of Least Resistance

Gandhi lived in South Africa for twenty years and fought the system of apartheid with passive resistance. He learned about this philosophy from the writings of Russian writer Leo Tolstoy, American Henry David Thoreau, and no less a personage than Jesus Christ himself (profiled in Chapter 3). Although Gandhi was a Hindu, he was not averse to plumbing the secular and spiritual traditions of other cultures to find wisdom.

Passive resistance is the nonviolent protest of unjust social and legal conditions, and the awareness that resistance may not only be futile, it might be extremely painful. Gandhi was often beaten and spent a lot of time behind bars, but he steadfastly faced down his foes without fighting back. The South African government eventually, and reluctantly, acceded to many of his demands. Although it was a hard-won battle, he proved that passive resistance could effect change. Gandhi returned to his native India, determined to take on the mighty British Empire.

QUESTIONS?

What is *Satyagraha*?

Satyagraha is the Sanskrit word that Gandhi used to describe his version of passive resistance. It gives the movement a firmer, more resolute meaning than the English word *passive* implies. There is a profound spiritual strength inferred in Gandhi's phrase.

Gandhi called his version of passive resistance *Satyagraha*, and it became the rallying cry of the Indian people under Gandhi's guidance. The British government began to aggressively suppress the rebellious spirit of the natives, and this inevitably led to a massacre of protestors by British soldiers. The population got behind Gandhi in a massive nonviolent attack on British rule in the form of boycotts of British courts, schools, government agencies, and British products. This hurt the British in the wallet, always an effective means of protest.

Gandhi's Truth

Gandhi also practiced what he preached. He encouraged a return to the native customs and clothing. This is when he became the Gandhi we know from old photographs and newsreels. He doffed his Western clothing and made his own robes with a spinning wheel. He became a true spiritual leader, living a humble and simple life. It was during this period that he became an international figure and the Indians reverentially called him Mahatma.

Gandhi's first attempt to orchestrate a civilly disobedient revolution was a failure. Human nature being what it is, the people still resorted to violence in their rebellion. He was imprisoned for two years for his activities during those dark days. On his release from jail, he retired from public life, but as the old saying goes, you can't keep a good Mahatma down.

Gandhi led more civil disobedience protests, including a refusal to pay taxes on salt. He led a celebrated march to the sea where thousands of Indians extracted salt from seawater. He was again locked up and launched a series of hunger strikes that alarmed the British. If he were to die in their custody, it would have unleashed an unrestrained violent rebellion among the people.

India was granted a limited "home rule" in 1935, but this was still short of full independence. Gandhi continued to work for freedom and also sought to eradicate the rigid Indian caste system, far more intractable than any Western class system. He particularly felt for the Untouchables who, as the name implies, were the lowest and most maligned caste.

In addition to their struggle against the British, India was divided into two religious groups, the Hindus and Muslims, who were usually at each other's throats. Gandhi, a Hindu, tried to achieve a rapprochement between the two rival religions. Britain demanded a cease-fire before they would consent to allow home rule to become outright independence. Gandhi reluctantly agreed, and this is how India and Pakistan became separate states. Although the people are all ethnically Indians, they are now two neighboring nations that have often been at the brink of war since the 1940s. This is not a situation Gandhi would have endorsed.

Gandhi was assassinated in 1948. Thus ended the life of one of the most influential men of the twentieth century. His principles live on and were practiced by our next subject, a great American civil rights leader.

Martin Luther King Jr.

The legacy of Martin Luther King Jr. (1929–1968) took the same philosophy of civil disobedience and passive resistance that Gandhi had used in India and brought it to the United States. He changed the nation by helping to end the brutal racist discrimination that was inflicted upon black American in the century following the Civil War.

King was the son of a preacher who in turn became a preacher himself. A powerful and passionate orator, he was outraged by the injustices he saw around him. He spoke from the pulpit and eventually took to the streets. Action speaks louder than words, no matter how eloquent the words may be.

The Battle Against Discrimination

The first cause that brought King into the national spotlight was the Montgomery Bus Boycott. Montgomery, Alabama, was indicative of most Southern cities and towns in the mid-1950s. There were segregation laws that kept blacks and whites apart. There were separate restaurants, public restrooms, water fountains, and other public facilities for black citizens and white citizens. On the public transportation system, blacks were required by law to sit at the back of the bus and to surrender their seats to white people should the bus become crowded. One day a woman named Rosa Parks refused to give up her seat to a white man. This simple act of self-respect created a firestorm. She was arrested, found guilty of disorderly conduct, and fined. That evening the black community decided that a protest was needed to draw attention to this injustice and, they hoped, bring it to an end.

ESSENTIALS

The very bus in which Rosa Parks refused to surrender her seat was auctioned off recently for many millions of dollars. The owners plan to make it a mobile museum in the continuing effort to educate the public about the civil rights movement.

King led the protest and through the media attention brought his case not only to the locals but also to the whole country. The Montgomery black community boycotted the bus service for over a year. For the first time, many Americans were made aware of the depth of the discrimination in the Deep South. Or perhaps the attention that was generated made the situation no longer possible to ignore. The protestors encountered violent reprisals and King's home was bombed during the protest.

King went on to establish the Southern Christian Leadership Conference, which brought together black religious leaders throughout the South in a unified effort to continue the battle against discrimination. The increasing violence compelled the federal government to get involved at the state level. The dirty little secret of discrimination was becoming a very public disgrace, and the momentum was growing for radical and sweeping civil rights reform.

King visited India in 1959 to experience firsthand Gandhi's land. He wanted to talk to those who knew Gandhi in an effort to get a better understanding of how he had achieved the social upheaval that changed the course of a mighty empire. King returned home determined to bring about similar changes in America.

A major test in incorporating the teachings of Mahatma Gandhi into the same culture that gave us *Hee Haw* occurred in Birmingham, Alabama, in 1963. King's nemesis was a police chief with the bellicose name of "Bull" Connor. King urged schoolchildren and teens to join in the nonviolent marches, and the world saw the peaceful marching of singing children met by police with attack dogs and firefighters with high-power hoses. Not exactly the finest hour for these two noble professions. King was locked up after the chaos ensued. It was from jail that he wrote one of his most famous civil rights pieces, "Letter from a Birmingham Jail," to his colleagues, smuggling it out on whatever bits of paper were available to him.

The Dream Lives On

King's most remembered moment came during the March on Washington in 1963, with his eloquent "I Have a Dream" speech. No decent man or woman could deny that this was a dream that had to be realized, not only for African-Americans but for all Americans. King's efforts were directly responsible for the passage of the Civil Rights Act in 1964. He received the Nobel Peace Prize in the same year.

King did not rest on his laurels. He and his followers marched in Selma, Alabama, for voting rights for the black citizens. The protestors were again met with police brutality, and again it was recorded for the entire world to see. Public outrage brought sympathizers into the region, and additional federal legislation—in the form of the Voting Rights Act of 1965—outlawed the illegal and immoral tactics that had been used to discourage blacks from going to the polls.

In his last years of life, King branched out to protest the Vietnam War. He also shifted his focus slightly to speak of socioeconomic discrimination and inequality as well as racial injustice. The younger and more militant men of the Black Power movement began to criticize King, suggesting that the nonviolence he had always advocated was not the way. They believed, in the words of another civil rights leader who had recently been slain, Malcolm X, that they must achieve their goals "by any means necessary."

FACTS

The Kennedys have created quite a myth around themselves. One is that they were champions of civil rights. Their record is not exemplary on that score. In fact, while serving as attorney general under his brother, President John F. Kennedy, Robert Kennedy illegally wiretapped King, violating his civil rights and skirting the U.S. Constitution.

On April 4, 1968, Martin Luther King Jr. was assassinated while standing outside his room at the Lorraine Motel in Memphis, Tennessee. A man named James Earl Ray was caught, convicted, imprisoned, and later recanted his confession. The King family, many years later, had a victory in court in their efforts to prove that there had been a conspiracy to assassinate King. All the 1960s "lone gunmen" were probably not as "lone" as once believed. Thus ended the life, but not the dream, of one of the great social activists and thinkers of recent times.

CHAPTER 16

Champions of Women's Rights

The feminist movement began long before women burned their bras in the 1960s. Over a century earlier, women with petticoats beneath their ankle-length dresses brandished hatchets against kegs of "demon rum." They also fought for the abolition of slavery and for the rights of women to shatter the glass ceiling and take their rightful place as equal beneficiaries of the American dream.

The Feminist Movement: Then

Although the feminist movement is usually associated with the modern era, it has existed in many forms and under many names since ancient times. It did not achieve great success until the twentieth century. However, lone voices in the wilderness have been lobbying for equal rights between the sexes for a long, long time.

ESSENTIALS

The early feminist movement was called *suffrage*, which specifically meant securing equal rights in the political arena; that is, the right to vote. Hard as it is to believe, women did not have the right to vote in national elections until 1920, only eighty-some years ago.

Until comparatively recent centuries, most men did not have many rights, either. In the "enlightened" civilizations of the Renaissance, even in those cultures that held elections, the electorate consisted of wealthy men with property. The peasant class had little or nothing to say about anything. It was not until the eighteenth and nineteenth centuries that the idea of equal rights was bandied about as something that had potential, and it was not until the twentieth century that it became a reality. And even in the early days of the twenty-first century, there are those who believe we still have a long way to go.

Earliest Supporters

One of the first supporters of feminism in the modern age (modern meaning the past 300 years) was a man. British philosopher John Stuart Mill wrote eloquently on the subject in 1869 in his book, *The Subjection of Women*. He argued that a woman's lot in life was akin to slavery and that the poor treatment of women also adversely affected men, and thus society as a whole. He wrote:

There was a time when the division of mankind into two classes, a small one of masters and a numerous one of slaves, appeared, even to the most cultivated minds, to be natural, and the only natural, condition of the human race. . . . But, it will be said, the rule of men over women differs from all these others in not being a rule of force: it is accepted voluntarily; women make no complaint, and are consenting parties to it. In the first place, a great number of women do not accept it. Ever since there have been women able to make their sentiments known by their writings (the only mode of publicity which society permits to them), an increasing number of them have recorded protests against their present social condition: and recently many thousands of them, headed by the most eminent women known to the public, have petitioned Parliament for their admission to the Parliamentary Suffrage. The claim of women to be educated as solidly, and in the same branches of knowledge, as men, is urged with growing intensity, and with a great prospect of success; while the demand for their admission into professions and occupations hitherto closed against them, becomes every year more urgent. Though there are not in this country, as there are in the United States, periodical conventions and an organised party to agitate for the Rights of Women, there is a numerous and active society organised and managed by women, for the more limited object of obtaining the political franchise. Nor is it only in our own country and in America that women are beginning to protest, more or less collectively, against the disabilities under which they labour. France, and Italy, and Switzerland, and Russia now afford examples of the same thing. How many more women there are who silently cherish similar aspirations, no one can possibly know; but there are abundant tokens how many would cherish them, were they not so strenuously taught to repress them as contrary to the proprieties of their sex.

Another early feminist was Mary Wollstonecraft (1759–1797), a truly enlightened woman of the eighteenth century. She wrote a nonfiction work called *Vindication of the Rights of Woman* in 1792. She wrote:

Women are told from their infancy, and taught by the example of their mothers, that a little knowledge of human weakness, justly-termed cunning, softness of temper, outward obedience, and a scrupulous attention to a puerile kind of propriety, will obtain for them the protection of man; and should they be beautiful, every thing else is needless, for, at least, twenty years of their lives.

Thus Milton describes our first frail mother; though when he tells us that women are formed for softness and sweet attractive grace, I cannot comprehend his meaning, unless, in the true Mahometan strain, he meant to deprive us of souls, and insinuate that we were beings only designed by sweet attractive grace, and docile blind obedience, to gratify the senses of man when he can no longer soar on the wing of contemplation. . . . I may be accused of arrogance; still I must declare, what I firmly believe, that all the writers who have written on the subject of female education and manners, from Rousseau to Dr. Gregory, have contributed to render women more artificial, weak characters, than they would otherwise have been; and, consequently, more useless members of society. I might have expressed this conviction in a lower key; but I am afraid it would have been the whine of affectation, and not the faithful expression of my feelings; of the clear result, which experience and reflection have led me to draw. When I come to that division of the subject, I shall advert to the passages that I more particularly disapprove of, in the works of the authors I have just alluded to; but it is first necessary to observe, that my objection extends to the whole purport of those books, which tend, in my opinion, to degrade one half of the human species, and render women pleasing at the expense of every solid virtue.

Strengthen the female mind by enlarging it, and there will be an end to blind obedience; but, as blind obedience is ever sought for by power, tyrants and sensualists are in the right when they endeavour to keep women in the dark, because the former only want slaves, and the latter a play-thing. The sensualist, indeed, has been the most dangerous of tyrants, and women have been duped by their lovers, as princes by their ministers, whilst dreaming that they reigned over them . . .

I will allow that bodily strength seems to give man a natural superiority over woman; and this is the only solid basis on which the superiority of the sex can be built. But I still insist, that not only the virtue, but the knowledge of the two sexes should be the same in nature, if not in degree, and that women, considered not only as moral, but rational creatures, ought to endeavour to acquire human virtues (or perfections) by the same means as men, instead of being educated like a fanciful kind of half being—one of Rousseau's wild chimeras . . .

These pioneers did not gather enough support to dramatically change the status quo, but their words rang loud and clear to the generations that followed.

FACTS

The phrase "all *men* are created equal" was taken literally in colonial America. Women were simply regarded as inferior to men—physically, intellectually, and in every other way. Still, women in the colonies and later in the United States did have a few more rights than their counterparts on other continents.

The real feminist advances began in the early 1800s. Women became socially involved in causes such as the fight for the abolition of slavery and the temperance movement (an early effort to prohibit the distribution and consumption of alcohol). The women in these movements were treated as second-class citizens even as they fought for the civil rights of others. Enough was enough, they said, and a separate women's movement was born. The early feminists were Lucretia Coffin Mott, Elizabeth Cady Stanton, Susan B. Anthony, Lucy Stone, Abby Kelley Foster, and Ernestine Rose. There were also some men who got in the ladies' corner, among them poet Ralph Waldo Emerson. Let's look at the two most renowned suffragette sisters.

Susan B. Anthony

Susan B. Anthony (1820–1906) spent her entire adult life crusading for women's rights. She was also an abolitionist and temperance activist. She teamed with Elizabeth Cady Stanton and exhibited a nineteenth-century version of "girl power" that eventually won women the right to vote, although neither woman lived to see it.

They worked to change the laws, rally other women and sensitive men around their cause, and published a newspaper called *Revolution.* Anthony often delivered the speeches that Stanton wrote. Anthony was the more flamboyant of the two and the more inspiring public speaker, but she always gave Stanton the lion's share of the credit.

Susan B. Anthony was a great feminist leader who was instrumental in creating the sweeping changes that she never actually witnessed. She was eventually honored with the Susan B. Anthony dollar coin. She should be remembered for much more than this coin that most people continue to confuse with a quarter.

Elizabeth Cady Stanton

Elizabeth Cady Stanton (1815–1902) was the daughter of a judge and congressman; as a result, she was exposed to a higher level of education than most women of her age. She married abolitionist Henry Brewster Stanton, and the couple had seven children.

When she and her husband attended the World Anti-Slavery Convention in 1840 in London, England, she discovered that women were not allowed to attend. The reformers in attendance did not see the irony and hypocrisy of this discrimination. She met another suffragette at the convention, Lucretia Coffin Mott, who was one of the founding members of the American Anti-Slavery Society. The enlightened men at the convention finally allowed the women to attend and address the assembly—from behind a curtain!

Stanton was a more radical thinker than many of her contemporaries. She spoke openly of reproductive rights for women, reforming the unfair divorce laws, and other topics that even some of her fellow suffragettes found extreme. Although she was instrumental in introducing a constitutional amendment for women's suffrage in 1878, it did not see the light of day until many years after her death. Her book, *The Woman's Bible*, which was essentially an annotated edition of the Good Book with feminist notes in the margins, alienated her from most of her fellow activists.

With Lucretia Coffin Mott, she organized the first feminist convention in 1848, held in Seneca Falls, New York, where Stanton was living. They adopted what they called a Declaration of Sentiments, modeled on the Declaration of Independence. It detailed eighteen grievances that women suffered, among them limited economic and educational opportunities. Press coverage was mostly hostile, with the famous journalist Horace ("Go West, young man") Greeley one of the rare supporters. Former slave and abolitionist orator Frederick Douglass (see Chapter 15) was also in attendance.

ESSENTIALS

The vicious attacks would follow the feminists through the decades. Not-so-subtle intimations were made about their moral character and sexual preferences. Violence from street hoodlums often accompanied subsequent conferences and rallies. Despite the obstacles, they persevered.

The suffragettes and the abolitionists eventually went their separate ways to pursue their distinctive agendas. The abolitionists were having enough trouble ending slavery and fighting for the rights of black men. Adding women into the equation, they felt, was hindering their cause. Stanton and Anthony established the National Woman Suffrage Association; a rival faction, the American Woman Suffrage Association, was also formed. The former sought to change the laws in one fell swoop at the federal level. The latter's mandate (or *womandate*, if you will) sought to effect change gradually, one state and territory at a time. (In fact, Wyoming women got the vote in 1869. Wyoming was a territory, not a state at the time.)

In 1872, Susan B. Anthony persuaded a few sympathetic election officials at a polling place into letting her and a few friends vote. When it was discovered, they were all arrested. Anthony was fined $100, which she refused to pay. Some time later, she gave this speech about the experience:

> Friends and fellow citizens: I stand before you tonight under indictment for the alleged crime of having voted at the last presidential election, without having a lawful right to vote. It shall be my work this evening to prove to you that in thus voting, I not only committed no crime, but, instead, simply exercised my citizen's rights, guaranteed to me and all United States citizens by the National Constitution, beyond the power of any state to deny. The preamble of the Federal Constitution says:
>
> "We, the people of the United States, in order to form a more perfect union, establish justice, insure domestic tranquility, provide for the common defense, promote the general welfare, and secure the blessings of liberty to ourselves and our posterity, do ordain and establish this Constitution for the United States of America."
>
> It was we, the people; not we, the white male citizens; nor yet we, the male citizens; but we, the whole people, who formed the Union. And we formed it, not to give the blessings of liberty, but to secure them; not to the half of ourselves and the half of our posterity, but to the whole people—women as well as men. And it is a downright mockery to talk to women of their enjoyment of the blessings of liberty while they are denied the use of the only means of securing them provided by this democratic-republican government—the ballot.

The 1890s through 1918 saw gradual victories for the suffrage movement and a gradual change in the popular zeitgeist. More and more states were granting women suffrage but there was still no change at the national level. Women could now vote for governors in many states, but not for the president.

Neither Susan B. Anthony nor Elizabeth Cady Stanton lived to see it, but their efforts on behalf of American women were rewarded when the

Nineteenth Amendment to the United States Constitution was ratified on August 18, 1920, granting women the right to vote. The second phase of the women's movement would be equally tumultuous and eventful.

First Lady of the World

Eleanor Roosevelt (1884–1962) was a remarkable woman who changed the role of the First Lady and public wife. But even prior to her husband Franklin D. Roosevelt's years in the White House, she was a formidable and forward-thinking woman.

Born into America's wealthy ruling class, she was orphaned at an early age. She did not have to change her monogrammed towels when she married, for the man was her fifth cousin once removed, Franklin Delano Roosevelt. And the man who gave the bride away in their 1905 wedding was her uncle, President Theodore Roosevelt.

QUESTIONS?

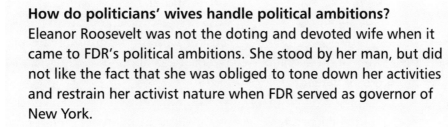

How do politicians' wives handle political ambitions?
Eleanor Roosevelt was not the doting and devoted wife when it came to FDR's political ambitions. She stood by her man, but did not like the fact that she was obliged to tone down her activities and restrain her activist nature when FDR served as governor of New York.

Eleanor Roosevelt had an activist streak and an independent nature long before she became First Lady. During World War I, she did volunteer work for the Red Cross and championed the cause of compassionate treatment for veterans suffering from "shell shock." In those days, the condition was not understood or called by the now familiar diagnosis of post-traumatic stress disorder.

The marriage of the Roosevelts was tested by FDR's affair with his secretary, and perhaps other factors. She stayed married to FDR until his death. Although there was no doubt deep affection and mutual respect between the two, in many ways they led separate lives. Eleanor spent more and more time living alone in New York City, often with two close female friends. She was involved with the League of Women Voters, several Democratic women's groups, she wrote for a paper called *Women's Democratic News*. When not in New York City, she lived in the house she had built on the Roosevelt's sprawling Hyde Park estate with her female friends.

Though she may have curtailed her activism during FDR's political career, she still managed to be a new kind of First Lady when he

Eleanor Roosevelt

became president of the United States in 1933. She did things no president's wife had ever done before she held regular press conferences, championed the causes of the downtrodden suffering during the Great Depression, and was especially sensitive to the plight of African-Americans. This caused the Ku Klux Klan to put a price on her head. Old boys and their network also resented this outspoken, upstart woman, fearful that she might give their wives and daughters dangerous ideas about the woman's place in the order of things.

After FDR's death in 1945, she continued to play in active role in social and political affairs. President Harry Truman appointed her the U.S. representative to the United Nations and proclaimed her "First Lady of the World." She remained an outspoken champion of women and other disenfranchised groups until her death in 1962.

The Feminist Movement: NOW

The organization most associated with the modern feminist movement is the National Organization for Women (NOW). It has been a politically and socially activist organization since its inception in 1966. With half a million contributing members and hundreds of chapters across the country, NOW is the largest organization of feminist activists in the United States.

Betty Friedan

One of the founders of NOW was Betty Friedan (b. 1921). She also served as its first president, from 1966 to 1970. Friedan is the author of the modern feminist tract, *The Feminine Mystique* (1963), considered by many to be the document that indoctrinated the modern feminist movement. The title refers to the traditional female role of wife and mother as the ideal. To attempt to forge a destiny in the "man's world" made women somehow less than women, mutant creatures trying to be men yet lacking neither the tools nor the talent. This attitude, said Friedan, was nothing short of a global patriarchal conspiracy to keep women powerless; or, as the cliché says, "barefoot and pregnant."

Betty Friedan continues to be a popular and prolific writer, lecturer, and activist. Her other major works include *It Changed My Life* (1976), *The Second Stage* (1981), *The Fountain of Aging* (1993), and *Life So Far* (2001).

Gloria Steinem

Another well-known voice in the modern feminist movement is Gloria Steinem (b. 1934). Ironically, her career as a feminist began with a stint as a Playboy bunny. As a struggling journalist, she went undercover in one of the Playboy Clubs owned by Hugh Hefner, founder of *Playboy* magazine. Her writing career and her feminist perspective took off after she had a taste of what it was like to be regarded as a sex object and not as an individual with thoughts and feelings and ideas.

FACTS

Steinem's story of her experience as Playboy Bunny not only launched her career as both a writer and a feminist, but the story was later made into a TV movie called *A Bunny's Tale*, starring Kirstie Alley.

Steinem worked with Betty Friedan and politicians Bella Abzug and Shirley Chisholm to found the National Women's Political Caucus in 1971. She also founded *Ms.* magazine, a periodical devoted to women's issues.

She has been in the public eye ever since. Her books include *Outrageous Acts and Everyday Rebellions* (1983), *Revolution from Within: A Book of Self-Esteem* (1992), *Her Story: Women Who Changed the World* (1995), and *Moving Beyond Words* (1995), a collection of her essays on women's issues.

Gloria Steinem has said, "If the shoe doesn't fit, must we change the foot?" She and other feminists remain committed to shaping a world that better fits the needs of its people and achieving equality for all women.

Feminist Fatale

In her books *Sexual Personae: Art and Decadence from Nefertiti to Emily Dickinson; Sex, Art and American Culture: Essays;* and *Vamps & Tramps: New Essays*, Camille Paglia (b. 1947) tackles a variety of hot-button issues, and her opinions are nothing if not explosive. She is a lesbian, yet she rejects political correctness with passion and acerbic wit. She calls it nothing more that "fascist speech codes." Her contemptuous dismissal of "white middle-class college girls" as the purveyors of the sexual harassment witch hunt and her suggestion that "date rape" is highly exaggerated and based on bourgeoisie prudery has raised the eyebrows and the blood pressure of many.

A frequent guest on talk shows, Camille Paglia also has a regular column in the e-zine Salon.com. She resents being called a conservative. She thinks of herself as a libertarian Democrat. She sees the political feminist Left as naïve. Men and women are different and the differences are hardwired and instinctual. In primordial times, women sought the cavemen with the biggest club, and now if women seek a man with a humongous portfolio, the principle is biological. Nothing to be ashamed of, it's simply nature, she insists. Paglia suggests that militant feminists would prefer to "lobotomize the village in order to save it." She calls them "bellyachers," "anorexics," "bulimics," "sob sisters," and other less than laudatory monikers. She lauds Madonna for bringing the "beauty and pleasure and sensuality back into feminism." Paglia is a true original, not to everyone's taste, but as cage rattlers go, she is one of the more provocative and entertaining.

The Equal Rights Amendment and Other Campaigns

NOW marched in support of the Civil Rights Act of 1964. They marched (unsuccessfully) for the Equal Rights Amendment (ERA) in the 1970s. They have marched for women's lives, abortion rights, lesbian rights, increased protection for abused women, equal pay for equal work, affirmative action, and many women's rights and civil rights causes.

The failed attempt to add an Equal Rights Amendment occupied NOW during the 1970s. They hoped the addition of the ERA to the United States Constitution would make their agenda the law of the land. Among other grievances, it was determined that women in the workplace made just fifty-nine cents for every dollar paid to men.

FACTS

First proposed in 1923 by Alice Paul, suffragist leader and founder of the National Woman's Party, the Equal Rights Amendment says that "equality of rights under the law shall not be denied or abridged by the United States or by any state on account of sex." The ERA is still not part of the U.S. Constitution. It has been ratified by thirty-five of the necessary thirty-eight states. For the ERA to become the Twenty-Eighth Amendment, three more states must vote yes.

NOW's campaign in the early 1990s was called "Elect Women for a Change." The campaign was a success; many women and feminist-minded men went to their respective state houses and the nation's capital in the 1992 elections. In addition, NOW has tried to eradicate sexual harassment and violence against women. They were instrumental in helping to pass into law the Violence Against Women Act of 1994.

Now supports a wide range of women's rights campaigns, from safe and legal abortions to economic equality to eradicating domestic violence. Visit *www.now.org* for more information.

CHAPTER 17
Explorers into the Human Psyche

Sigmund Freud and Carl Jung are the two most famous psychiatrists and researchers into the human mind of the twentieth century. Even those with bare-bones knowledge of Freud and Jung are vaguely familiar with some of their concepts and catch phrases that have entered the language.

Sigmund Freud

Sigmund Freud (1856–1939) is perhaps the best-known and most prominent psychologist of the twentieth century. He is one of the founding fathers of modern psychology and psychotherapy, introducing the fifty-minute hour, free association, and theories on the unconscious, the Oedipus complex, and the interpretation of dreams that continue to fascinate both professional and armchair psychologists.

Even those who know nothing of history or psychology have some knowledge of Freud. His psychological terminology has entered the language. Most people have heard the expressions *Oedipus complex* and *Freudian slip.* People talk of rampaging "egos" and equally rampaging "ids."

QUESTIONS?

Why did Freud sit behind his patient?
During a psychotherapy session, the patient would lie on a couch while Freud sat in a chair behind the patient, trusty notebook in hand. Freud chose this arrangement because he did not want the patient to be influenced by his facial expressions or body language.

In popular culture, the stereotype of a psychologist is usually a cigar-smoking, bearded man with a thick German accent. This is a caricature of Sigmund Freud. In fiction, films, and television, Sigmund Freud has treated Nietzsche (Chapter 2), as well as Sherlock Holmes for his cocaine addiction, and attended a cocktail party held by Major Tony Nelson and his mischievous genie, Jeannie.

Dreams and the Unconscious

Freud was a doctor in Vienna, Austria, in the late nineteenth and early twentieth centuries. Trained as a neurologist, he began to explore the workings of the human mind. Freud had many patients who had physical symptoms, but they did not have anything physically wrong when he examined them. The doctor determined that their ailments were psychosomatic; that is, the physical problems were caused by a mental problem. If the patient could get a grasp on what was bothering him or her, Freud reasoned, perhaps the physical symptoms would disappear.

Freud began to treat these patients with hypnosis. By placing a patient in a trancelike state, the person's defenses would come down and Freud

Sigmund Freud

would have access to the patient's unconscious. And in that buried and mysterious mental realm, the problem could usually be identified and thus cured.

Freud likened the mind to an iceberg. The conscious mind, that part that we are aware of, is the tip of the iceberg. The other nine-tenths of the iceberg is our unconscious mind. The unconscious exercises a far greater control over our actions that we realize. Why do people get psychosomatic illnesses, sabotage relationships, arise bright and early on a holiday but drag themselves out of bed on Monday morning? Freud proposed that this was the unconscious at work.

Freud called the forces that fill the unconscious world *drives*. The main drives that we bury are ironically—or perhaps quite logically—the things we seek out in entertainment: sex and violence. We repress these impulses because our upbringing and the constraints of society compel us to do so. Those who allow these drives to run amok usually end up in jail or dead.

FACTS

All people dream during the night, even if they do not remember their dreams. Most dreams occur during the deepest stage of sleep, called REM (rapid eye movement) sleep. The brain is active, but the muscles are in a state of near paralysis. If this did not occur, people would be acting out their dreams while still asleep!

Two ways in which Freud explored the depths of the unconscious were dream interpretation and a technique he called free association. Ancient people believed in the profound significance of dreams. They believed that dreams were signs from the gods or prophecies of things to come.

God communicates to people through dreams in the Old Testament on a regular basis. Freud, being a secular-minded scientist, did not put much mystical stock in dreams, but he firmly believed in their ability to tell us things about ourselves that we did not know or were unwilling to accept.

Freud believed that dreams spoke to us though symbolism, imagery, and allegory. They are a cinematic and poetic expression of our unconscious. Modern dream researchers have compared the mind during sleep to a computer that is going through a "scan disk" and "defrag." That is, extraneous data that has been accumulated during the course of the day is summarily dispatched to the "recycle bins" of our psyche, providing some vivid dreams in the process.

In free association, the patient is encouraged to ramble at length about anything that comes to mind. It may have no apparent meaning and not make very much sense. Freud's job was to sift through the gabbing and find recurring themes and motifs and piece together a puzzle. When all the elements were correctly assembled, he would have a clear picture of the problem.

A Love/Hate Relationship

Freud is also famous for the infamous Oedipus complex theory, which makes most men writhe and cringe in deep discomfiture. Oedipus is a character in a Greek tragedy by Sophocles. Oedipus is a traveler who kills a man on the road in an ancient equivalent of road rage. He then answers the "riddle of the Sphinx" and is made king, marrying the widowed queen. Many years later, Oedipus learns that the man he killed was actually his father and the woman he married is his mother. Horrified, he gouges out his eyes and wanders off into the wilderness.

QUESTIONS?

What is the Electra complex?
Freud assumed girls had the same kind of love/hate relationship with their mothers that boys had with their fathers. He did not give it a name, but this version was later called the "Electra complex," for another character from Greek drama who murdered her mother.

Freud theorized that every young man goes through an internalized Oedipus complex. He unconsciously wants to remove his father from the picture and possess his mother. Freud believed that a young man who does not successfully pass through this stage will indeed be a truly disturbed fellow. He will have big-time issues with authority, and, of course, with women.

Freud, a product of Europe of the nineteenth century, believed that the Oedipus complex was a universal phenomenon. Other researchers believe that it is not an archetypal condition that spans all cultures.

Ego, Superego, and Id

Freud theorized that there are three components to the human personality. He called these the ego, the superego, and the id. The ego is the part that we are aware of and that the rest of the world can easily see; it is the conscious personality. The superego is what other people would call the conscience. This part contains all the codes of conduct and the sense of right and wrong that have been imprinted on our minds by both our parents and society at large. The id is the mostly unconscious, "naughty" part of the personality. It is composed of those sex and violence drives that civilized people have learned to keep under wraps.

Freud also categorized the following stages of psychosexual development:

- The oral stage is from birth to eighteen months. During this stage the baby embarks on the adventures of discovering the world via its oral sensations.
- The anal stage, from eighteen to thirty-six months, coincides with the toilet-training period. Children who get psychologically stuck in this stage can become either anal retentive or anal expulsive as adults. This means that the person is either a complete control freak or a total slob.
- The phallic stage is from approximately ages three to six years old. The child becomes fascinated with his or her genitals and the Oedipus complex begins to rear its incestuous head.

- Sexual feelings are suppressed in the latency stage, according to Freud. Its duration is from age six to puberty. During this stage, girls think all boys have cooties and vice versa.
- The final stage is the genital stage, which starts at puberty and continues for the remainder of the life span. The well-adjusted individual commences what should be a "normal" life.

Freudian psychoanalysis became enormously popular in medical and scientific circles. Over the decades, Freud has fallen in and out of favor. Many critics think that he was preoccupied with sex and that what he treated as universal traits may have been specific to nineteenth-century Europe. Freud had many protégés. One of the most famous is Carl Jung.

Carl Jung

Swiss psychiatrist and psychologist Carl Gustav Jung (1875–1961) was a devoted disciple of Freud, but as often happens in coaching and mentoring relationships, the protégé breaks from the mentor and goes off in another direction. Jung broke with Freud and took his psychological speculations in a different and somewhat spiritual direction. Jung is very popular today, not only among armchair analysts but also with the New Age crowd. They enjoy his mystical musings and share his interest in Eastern philosophy.

Jung's Take on the Unconscious

Freud and Jung parted in their theories on the nature of the unconscious. Jung did not put the emphasis on the sexual drives of which Freud was so fond. Jung initially used Freudian analytic techniques in his practice, and Freud was looking for a younger man to become his successor and maybe even a surrogate son. But the break went beyond theoretical division and their friendship ended bitterly.

Jung's break with Freud also isolated him from the rest of the psychiatric circles in Europe. He took a lengthy sabbatical and engaged in the dubious, possibly even dangerous practice of self-analysis. This process is akin to the cliché that a lawyer who represents himself has a fool for a client. Jung chronicled this journey in his memoir *Memories, Dreams, Reflections* and called it a "confrontation with the unconscious." Jungian theories and the Jungian school of thought were the result of this inward journey, and his ideas are a major contribution to psychology, transcending it to embrace the worlds of mythology, folklore, astrology, Eastern spirituality, and alchemy.

Where Freud used an iceberg analogy to explain the unconscious (the unconscious part of our mind and personality is the 90 percent of the iceberg that is below the surface), Jung made the comparison of a cork floating on the ocean. The cork is our conscious mind and the ocean is the unconscious. The cork is tossed about at the whim of the cruel sea unless we can gain a better understanding of the nature of our true Self (of which we are only dimly aware, if at all) via the psychotherapeutic process he called *analytical psychology*.

FACTS

The best modern example of the Hero's Journey is the first *Star Wars* trilogy. George Lucas (whom you'll read about in Chapter 21) has acknowledged that Campbell was a big influence on him and his writing. One of the possible reasons for the enormous success of *Star Wars* is that it taps directly into the collective unconscious and appeals to people on an archetypal, unconscious level.

People who may not be well versed in Jung probably have heard the phrase *collective unconscious*. Jung describes this as a shared memory of symbols, imagery, and memories that he called *archetypes*. These go way back to the dawn of time and are very similar if not exactly the same in all cultures and civilizations. The famous mythographer Joseph Campbell endorses this theory of the collective unconscious in his book *The Hero with a Thousand Faces*. By cataloguing and cross-referencing myths from a broad spectrum of cultures and time frames, Campbell came up with the notion of the *monomyth*. There is basically one story with the same cast of archetypes that Campbell called "The Hero's Journey."

Male and Female Energy

Jung encountered a wide array of archetypes in his journey within. For many of his contemporaries, this speculation bordered on fantasy. Men of science found the idea of mythical energies springing forth from a primordial reservoir and dwelling within every human a little too poetic a principle to withstand empirical scientific critique.

Jung spoke of "getting in touch with your feminine side" many years before it became a New Age cliché. Jung suggested that within every man and woman there is counterpart male and female energy. The female energy in a man is called the *anima,* and the male energy in a woman is called the *animus.*

Jung was big on the necessity of what he called individuation. This term means integrating all the disparate elements of the psyche and the personality into something resembling wholeness (or as close as we mere mortals can get to wholeness). Awareness of your internal "better half" is a key component of the individuation process.

ESSENTIALS

The anima/animus theory is a modern spin on Plato's retelling of an ancient myth. The myth explains the nature of love by saying that humans were once a giant androgynous ball that the gods split in two. As a result, men and women feel incomplete until they find their other half.

For all his enlightened mystical ruminations, Jung is often accused of being a stodgy Old World coot. His theory of the anima and animus describes what it is like when your inner man or woman is too powerful. A man with a powerful anima becomes an annoying whiner, and a woman with a pumped-up animus becomes overbearing and unpleasant.

The Shadow Knows

Another interior component of the personality is Jung's notion of what he called *the shadow.* Jung had his own version on Freud's theory of the ego, superego, and id. Jung's definition of ego is the conscious part of the mind. The ego is the cork bobbing on the ocean. Jung called his counterpart of the id and superego combined the shadow. Simply put, this is a person's dark side, the impulses and desires that are lurking beneath the surface. Jung believed that people have a tendency to project those negative elements on people that they dislike. Jung maintained that the ideal was to embrace the shadow and try to integrate it into the self. Burying the shadow never works. The shadow will be heard, usually when least expected, if it is not controlled.

In the *Star Trek* episode called "The Enemy Within," Captain Kirk is split in two because of a transporter accident. His "good" half is gentle and passive; his "bad" self is lustful and aggressive. The "evil Kirk" is a pop culture representation of Freud's theory of the id and Carl Jung's shadow.

The mask that we show the public is what Jung called the *persona*. The persona is both revealing and concealing. We act differently around different people. They see different sides of us and we may never let one see the other. Your boss does not see your stud muffin side, and your sweetheart should not be exposed to your inner S.O.B.

We all have multiple personae, which is not the same as multiple personalities. Problems arise when one aspect of the psyche dominates the others. The ideal is to know your persona and use it as necessary, but also to know that it is only a small piece of your self.

Jung also wrote extensively on the subject of alchemy. Alchemy was the medieval quasi-scientific belief in which practitioners endeavored to turn base metals into gold. Jung, historian and psychologist, interpreted their efforts as those of primitive therapists. The attempt to turn lead into gold was really a metaphor for attempts at individuation.

Jung was a great thinker whose psychological theories crossed academic disciplines to include philosophy, spirituality, folklore, and more. Nobody's perfect, however. He is also deeply criticized in other circles for his failure to denounce the rise of Hitler and the Nazis in Germany in the 1930s. He ultimately did so, but many believe it was too little, too late.

CHAPTER 18

Pioneers in Research and Healing

Energy is all around us, whether it be lightning in the sky or fossil fuel deep in the earth. These two scientific pioneers were both martyrs to their discoveries. One was killed by the very force she discovered, and the other is one of the least-known yet most misunderstood and unfairly maligned visionaries of this or any age.

Marie Curie

Marie Curie (1867–1934) was a chemist, who along with her husband, Pierre Curie, was a pioneer researcher in the field of radioactivity. She won two Nobel Prizes but did not profit financially from her work, and her work ultimately killed her. Such dedication is seldom seen in the medical community.

Top of Her Class

Marie Curie (nee Sklodowska) was born in Poland at a time and in a place where the opportunities for women were severely limited. Although she excelled in school, she took a position as a governess after

Marie Curie

graduation. She had an older sister who was studying medicine in Paris, France, where things were a little more enlightened. Her sister became a doctor and married a doctor. They invited Marie to come live with them. It was a great break for a gifted young woman. She attended the celebrated Sorbonne and graduated at the top of her class. She met and married her husband Pierre in 1894. Together they began their groundbreaking research.

All who have taken chemistry in high school are familiar with the imposing Periodic Table of Elements that probably adorned a wall in the classroom. It would have been a little smaller without Marie Curie's input. Radium and polonium would be missing from the chart had the Curies chosen another profession.

The Curies expanded upon the findings of a German physicist named Wilhelm Röntgen, who discovered x–rays, and a French scientist named Henri Becquerel, who discovered that uranium in its solid form discharges radiation. Marie Curie ascertained that the element thorium emitted radiation as well. She learned that a mineral called pitchblende released even more radiation than these other elements. Working with these existing substances, the Curies conducted extensive research and discovered two new elements, radium and polonium (which she named for her birthplace of Poland). They accumulated one gram of radium from eight tons of pitchblende.

FACTS

Marie Curie won her first Nobel Prize in 1903. She shared it with her husband and Henri Becquerel for their early work with radioactivity. Her second was awarded in 1911 for her discovery of the elements radium and polonium, the latter being named for her birthplace of Poland. The Curies' oldest daughter Irène became a scientist and Nobel Prize winner herself. Rarely are Nobel Prizes a family affair.

Tragedy struck the Curies in 1906, when Pierre was struck and killed by a horse and carriage. Marie took over his position at the Sorbonne, becoming the first woman to teach in this exalted European institute of higher learning.

The Advent of X-rays and Radiation Therapy

In 1910 Marie Curie isolated pure radium, and in 1914 the Institut de Radium was built specifically to accommodate Curie's continuing research. During World War I, Marie Curie worked to see that ambulances on the front lines had x-ray machines to aid the army surgeons in treating the wounded. She courageously brought the machines to the front lines herself. She taught a new generation of doctors and nurses how to use this new equipment and also worked with the International Red Cross.

ALERT

Those of us who visit the doctor and dentist are exposed to small amounts of radiation every time we have an x-ray. You will notice that the doctor and the assistants leave the room. Prolonged exposures to x-rays can be fatal, and sadly, this is what happened to Marie Curie. She developed leukemia and died in 1934.

The Curies never sought to patent any of their discoveries. They believed that their work should be freely given to all to benefit the world. Profoundly altruistic, they lived modestly, often in near poverty as a result.

The x-ray and radiation therapy to treat cancer have been in standard practice for decades. Though undeniably helpful, both are also indisputably harmful. Radiation treatment is a profoundly unpleasant affair, as anyone knows who has experienced it or watched a loved one go through the ordeal. For years these were the best options we had for treating cancer. It is hoped they will soon become obsolete as new technologies are discovered and implemented. There are now, albeit very expensive, computer imaging facilities that can examine your insides from head to toe without invasive treatments or any deleterious side effects.

This was not available in the early years of the last century. Marie Curie saved lives at the expense of her own and did not grow rich while exposing the world to the positive effects of radiation. She was an exemplary combination of brilliance and decency, qualities that do not always go hand in rubber glove.

Wilhelm Reich

Most people have never heard of Wilhelm Reich (1897–1957), and those who have heard of him are probably only aware of the wealth of erroneous information that has been accepted as fact. Many of these inaccuracies are deliberate attempts to discredit and misrepresent his work. Like the great thinkers of the Renaissance who were hounded by the political and religious authorities of the day, only to have their work posthumously validated, it is likely that future generations will regard Reich the way we look at Giordano Bruno and Galileo (see Chapter 6). As we've seen, men and women who are ahead of their time usually inspire criticism—and worse—when they rattle the collective cage.

Sexual Healing

Reich was a psychiatrist and scientist on the younger end of the generation that produced Freud and Jung. He studied medicine at the University of Vienna and as a member of the Vienna Psychoanalytic

Institute. He varied from typical Freudian analysis by sitting across from the patient, not behind him or her, as the patient lay on the now-stereotypical couch. Freud hailed him as a genius, but as was always the case with Sigmund, he had an inevitable falling out with his protégé.

Reich's emphasis on sexuality and the energy behind it made him unpopular among his colleagues and anathema to the self-righteous. He was labeled a sex maniac. Reich believed that a healthy sex life was the best cure for neurosis. By a healthy sex life, he meant a fully expressed, gratifying experience, not promiscuity for its own sake. The libertine and the celibate were often equally maladjusted. The Rolling Stones sang "I Can't Get No Satisfaction." This is a rock-and-roll distillation of Reich's theory: It's not quantity; it's quality.

QUESTIONS?

What is *body armor*?
According to Reich, the unhealthy person is rigid in face and form. We are all born innocent babes, but as we grow all manner of dysfunction creates a shell—what Reich called *body armor*—around us that prevents healthy expression of our normal bodily functions.

We can turn on almost any radio talk show to hear a frank discussion of how many women rarely have a satisfactory orgasm, and some never have them at all. Reich argued that men do not have a fully realized experience either. We are all sexually blocked to varying degrees, and this blockage can create more than sexual frustration. Given the teachings on sex as taboo, slightly naughty, or downright sinful, there is a lot of energy building up in the world that is not finding expression. It can cause physical and mental illness, from a mild case of obsessive-compulsive disorder to terminal cancer.

May the Orgone Be with You

These teachings were controversial stuff in the 1920s. Reich also coined the phrase *sexual revolution* long before the swinging 1960s.

This kind of talk was not well received, to say the least. He was attacking nothing short of society itself. Society denied the natural expression of sexuality, and the ramifications of this repression extended far beyond the bedroom. With this denial, people sublimated their sexual energy and transferred it to every other facet of life. Sexual repression, said Reich, could create everything from religious fanatics to fascist dictators.

In fact, his book *The Mass Psychology of Fascism* did not endear him to Hitler and the Nazis, who had just come into power in Germany. Reich also flirted with communism, but the Communists did not like his theories either. In later life, Reich was a staunch opponent of communism and all totalitarian states. The stock-in-trade of such governments was repression in every form: body, mind, and spirit.

FACTS

Look at the sky on a clear day and you can see tiny white specks spiraling around in the air. This is orgone energy. It is ubiquitous. It is in the birds and the bees and the flowers and the trees. A twentieth-century scientist and medical man discovered in a laboratory what the mystics had been talking about for millennia. Some call it *chi;* others call it *reiki.* Pop culture gurus call it *the force.*

Reich's work studying sexual energy—and the repression of sexual energy—led him to believe that there was a life force that was everywhere and in everything. Through scientific experimentation he identified this energy and called it *orgone energy.*

Reich fled Europe in the days before World War II and settled in New York City. There he continued his controversial experiments. He believed that orgone energy had enormous untapped potential. It could conceivably do everything from curing a headache to becoming a free and clear source of energy that would make fossil fuels obsolete. Theories like these made Reich enemies in high places and would later have tragic ramifications.

He constructed a device, the orgone accumulator, that could harness the energy, and if concentrated and applied to the body, often had marvelous healing properties. Reich adapted his psychiatric practice to include orgone work with more traditional psychotherapy. Though not as commonly practiced as more traditional Freudian and Jungian therapies, the likes of Sean Connery and Jack Nicholson are on record as having explored orgone therapy.

When Reich constructed a small motor that operated with orgone energy as its fuel, people outside the medical community began to take notice. If there were energy all around us that could provide a free, limitless, and nontoxic power source, a certain section of the business community and ruling class would find themselves out of business. And, to them, the business of America *is* business. One day, if the world survives, there will be alternative sources of energy in use, perhaps even orgone energy, but not until the last drop of fossil fuel is taken out of Mother Earth's hide.

Always a maverick and even a pariah, the attacks upon Reich now came in full force. Ironically, after fleeing Hitler's fascism, Reich's downfall came from forces within the United States.

The first salvo came from the Food and Drug Administration. They began to investigate the orgone accumulator. Scurrilous smear tactics had always branded Reich as a pervert, and there were accusations that the device was some kind of pornographic sex toy.

ESSENTIALS

Book burning in America? Yes, it happened. Before *Harry Potter*, Reich's books were banned and even burned. The establishment decided that orgone energy should not be discussed, because it did not exist. Yet no one was interested in reviewing Reich's findings, which sounds a lot like the pope's refusal to peer into Galileo's telescope (see Chapter 6).

Reich was eventually brought to trial on the charge that he was a charlatan. It was alleged that the orgone accumulator was a fraud and Reich's books were merely meant as publicity material to promote sales of this dubious device. A U.S. court deemed the accumulator a fraud, determined that orgone energy did not exist, and ordered Reich's books burned. Strange jurisprudence in the land of the free and the home of the brave. It is clear that powerful forces behind the scenes were manipulating events to railroad Reich.

The harassment didn't stop. Reich was eventually convicted of violating the injunction against him and sentenced to two years in prison. He died in jail just one week before he was to be released, ending the life of an innovative thinker whose controversial theories are gaining more popularity everyday.

CHAPTER 19
Great Inventors and Scientific Minds

Two of these men of science and invention amaze and baffle us with their theories, and one is largely responsible for the home entertainment center you cannot live without. From explaining the mechanics of a singularity in the space-time continuum to providing the lights, camera, and action that we take for granted, these men have greatly enriched our world.

Thomas Edison

Thomas Alva Edison (1847–1931) is the one of the most prolific and influential American inventors of all time. You use the items he devised everyday. In fact, you would feel a great loss if you were suddenly deprived of them. They are the conveniences you take for granted, probably never realizing that one man was responsible for developing them. Your home entertainment center would not exist without the hard work of Thomas Edison.

The Wizard of Menlo Park

Thomas Edison was a man of big ideas. Do you recall that ubiquitous cartoon image of a light bulb going off over a person's head to signify an idea? That happened to Edison all the time and had never happened to anyone else before that. Why, you may ask? Because Edison invented the light bulb.

As a boy, Edison learned about the telegraph, one of the earliest forms of mass communication. The telegraph transmitted clicks over wires that were received and interpreted by the operator at the other end. These dots and dashes were called Morse code, named for their creator Samuel Morse. Edison built on this technology to invent a voting machine and a stock ticker and a new and improved telegraph that could send four messages simultaneously.

QUESTIONS?

How many geniuses does it take to change a light bulb?
The answer: one, in his Menlo Park, New Jersey, shop. With the invention of the light bulb, Edison became internationally famous and was known throughout the world as the Wizard of Menlo Park.

He also improved on Alexander Graham Bell's telephone, increasing the distances over which calls could be made. Bell's device was limited; Edison made it limitless. During Edison's fiddling around with the telephone, he stumbled onto the idea that he could permanently record sounds and voices. Thus the early phonograph was invented.

In short order, Edison had revamped the telegraph and the telephone and invented a device that would make possible the music industry of today. It was after this work that the light bulb literally illuminated over his head, and he invented the incandescent lamp. After much trial and error, he came up with a prototype that burned for forty hours. There is an urban legend that Edison originally invented a light bulb that would never burn out, but changed it to a forty-hour bulb when he realized that not much money would be made selling an eternal flame.

ESSENTIALS

Edison was the first movie mogul. He built a small movie studio and began a career as a director. His films were short subjects that featured celebrities of the day, including Buffalo Bill and his Wild West Show. Charles Ogle was the first man to play Frankenstein's monster in a 1910 movie produced by Edison's studio.

Of course, you need a central source to illuminate a home or an office building and eventually a city, so Edison invented the generator, then called a dynamo.

Edison later built on the work of an Englishman named Eadweard Muybridge, whose specialty was stop-motion photography. This kind of

Thomas Edision

photography was similar to those little books in novelty stores that you flip quickly through to create the illusion of a "moving picture." Edison took this notion to the next level, and in 1890 introduced the first movie camera. The projection device that was the companion of this amazing invention was called the Kinetoscope.

Next on Edison's hit parade was the invention of what would become the modern battery. Battery power, of course, made things portable. Devices no longer had to be plugged into a power source.

Edison the Man

Edison's private life was full of ups and downs. He lost his first wife to typhoid fever at a young age. He remarried and moved his laboratories to another town in New Jersey, where he lived and worked for the remaining forty-five years of his active life. He had children from both marriages, but he was something of an absentee father, routinely spending eighteen-hour days toiling in his lab, churning out devices and creating a brave new twentieth century. Edison was the classic absent-minded professor who lacked social graces and often toiled in his soiled work clothes for days on end. But where would we be without his Herculean efforts?

ESSENTIALS

Edison embodied the American traits of rugged individualism, entrepreneurship, and a "can do" spirit. His life was the subject of two film biopics: *Young Tom Edison* starring Mickey Rooney and *Edison the Man* with Spencer Tracy in the lead.

From age twelve, Edison was partially deaf as a result of a bout of scarlet fever. Instead of succumbing to despair and self-pity, he often remarked that his hearing impairment increased the intense focus and concentration needed for his work.

Today his name is associated with the unhappy reality of paying the monthly bills. Many Americans have to make checks payable to Con Edison to keep the home fires burning. Edison is largely forgotten as a man these days, but his influence is felt in almost everything we do: turning on the lights, listening to music, watching television and movies, gabbing on the phone. His legacy permeates our culture; we would literally be in a dark age without Edison.

Albert Einstein

Even those who know next to nothing about Albert Einstein (1879–1955) are familiar with the visual representation of him: the old guy with the unruly white hair and bushy mustache in a white lab coat. This image has entered the pop culture consciousness and been lampooned in movies and cartoons for decades. Einstein's image has come to be associated with the stereotype of the scientist, both "mad" and otherwise.

Young Einstein

However, Einstein was not the eccentric crackpot sputtering incomprehensibilities in a German accent that his portrayal perpetuates. He was born in Germany but eventually came to the United States, and was the best known and arguably the most brilliant scientist of the first half of the twentieth century.

A child math whiz and all-around prodigy, Einstein often cut class but not to go to a keg party. He was smarter than his teachers and learned more through independent study. Hence he was not highly thought of by his professors at the Swiss Federal Institute of Technology in Zurich. The stuffy academics did not give Einstein any references or recommendations, so he struggled, finding the odd job here and there as a tutor and a substitute teacher. He married, had two sons, and continued studying, getting a doctorate from the University of Zurich in 1905.

FACTS

Einstein's third paper of the period is the one we are probably most familiar with, at least by the name of the theory he proposed. The paper was titled "On the Electrodynamics of Moving Bodies," and in it he outlined his famous theory of relativity.

Einstein published three significant papers in the first years of the twentieth century that changed the way the scientific community looked at physics. The first two challenged long-held beliefs about Brownian motion and the nature of light. His paper on light proposed that light is composed of particles, called photons. This radical notion did not sit well with the academics of the day. Radical notions never do. Nevertheless, Einstein's theory was proved to be correct.

Einstein was trying to understand and explain the nature of and interrelation between matter and radiation. Two laws had been established and were deemed immutable. The *mechanical worldview* dealt with the material world, and the *electromagnetic worldview* addressed light and radiation and electricity, the nonphysical yet very real elements in the universe. There had been no satisfactory worldview showing the interaction of these two laws.

Relatively Speaking

Einstein started with the premise that there is no such thing as "absolute motion." Does a car drive past a stop sign or does the stop sign move past the car? Huh? That's a no-brainer. Or is it? The stop sign is moving. It is on Earth, which is not only rotating on its axis but also revolving around the sun. In fact, we are all moving at many thousands

Albert
Einstein

of miles an hour. So you see, everything is relative. But Einstein also said that the speed of light is a constant 186,000 miles per second whether the observer of the traveling light is at motion or at rest. This is a difficult concept to explain, let alone to understand, but suffice it to say it created quite a buzz.

Einstein had to keep a day job while he continued to gain support and respectability. He got his first professorial job at the University of Zurich in 1909. He bounced around to various universities in Europe for the next few years, ending up as director of the Kaiser Wilhelm Institute for Physics in Berlin.

FACTS

As a scientist, Einstein believed in experimentation and observation of empirical data. But as a genius, he believed in intuition and in leaps of the mind that could explain things that were not necessarily easy to prove. In other words, he relied on faith that was based on his unique mind and its ability to decipher mysteries of the universe.

He continued to work on his theory of relativity, publishing the full general theory of relativity in 1916. In it, he tackled the concept of gravity.

There is more than mere gravity influencing the movement of celestial bodies. He defined time as the fourth dimension, along with the familiar three dimensions defined by the ancient math whiz Euclid. These four dimensions create the new concept of the *space/time continuum*. Those who are science fictions fans always hear that phrase bandied about.

Another familiar science fiction device attributed to Einstein is that astronauts who travel far into outer space and return will only have aged a few months or years while planet Earth will have aged decades if not centuries. "Einstein was right," says one character in the final scenes of the movie *Close Encounters of the Third Kind*, when young World War II pilots who were abducted by aliens return to 1977 America still young.

ESSENTIALS

The introduction of the fourth dimension of time proves Einstein's belief that the universe is not one of lines and planes but rather of curves. For example, light can bend as it travels, and the orbits of planets are elliptical. According to Einstein, the shortest distance between two points is not necessarily a straight line.

The theory that says that more than gravity affects motion is called the *principle of equivalence.* In this theory, equivalence means the equivalence between forces produced by gravity and acceleration. Gravity is, of course, the force that, among other functions, keeps our feet on the ground, and acceleration is, of course, increasing speed. It is impossible to determine which factor, gravity or acceleration, is impacting the object in question. Einstein maintained that if a passenger in a railroad car on a flat track was deprived of sound and the windows were covered, he or she would not be able to tell whether the train was moving or stationary. And if the car made a discernible turn, the passenger would be unable to determine if the movement was caused by gravitational pull or a change in acceleration.

Einstein spent the latter part of his life working on what he called the *unified field theory*. In other words, he sought to link every type of physical interaction within the space/time continuum. It was to be the physics version of the Buddhist principle that we are "one with everything."

Man of Peace

Einstein was awarded the Nobel Prize for physics in 1921. He was an international celebrity and spokesman for social causes, most notably pacifism and Zionism (a movement that sought to establish a national homeland for the Jews in Palestine). He opposed Germany's involvement in World War I and when Hitler came to power in 1933, Einstein left Germany for good. He came to the United States and got a job at Princeton University in New Jersey. Einstein continued to work on behalf of Zionism, but he gave pacifism a rest, given the growing Nazi menace.

FACTS

Einstein and some other physicists contacted President Franklin Roosevelt to advise him that Germany was most likely working on an atomic bomb and if the United States did not develop one first, Germany could conquer the world. Based on this warning, the race to develop the A-bomb was on. Einstein took no part in its development and testing.

Einstein returned to his pacifist leanings after the war. His Zionist nature was pleased when the state of Israel was founded in 1948, but he declined an offer to become the new nation's first president. He was a doctor, not a politician. As a man whose theories helped others develop nuclear weapons, he spent much of his energy in the postwar years preaching disarmament. Einstein died in 1955.

Stephen Hawking

Stephen Hawking (b. 1942) is a man who studies and speculates on things that can make the average person's brain hurt. He has spent his adult life trying to make things like black holes comprehensible to the general public. Not many academic eggheads can boast to having appeared on *Star Trek: The Next Generation*. Hawking played a holodeck program of himself conjured by the ever-inquisitive android Data.

A Singular Understanding

Hawking was born and educated in Oxford, England. His area of interest and expertise is the heady study of space and time, including singularities, black holes, quantum physics, and other concepts that leave most of us scratching our heads.

During his academic career, Hawking learned that he had the degenerative disease called Amyotrophic Lateral Sclerosis (ALS). He is wheelchair bound, and his speech and movement are severely impaired. Nevertheless, he has continued to work and his handicap has not thwarted his fertile mind from contributing to our understanding of the cosmos.

Hawking was fascinated by singularities. A singularity is an anomaly in the space/time continuum, something where the normal laws of physics do not apply. The best-known example of a singularity is a black hole. A black hole is the last gasp in the long life of a star. Our own sun will eventually burn out and die, collapsing and creating a void in the fabric of the universe.

FACTS

There has been much speculation about what goes on inside a black hole. Some say they are gateways to other dimensions or shortcuts to the other side of our own universe. Others suggest that, since the laws of space and time do not apply, a spaceship sucked into one would be caught in a cosmic hell, a bleak eternity in which you could take millions of years to die.

Hawking built on Albert Einstein's theory of relativity. He proved that along with the creating of the universe at the moment in time called the big bang, singularities were also created.

Fixing a Hole

Some people make a fuss over nothing, and some might suggest that the ultimate nothing is a black hole. Hawking's extensive studies revealed that a black hole is far from a void. By looking at the rim of a black hole, called an event horizon, Hawking concluded that it could either stay the same size or get bigger. Black holes never shrink. If two black holes combined, the surface would be more than simply the combined size of the two. Black holes are like the incurable disease of the cosmos; they never get "better," only "worse"—worse being a bigger ominous void capable of sucking in stars and planets. Not something that you want in your celestial neck of the woods.

Hawking corroborated the work of an American physicist named John Wheeler when he confirmed through mathematical certitude that matter that enters a black hole is not destroyed but loses its shape and chemical composition while retaining its mass.

FACTS

Hawking has written several books that try to make his theories accessible to the general public, including *Black Holes and Baby Universes and Other Essays* (1994), *A Brief History of Time* (1998), and *The Universe in a Nutshell* (2001). A documentary about his life and work based on *A Brief History of Time* may be available at your local video store or is sure to pop up periodically on PBS.

Hawking became very interested in the areas of space near black holes. Studying these unstable regions helped him refine the scientific school called quantum mechanics. For many centuries, since the days of the ancient atomists, it was believed that the atom was the smallest particle possible, and that it was indivisible. The invention and deployment of the atom bomb put an end to that theory, and since then much more had been learned about this amazing micro-universe where many of the laws of conventional science do not apply.

We have all heard of virtual reality as it relates to technology. Hawking found that there is a virtual reality within reality. Black holes were believed to be a void; and like the Roach Motel, once something checks in, it never checks out. Closer examination revealed that black holes appear to discharge heat. One explanation Hawking came up with is that "virtual particles" were being created. Space itself, also long thought to be a void, was full of spontaneously created virtual particles. These particles cannot be detected through scientific equipment, only through the way they affect those particles that we can identify through a particle detector. Hawking called these mystery particles.

In addition to matter, we have antimatter. If you're a fan of *Star Trek*, you probably know that the Starship *Enterprise* runs on a delicate balance of matter and antimatter. There is also the mind-blowing theory that there are myriad parallel universes that coexist with our universe and that occupy the same space but in another dimensional plane. These universes interact at a subtle subatomic level. To those denizens of the parallel universe, we are the antimatter.

Parents and teachers have always encouraged children to "reach for the stars." Stephen Hawking not only reached out into the cosmos, he continues to unravel its riddles and explain its many mysteries, boldly going where no scientist has gone before.

CHAPTER 20

Pop Culture Visionaries

In the twentieth century, with the explosion of the film and recording industries, and the ability to mass-produce their products for widespread consumption by the ever-eager populace, a new breed of thinking entertainers emerged. Moviemakers, sci-fi thinkers, musicians, and animators had artistic visions that would became an integral part of our pop culture consciousness.

Walt Disney

Who can deny that the man who gave the world Mickey Mouse and other beloved characters is an entertainment great thinker nonpareil? Walt Disney (1901–1966) was a maverick in the early days of movie animation. Disney was born and raised in Chicago. When he was sixteen, he lied about his age to serve with the American Red Cross during World War I. On his return to the States, he received a scholarship to the Kansas City Art Institute. His pre-Mickey endeavors included a series of animated short features for a movie theater chain called Newman's Laugh-O-Grams. It was not long before he heard the seductive call of the siren that led him westward-ho to Hollywood.

With his brother Roy O. Disney as his business partner, Disney began to produce animated short subjects—cartoons, as they are also called. His early effort was a series called *Alice Comedies*. They were a combination of a live character, Alice, thrown into an amazing animated world. Clearly he was using *Alice in Wonderland* as his inspiration. The *Alice Comedies* were very popular, as was the now-forgotten animated character of "Oswald the Lucky Rabbit."

Disney was partnered with some unscrupulous associates who stole the rights to the Oswald character, wooed most of his staff of animators away from him, and basically left him high and dry. What does a person do in a situation like that? Some may be so despondent that they would buy a one-way ticket to Palookaville and give up. Not a great thinker, however. Walt Disney went on to make pop culture history.

Disney, with his wife and the friends who stood by him, created a series of cartoons featuring a new character. One of these was the first short animated film to include a soundtrack—the 1928 masterpiece *Steamboat Willie,* which originated the concept of making a separate cartoon for each animated action. It also introduced a certain rodent that would take his place as the most famous vermin of all time. Disney even provided the voice for the character in this landmark in animation. You all know his name, and those of you of a certain age can spell it in tune: and a-one, and a-two—M-I-C-K-E-Y M-O-U-S-E!

Disney also introduced *Silly Symphonies*, a series of cartoons that did not have a star character but introduced to the world the celebrated pantheon of Donald Duck, Goofy, Pluto, Minnie Mouse, and the rest.

The first color cartoon, released in 1932, was called *Flowers and Trees*. It was also the first cartoon to win an Academy Award. Disney wanted to ambitiously push the animation envelope and make the first feature-length cartoon. He did so in 1937. *Snow White and the Seven Dwarfs* has been a perennial classic for more than sixty years. Its 2001 release in a spiffy, remastered DVD edition broke sales records, eclipsing much of the popular entertainment of today.

Most of us grew up with Disney in the periphery of our lives. We have probably all seen *Pinocchio, Bambi, Dumbo, Fantasia, Jungle Book, Sleeping Beauty, Lady and the Tramp, 101 Dalmatians*, and the many other animated classics that Disney gave us.

Disney never stopped producing animated films, but he expanded into the arena of live action in the 1950s. *Treasure Island, Swiss Family Robinson,* and *20,000 Leagues under the Sea* were early classics. This list is legion, and most of us have seen at least a few of these movies: *The Absent-Minded Professor, Son of Flubber, The Shaggy Dog, The Shaggy D.A., The Love Bug* (and its sequels), *The Computer Wore Tennis Shoes, The World's Greatest Athlete, The Parent Trap, Pollyanna,* and many more.

Disney also ventured into television with *The Mickey Mouse Club* in the 1950s. A much later incarnation introduced a very young Britney Spears and Christina Aguilera, who went on to grow up and become pop music sensations. Disney Productions also gave the world *Davy Crockett, Daniel Boone, Zorro, The Wonderful World of Disney,* and many other fondly remembered television shows.

Disney was most proud of *Mary Poppins* (1964). It was one of the most innovative films of its time, and its combination of live action and music amazed its audience. Julie Andrews won the Academy Award as Best Actress, although many believed this was to punish Audrey Hepburn and offer a consolation prize to Andrews. (Hepburn lobbied for and won the role of Eliza Doolittle in *My Fair Lady* that most felt should have gone to Andrews, who originated the role on stage.)

In 1955, Disney opened his first theme park, Disneyland, in California. It was a place where families could enjoy wonderful scenery and amusement park rides and could meet their favorite Disney characters. Disney did not live to see Walt Disney World open in Florida in 1971, but he was involved in the planning stages of this bigger and better entertainment center. An attempt to send the magic abroad, Euro Disney, was less successful.

Disney won an astounding thirty-two Academy Awards, a record that is unlikely to ever be broken. He rewrote the rules in Hollywood, and his legacy and even his name have become enmeshed in the collective consciousness of popular culture.

QUESTIONS?

Is he or isn't he?
Disney died of lung cancer in 1966 and was cremated and buried in Forest Lawn Cemetery in Los Angeles. Or was he? A bizarre urban legend that appeared after his death maintains that his body is really frozen in suspended animation, and that one day he will rise again to entertain future generations.

Walt Disney is still a thriving entertainment conglomerate with tentacles reaching into every facet of entertainment and communication. Disney owns the ABC television and radio networks. A Disney store selling all kinds of Disney merchandise can likely be found in your local mall. And the company keeps the animation tradition alive with contemporary classics like *The Lion King, Beauty and the Beast, Aladdin,* and *Tarzan.* The magic of Walt Disney is a true global phenomenon.

Leni Riefenstahl

Not every great thinker accomplishes greatness in the good sense. Some have great ideas that either directly or indirectly contribute to bad things. It is difficult enough now for a woman to have an independent and successful career in the entertainment field. It was exceedingly rare in the 1930s. Certainly there were movie stars, but they were usually under contract to a studio and had little creative control over the projects on which they worked. It was unheard of for a woman to become a movie director and to be hailed, even by her enemies, as a genius.

German Leni Riefenstahl (b. 1902) was such a woman. She is universally acclaimed as an arresting filmmaker. She was gifted in so many ways, but she did not show sound judgment in her choice of subject matter: namely, Adolf Hitler and his Nazi regime.

So many people correctly associate Hitler and fascism with cruelty and barbarism of the worst sort. They don't realize that Germany was a civilized European nation with a rich artistic and cultural reputation. This fact makes it all the more shocking and horrific that such savagery could rise amidst such civility.

Riefenstahl was a talented and beautiful actress who was a rising star in the German film industry. Given the opportunity to direct, she displayed formidable talent in what was, and to a degree still is, regarded as a man's milieu. It is no surprise that actress Jodie Foster has expressed interest in making a biopic on Riefenstahl's life.

Unfortunately for her, one of her biggest fans was Adolf Hitler. It was not wise to say no to *der Führer*, and thus she embarked on the greatest triumphs of her career, much to her future detriment.

Riefenstahl made several documentaries about Hitler and the Nazis, most notably *Triumph of the Will* (1935) and *Olympia* (1938). *Triumph of the Will* is considered the best and most notorious propaganda film of all time. It records the 1934 Nuremberg Rally. Inventive camerawork and editing create a hypnotic mood. The film whipped the Germans into a patriotic frenzy and horrified those who had the foresight to see what havoc Hitler and his henchmen would wreak upon the world. But everyone admitted that Leni Riefenstahl was a cinematic genius. It was her subject matter that was abhorrent.

Olympia is a two-part documentary about the 1936 Olympics held in Berlin. This was an equally inventive and powerful propaganda piece that was praised for its lyrical style. The film set the standard for how to cover a sporting event. She did things no one had ever done before when filming athletics, such as using slow motion, underwater photography for the swimming competitions, and other techniques that are now standard. Everything that we see in sports coverage today was inspired by the moviemaking of Leni Riefenstahl.

FACTS

Ironically, the real star of the 1936 Berlin Olympics was American track star Jesse Owens. He was indeed a stranger in a strange and unholy land. Owens, an African-American, was a gold medal winner at those games, where he also broke world records in the 200-meter race and the broad jump.

Although she was hailed as a genius, Riefenstahl made no friends outside Germany. She went to Hollywood, where she was treated cordially at best, but there was no warm welcome or offer to emigrate to Tinseltown. After World War II, the Americans briefly arrested her for her association with the Nazis, and later the French did the same, but she was released and never charged with any war crimes. In later years, she worked mostly as a still photographer in Africa. She was dismissed in the American press after the war as a "Nazi pinup girl" and blacklisted from the film industry.

Riefenstahl never shook off the stain of Nazi sympathizer, although she has denied any such leanings and considers herself a filmmaker chronicling an event. In reality, she rolled the dice and lost. Had Germany won the war she would probably have been hailed as the greatest moviemaker of the twentieth century. She wrote her unapologetic autobiography in 1993. As of this writing, she is still alive. She has had a long, long time to reflect upon what might have been.

Orson Welles

The story of Orson Welles (1915–1985), American actor, director, and producer, is a frustrating tale of genius never fully realized. To paraphrase Welles himself, he started at the top and went steadily downhill. Some attribute this to his quixotic, mercurial personality; others say it was Hollywood's resentment of and inability to handle this Colossus in their midst.

The man who directed *Citizen Kane*—unilaterally regarded by film buffs worldwide as the greatest movie ever made—ended his career as a frequent guest on the *Dean Martin Celebrity Roasts* and performing magic tricks on the *Merv Griffin Show* in his ubiquitous black suit. He spent his later years receiving lifetime achievement awards, but studio heads would not give him what he really wanted—a directing assignment.

ESSENTIALS

Hollywood began taking an interest in this brash young dynamo. Legend has it that when he first walked on to a movie set, he commented that it was the best electric train set a boy could have.

Born in Kenosha, Wisconsin, Welles was a child prodigy who began exploring his artistic bent practically from the cradle. In his late teens, he traveled to Ireland and worked in the fabled Abbey Theatre. By the time he was in his early twenties, he was a radio star in New York City, where he founded the Mercury Theater. This troupe performed radio shows and theatrical productions. Welles was the first man to ominously intone the now famous words, "Who knows what evil lurks in the hearts of men— The Shadow knows!" And on Halloween 1938 he scared the collective pants off America with his radio adaptation of H. G. Wells's *The War of the Worlds*, done in a news-broadcast style. Millions actually believed that Martians had landed in New Jersey!

Welles chose as his first project a film called *Citizen Kane* (1941), which was a fictionalized account of the life and times of the powerful and controversial newspaper tycoon, William Randolph Hearst. Welles had unprecedented freedom for a fledgling director and made a masterpiece that broke all the rules and changed moviemaking forever. Not bad for a twenty-five-year-old.

His next film also pops up on film critics' and historians' ten-best lists. Except for a brief cameo, Welles did not appear in *The Magnificent Ambersons* (1942), based on the novel by Booth Tarkington. Welles had a combative relationship with "the suits" in Hollywood and as a result never achieved the potential promised by *Citizen Kane* and *The Magnificent Ambersons*. He continued to take acting jobs in other people's movies, most memorably a small, yet crucial role in the suspense classic *The Third Man* (1949). The films he directed include *The Stranger* (1946), in which he played a Nazi war criminal hiding out as a college professor on an American campus. He teamed with his then wife, the sultry Rita Hayworth, in the thriller *The Lady From Shanghai* (1948), which climaxed with the now famous shootout in a carnival hall of mirrors.

FACTS

Welles directed and played the lead in a low budget version of Shakespeare's *Macbeth* and spent years filming *Othello* (1952) in Europe. He had to halt the filming many times when he ran out of money and took acting jobs in more traditional Hollywood fare to fund the ongoing project.

Welles's last great Hollywood film was the bizarre and moody film noir, *Touch of Evil* (1958). Originally hired as an actor in the movie, the film's star, Charlton Heston, lobbied to give Welles the directing job as well. Welles completely revamped the script and turned a grade-B thriller into a classic.

Welles continued to appear in other people's movies and had plenty of work as a narrator and voice-over artist. His dulcet tones were in great demand. His voice and literally larger-than-life personage were ubiquitous on television commercials and in small but memorable parts in feature films like *The Muppet Movie* (1979). Citizen Welles left us in 1985.

Gene Roddenberry

American Gene Roddenberry (1921–1991) boldly went where no screenwriter had gone before. He came up with an idea for a television show that had only marginal success in its initial run. This could hardly be deemed the work of a great thinker. Yet the idea eventually took on a life of its own, becoming a pop culture phenomenon that has grown and evolved and shows no signs of slowing down. It is mythology for the modern era. It has stalwart heroes, villains worthy of being hissed at, and as compelling a blend of camaraderie, philosophy, and derring-do as anything old Homer chipped on his tablets. It is, of course, *Star Trek*, and its creator Gene Roddenberry was a true pop culture visionary.

ESSENTIALS

Another television titan was the brain behind Desilu Productions (named for Desi Arnaz and Lucille Ball). Ironically, Lucille Ball is largely responsible for getting the original *Star Trek* series on the air. One television legend helped give birth to another.

Born in El Paso, Texas, Roddenberry came of age during the golden age of radio, when larger-than-life heroes literally stirred the imaginations of American youth, forcing listeners to fill in the pictures to match the words and sounds they were hearing. Radio forced people to think and to dream. (When things are presented in digitally remastered living color on a high-definition screen, the mind naturally atrophies. Hence the sorry state of pop culture today. But I digress.)

Roddenberry was a decorated pilot in the Army Air Corps during World War II, rising to the rank of captain. He was a civilian pilot after the war and survived a fatal crash. Of course, he would make household words out of fictional captains of flying craft later in his life. But writing was always his avocation, and eventually he went to Hollywood to follow his calling.

His calling was not readily forthcoming, however, so he joined the Los Angeles Police Department where his writing was limited to speeches and press releases. He continued to write television scripts in his off-duty hours under a pseudonym. Like most "overnight successes," Roddenberry toiled for many years and suffered the indignity and discouragement of mounting rejection letters.

His determination eventually paid off, and the writing jobs came. He wrote for many television shows, including the classic Western series *Have Gun, Will Travel*. But the nagging notion of something he called "Wagon Train to the Stars" continued to inflame his restless muse. *Wagon Train* was another Western show in which the titular caravan traveled across the untamed West encountering a different adventure each week. What if this notion was transferred to a spaceship traversing the limitless cosmos? This is how *Star Trek* was conceived in 1966.

FACTS

There are really only a handful of stories circulating in the collective consciousness. Literature, drama, television, and film are infinite spins on a few finite themes. It is the philosophical notion of thesis-antithesis-synthesis. Take an idea (*Wagon Train*); add a new element (science fiction) and you get the synthesis of the two (*Star Trek*). This simple formula is the essence of creativity.

The first *Star Trek* pilot, although considered a classic today, was regarded as "too cerebral" and not purchased by the network. Most science fiction of the day was juvenile in nature and the genre was not yet taken seriously by the "sophisticated" set. The only respected fantasy show at that time was the legendary *Twilight Zone*.

A second pilot was commissioned, and the main character was recast. William Shatner came aboard as the swashbuckling and histrionic Captain James T. Kirk (replacing Jeffrey Hunter's more muted Captain Christopher Pike). The pilot was purchased by Desilu Productions.

You probably know the story all too well. The crew of the USS *Enterprise* "boldly goes where no man has gone before." Captain Kirk, logical Mr. Spock, cantankerous Dr. McCoy, and the rest of the cast shared seventy-nine hour-long adventures from 1966 to 1969. Some episodes are masterpieces; others are serviceable entertainment; and many others are just silly. But an ineffable, elusive charm infused the proceedings.

Star Trek got off to a slow start. The show lasted just three seasons and was never a hit during its initial run. In fact, it was almost canceled more than once, saved only by a deluge of fan mail. It was only when it went into syndication in the 1970s and was shown as reruns that *Star Trek* really found its audience, spawning a devoted new following of Trekkies, a movies series, several spin-off television shows, and many hundreds of *Star Trek* conventions, which continue to be enormously popular. Today it remains a beloved classic.

The popularity of another sci-fi enterprise, *Star Wars*, made a *Star Trek* movie a highly anticipated inevitability. Six films with the original cast were made between 1979 and 1991: *Star Trek: The Motion Picture, Star Trek II: The Wrath of Khan, Star Trek III: The Search for Spock, Star Trek IV: The Voyage Home, Star Trek V: The Final Frontier*, and *Star Trek VI: The Undiscovered Country*. William Shatner returned for one more and earned the wrath of many a loyal fan by accepting a fat paycheck to kill off Captain Kirk in *Star Trek: Generations* (1994). This movie was a crossover film that introduced the cast of *Star Trek: The Next Generation* to the big screen, which starred Patrick Stewart as Captain Jean-Luc Picard.

ESSENTIALS George Lucas (b. 1944), along with Gene Roddenberry, gave contemporary times its modern mythology. All cultures have had their myths and legends, and most have survived the millennia and can still be read and enjoyed. But Lucas's contribution, the *Star Wars* universe, first captured the imagination of the world in 1977 and continues to enthrall us.

But the story does not end there. Lightning struck twice for Roddenberry with the creation of *Star Trek: The Next Generation*, which ran for seven seasons and has spawned, to date, three feature films.

Deep Space Nine, Voyager, and the new *Enterprise* make *Star Trek* one of the longest-running entertainment franchises and a source of joy for millions of fans worldwide.

Gene Roddenberry had the poignant opportunity to posthumously "boldly go." After his death, a canister of his ashes was given the rare honor of taking a flight aboard one of NASA's space shuttles. It was a fitting tribute to a man who inspired millions to look to the stars and dream.

George W. Lucas, Jr.

George Lucas (b. 1944) is the man who, along with Gene Roddenberry, gave contemporary times its modern mythology. All cultures have had their myths and legends, and most have survived the millennia and can still be read and enjoyed. But Lucas's contribution, the *Star Wars* universe, first captured the imagination of the world in 1977 and continues to enthrall us. It is no surprise, because Lucas, pop culture visionary that he is, employed ancient techniques to seduce his contemporary audience.

Lucas was born in Modesto, California. He was a racecar enthusiast and film student. His student films won him a scholarship from Warner Brothers. His first film was a low-budget science fiction movie called *THX-1138* (1970). It was an expanded version of an award-winning student film he had made. His first successful film was the enormously popular *American Graffiti* in 1973.

ESSENTIALS

If you recognize THX, it's because it became the name of a sound system Lucas's company, Lucasfilm Ltd., created. You have seen its logo appearing before movies in your local multiplex.

His next film was *Star Wars* (1977), and the rest is history. *Star Wars* became the first film to gross $200 million at the box office, and it set the bar for the future of filmmaking. Its enormous popularity is due not only to its dazzling special effects and technical wizardry, but also because its story and characters tap directly into our collective unconscious (see Chapter 18 and the profile on Carl Jung). This is not nefarious subliminal trickery; it is storytelling at its best.

George Lucas studied the work of another great thinker, the noted mythographer Joseph Campbell. As you may recall from Chapter 18, the venerable Campbell was a student of comparative mythology and wrote a book called *The Hero with a Thousand Faces*. In this seminal work, Campbell reduced all myths to what he called the "monomyth." All myths for all cultures have common themes and a similar cast of characters, similar to what Carl Gustav Jung called archetypes. Everyone from the Greeks and Romans to Africans and Chinese and Polynesians essentially tell the same stories to explain the universe and their place in it. Jung, Campbell, and Lucas believe these tales inflame the spirit at a subconscious level because they sprang from that spirit within all of us.

Whether you believe this theory or not, what it evident is that Lucas took the archetypes and found the makings of a story that tapped into the collective unconscious of moviegoers. The original *Star Wars* trilogy (*Star Wars* in 1977, *The Empire Strikes Back* in 1980, and *Return of the Jedi* in 1983) and now the prequel trilogy (*The Phantom Menace* in 1999, *Attack of the Clones* in 2002, and a third installment to be named at a later date) have been among the top-grossing films of all time and have made George Lucas and his collaborators a lot of money. They have also enthralled and mesmerized millions of loyal fans. What makes George Lucas a great thinker is his instinct and ability to tap into the rich tapestry of myth and legend and devise his own spin for a myth-starved, somewhat stale, pop culture landscape.

Steven Spielberg

Along with his friend George Lucas (they collaborated on the *Indiana Jones* trilogy), Steven Spielberg (b. 1947) stands as one of the most important modern filmmakers of the era. Despite the periodic misfire, his track record is nonpareil. And in his role as a producer, he has influenced a generation of fellow moviemakers.

Born in Cincinnati, Ohio, Spielberg was already a golden boy and wunderkind when he directed a now-cult-classic episode of the short-lived TV series called *Night Gallery*, which was created and hosted by Rod Serling and was an unsuccessful attempt to be the 1970s version of Serling's legendary *Twilight Zone* series. Spielberg directed former screen star and aging diva Joan Crawford in the tale of a wealthy blind woman who receives an eye transplant that will allow her to see for twelve hours. In typical Rod Serling fashion, there is a power blackout the night she opens her eyes. She wanders in the dark night and finally sees the sunrise before going blind again.

Spielberg also directed an acclaimed TV movie *Duel* (1971), in which a solitary motorist is terrorized and pursued on a desolate stretch of highway by a relentless truck. Spielberg's first feature film was the drama *The Sugarland Express*, starring Goldie Hawn. And then came *Jaws*, which became the first movie to make $100 million at the box office. (Spielberg later broke his own record with *E.T. The Extra-Terrestrial* and again with *Jurassic Park*, which grossed more than $900 million.)

You can hear the *Jaws* theme in your mind right now, can't you? It is the most recognizable few notes of music in a film that became the biggest hit of the day way back in 1975. Spielberg had nothing to do with the inexcusably inferior sequels that followed, including *Jaws 3D* and *Jaws 4: The Revenge*.

A list of Spielberg's films reveals his undisputed status as a cinematic great thinker, whose film characters are some of the most enduring of all time. Whether he had the uncanny ability to tap into the zeitgeist of the times, or whether the collective taste of the world conformed to his personal tastes, he has been an avatar of pop culture since *Jaws*. Consider this impressive list:

- *Close Encounters of the Third Kind* (1977)
- *Raiders of the Lost Ark* (1981)
- *E.T. The Extra-Terrestrial* (1982)
- *Indiana Jones and the Temple of Doom* (1984)
- *Indiana Jones and The Last Crusade* (1989)

- *Jurassic Park* (1993)
- *Schindler's List* (1993)
- *Amistad* (1997)
- *Saving Private Ryan* (1998)
- *A.I. Artificial Intelligence* (2001)

Of course, even pop culture visionaries don't hit a home run every time at bat. Anyone remember *1941*? Or *Hook*, a revisionist Peter Pan tale, with Robin Williams as the flyboy in green tights and Dustin Hoffman doing a mediocre Terry-Thomas imitation of the titular pirate?

Entertainers like Spielberg often encounter obstacles when they try to make "serious" films. *The Color Purple* (1985) and *Empire of the Sun* (1987) were not big hits or unilateral critical successes, but that changed with the masterful *Schindler's List* and *Saving Private Ryan*.

Viewers of *A.I. Artificial Intelligence* will notice something that dates the film if Spielberg does not decide to digitally delete the special effect from the video and DVD. In the future world of *A.I.*, Manhattan Island is in ruins, nearly submerged. Yet the ruins of the World Trade Center loom large.

With his production company Amblin Entertainment, and later Dreamworks SKG (which teams him with other big shots David Geffen and Jeffrey Katzenberg), Spielberg the producer has had a formidable impact on popular culture. Some of the films he produced but did not direct include the *Back to the Future* movies, *Gremlins, Men in Black, Twister, The Mask of Zorro, Gladiator,* and many others. He ventured into animation with the *American Tail* and *Land Before Time* movies, and the *Pinky and the Brain* television show.

The Beatles

All you may need is love, but the Beatles gave the world much more than that. Consistently named by fans and musicians alike as the most influential rock band in history, these four lads from Liverpool, England, did nothing less than change the face of music. In doing so, they also changed pop culture, the phenomenon of celebrity, hairstyles, and the impact of celebrities in social and political issues, and they helped introduce American and European youth to Eastern religions to boot. During their brief but eventful career, the Beatles released over 20 twenty original albums in the United States, including *Meet the Beatles, Rubber Soul, Revolver, Magical Mystery Tour, The Beatles* (also known as The White Album), *Abbey Road,* and *Let It Be.*

FACTS

The Beatles were heavily influenced by American rock and roll stars such as Little Richard and Chuck Berry. They also revered Elvis Presley, who, like many American singers, resented their intrusion into the pop culture world and it is believed offered to spy on them for the Nixon administration. Of course, this was the later Elvis of the jumpsuit and half cape era, when self-indulgence and abuse were taking their toll.

Just as America spearheaded the D-day invasion on June 6, 1944, England returned the favor—although many parents of the day were not particularly grateful—with something called the "British Invasion" twenty years later. "Beatlemania" officially reached American shores with the Beatles' appearance on *The Ed Sullivan Show* in 1964. Seventy-three million viewers tuned in to see what all the buzz was about. John, Paul, George, and Ringo immediately eclipsed Frankie Avalon, Fabian, and the other clean-cut American soft rock icons of the late 1950s and early 1960s were immediately eclipsed by John, Paul, George, and Ringo.

These mop-topped boys hailed from working-class backgrounds in Liverpool, England. From 1959 to 1962, their drummer was the "Mr. Asterisk" of rock and roll, Pete Best. Ringo Starr joined the band just before the band's wild ride into the swinging sixties.

The Beatles' body of work can be divided into two periods. The first half of their brief time together was pure pop magic—cute, clever, and eminently danceable tunes that evoked youth and playfulness. Mid-1960s songs such as "I Want to Hold Your Hand," "She Loves You," and "Love Me Do" are just plain fun, deceptively simple, and charming.

But what makes the Beatles great thinkers in their chosen field was their desire to reinvent themselves, leaping beyond the rewarding and lucrative success as pretty-boy pop stars. In the latter half of the 1960s, their music became more inventive and original. They stopped touring in live concerts about halfway through their life span and concentrated on studio recordings. They incorporated instruments beyond the usual guitars and drums, such as the sitar, and used the existing technology to make truly ground-breaking recordings. This made them bona fide "recording artists" rather than a mere "boy band."

Even the cranky parents of young Beatles fans warmed to later efforts such as "Let It Be," "Hey Jude," and "The Long and Winding Road." The 1967 album *Sgt. Pepper's Lonely Hearts Club Band* was arresting in its innovation and elevated pop music to a new level of artistry.

ESSENTIALS

Long before benefit concerts such as Live Aid or Farm Aid were in vogue, George Harrison organized and performed at an all-star charity concert in 1971 to raise millions for the famine-torn country of Bangladesh. The live album, *The Concert for Bangladesh*, won a Grammy Award.

Most of the Beatles' songs were written by John Lennon and Paul McCartney, but George Harrison contributed several of note, including the haunting hit "Something," a tune that Frank Sinatra recorded twice and called his favorite love song. He put his own twist on it by changing the original lyric of "You stick around now, it may show" to "You stick around, Jack, it may show." George Harrison later whimsically used Sinatra's rewritten lyric in his own performances of the song.

The Beatles also made a few movies, which enjoyed varying degrees of success. *A Hard Day's Night* (1964) and *Help!* (1965) were hits, revealing their flair for comedy and satire. They were a comedy team to rival the Marx Brothers as they cavorted around swinging London and other locales with a wit and irreverence that eclipses the "shagadelic" Austin Powers.

The Beatles split up in 1970 in a less-than-amicable break up. Each member has had a successful solo career, although we've lost two of the four members. John Lennon's life was cut short by his tragic murder in 1980 in New York City, and George Harrison succumbed to cancer in 2001. Paul McCartney is still active in the music industry and is now Sir Paul, having been knighted by Queen Elizabeth in 1997. Ringo went on to star in movies like *Caveman* and the miniseries *Princess Daisy*. He still tours regularly with his All-Starr Band.

Their original recordings continue to sell, and their many collections and anthologies always top the charts when they are released, outselling the current crop of pop stars and gaining the Beatles new generations of fans. Thirty Beatles tunes reached the Billboard Top 10 between 1964 and 1969. In 2000, twenty-seven of these number-one singles were released on one CD, appropriately called *1*, which became an instant bestseller in several countries. In 1988 the Beatles were inducted into the Rock and Roll Hall of Fame.

Madonna

She was born Madonna Louise Veronica Ciccone in 1958, one of eight children, in Michigan. In a classic show business rags to riches story, the woman we call simply Madonna left Middle America with little money and big dreams. After studying dance for years she incorporated a little warbling into her gyrations and the rest, as they say, is history.

ESSENTIALS

In the 1980s, Madonna burst on to the scene with songs such as "Like A Virgin" and "Borderline." Her first attempts to break into movies were unsuccessful, (anyone remember *Shanghai Surprise*?) as was her marriage to her co-star, Sean Penn.

Madonna has an amazing ability to reinvent herself and spring Phoenix-like from the ashes of her last incarnation. Madonna remains on the cutting edge of pop culture.

Madonna continually pushed the envelope and the boundaries of good taste. She got the Catholics angry with "Like a Prayer" and the pro-choice folks irate with "Papa Don't Preach" wherein she makes up her mind and is keeping her baby. When the performer decided she wanted a baby, she eschewed the traditional route but the second time around she was more conservative. She met and married British director Guy Ritchie and they produced her second child. Her kinky video "Justify My Love" had the distinction of being banned by MTV. She brought fetishism out of the dungeon with the song "Hanky Panky" and the generically titled coffee table photography book, *Sex*.

Now a wife and mother in midlife, one wonders what direction her career will take. One thing is for certain, she will remain in the public eye until, like Sinatra, she faces the final curtain.

CHAPTER 21

Great Entrepreneurial Minds

The men who made computers accessible, and made billions doing it, were the new wave of entrepreneurial and techno-revolutionaries. The fact that Granny spends much of her time surfing the Net is due in no small part to these men of vision. And lest you think all great entrepreneurial minds are computer types, don't forget the salesman extraordinaire in this chapter.

Ron Popeil

He did not say, "I think therefore I am," but he did invent such gadgets as the Pocket Fisherman, Chop-O-Matic, and the Rhinestone and Stud Setter, which he alleged would increase the value of your jeans at least fivefold. More people have heard of Ron Popeil than know who René Descartes was (and if *you* want to know who Descartes was, check Chapter 2). Unlike Popeil, the philosophers of yesteryear did not have the convenience of infomercials to spread their ideas.

Birth of a Salesman

Ron Popeil (b. 1935) is one of the most influential and successful entrepreneurs in the history of capitalism. He overcame humble beginnings and an unhappy childhood to create a peaceful empire as the "king of infomercials." Popeil does not make weapons of mass destruction or devise schemes to destroy the ecosystem. He helps you "cut the fat" and "set it and forget it" with his most recent contributions to Western civilization: the Showtime Rotisserie and BBQ, and the Pasta Maker.

After his parents divorced, young Ron lived the life of a virtual orphan, a Dickensian waif in a cold, cruel world. His career as a pitchman began when he went to live with his estranged father, Samuel J. Popeil, who was an inventor of gadgets. Young Ron functioned in a role akin to a magician's "lovely assistant" by helping his father demonstrate his products to potential buyers.

He quickly learned that he was a born salesman, and over the decades usurped his father at his chosen profession. This success gave him some satisfaction, perhaps, for the abandonment he experienced in his childhood. Like many performers, he found the adulation of the audience some compensation for the lack of parental affection.

With the advent of television in the 1950s, Popeil became more than a street corner barker. Rather than enthralling a handful of bemused and curious pedestrians, the entire nation became his audience, and his fertile mind concocted many an appliance: the Ronco Spray Gun, the Chop-O-Matic, the Dial-O-Matic, the Veg-O-Matic, the Mince-O-Matic, the afore-mentioned Pocket Fisherman, and the Rhinestone and Stud Setter, to name a few. His personal appearances were usually unscripted, and through repetition and trial and error he perfected the perfect pitchman shtick.

QUESTIONS?

Bass-O-Matic? What's that?
The classic "Bass-O-Matic" skit on *Saturday Night Live* was a twisted tribute to Popeil. Dan Ackroyd's manic pitchman puts a dead fish in a blender and then turns it on to create a nutritious and delicious "health shake." Popeil was said to be delighted. Such things are the sincerest form of flattery and make for great publicity.

Popeil is also a shrewd businessman who made a fortune, lost it in the shifting sands of capitalism, bought it back from a foreclosing bank, and enjoyed that rare "second act" that F. Scott Fitzgerald said did not happen in American life (not for him, certainly, further proof that people should avoid making sweeping generalizations).

Saturday-Morning Staple

Popeil is not resting on his laurels in the twilight of his life. His cheerful mug and contagious enthusiasm are all over the tube, where he's currently hawking his Showtime Rotisserie and BBQ, and the Pasta Maker. Popeil has it all—money, fame, and the requisite much-younger wife so common to the multimillionaire class. Yet he apparently has allowed the injustices of the past to repeat.

A valuable life lesson can be learned by watching the second Showtime Rotisserie and BBQ infomercial. First, it is not as engaging and charming as the original. Like the cute child who, upon realizing that grownups find him cute, begins to resort to cloying shtick and quickly becomes annoying, Popeil forgot a prime dictum of business—if it ain't broke, don't fix it. But the most psychologically intriguing moment comes when he introduces his middle-aged daughter. He ignores her gushing testimonial as he fusses with the device and is oblivious to her plaintive plea to allow her to utter his rallying cry, "Set it and forget it!" She does yelp the slogan, but with no acknowledgment from Daddy. Ron should recall his days hawking his father's wares before Woolworth salesmen in old Chicago. Even great thinkers often cannot prevent family dysfunction from crossing the generations.

Bill Gates

Alternately revered and reviled, prosecuted and praised, Bill Gates (b. 1955) has changed the way we look at the world, and the way the world can come to us. Take a closer look at the bespectacled guy with the pocket protector in a cubicle near yours. Bill Gates is either an angel or a devil to him, a role model to inspire him or a man who elicits profound envy. Gates is the poster boy inspiration of nerdy computer geeks everywhere.

Bill Gates is, of course, the man behind Microsoft, the computer giant with whom almost all of us have had some firsthand experience. These words are being typed in the Microsoft Word program. Chances are you use a Windows operating system on your PC, unless you are a MAC user. His innovative entrepreneurial spirit has made him one of the richest private citizens in the world, and his business practices made him the cyberdevil incarnate in the eyes of some competitors.

Computer Whiz Kid

Gates was born in 1955 in Seattle, Washington. His interest in the relatively new world of computers began at an early age. His journey began at age thirteen when he programmed the computer in Lakeside School, the private school he attended.

Gates began the Microsoft Corporation in 1974 at the age of nineteen, with his boyhood friend Paul Allen. They were classmates at Lakeside School in their native Seattle. In the late 1960s, this school had access to the primitive computers of the time. As Gates and Allen worked with these primordial machines, little did they know that the imaginations and passion of youth would make them rich and change the world. Their pre-Microsoft endeavor called Traf-O-Data was a company that was involved in computerized traffic analysis. Microsoft, originally hyphenated as Micro-soft, was formed later when they created and licensed a software program called MITS (Micro Instrumentation and Telemetry Systems). Their software became part of the new Altair microcomputer. Gates dropped out of college to focus on his fledgling business. No flipping burgers for this kid!

"Micro" Manager

Gates made a deal with IBM in which Microsoft would provide the operating system for their PC, or personal computer. MS-DOS quickly became the standard, and Gates was a billionaire by the age of thirty-one. Then came Windows. Other than the Mac users out there, every computer literate American is familiar with Windows. That's a lot of consumers. Gates became a rich and powerful man, and such men, whether through their actions or the envy of others, make enemies.

FACTS

A very thinly veiled caricature of Gates appears in the teenybopper conspiracy movie *Antitrust*. In the film, a computer tycoon from the Pacific Northwest steals the work of young geeks puttering in their parent's basements and then kills them. The movie did for Gates what Orson Welles did for William Randolph Hearst in *Citizen Kane*, but there the similarity ends.

Gates was accused of thwarting competition by wielding the might of Microsoft against his competitors. The allegations were that Gates exerted pressure on computer hardware companies like Compaq, Dell, Gateway, and others by making it clear that if they wanted the Windows operating system preloaded in their product, they must exclude competitor's products.

Bill Clinton and Attorney General Janet Reno's Justice Department decided to make a federal case of it. In 1999 Microsoft was found guilty of antitrust laws and ordered to break itself into two companies. This decision was overturned in an appeal, but the company was nevertheless chided for not playing fair. In 2001, Microsoft made $25.3 billion and has more than 40,000 employees. Gates's current title is chairman and chief software architect of Microsoft. He transferred his CEO duties to former executive vice president Steve Ballmer with the intention of focusing on the creative and development end of the business. Gates purchased some original sketches of Leonardo da Vinci for many millions of dollars, perhaps as a source of inspiration, not unlike the woman who tapes affirmations such as "You Go, Girlfriend" on her bathroom mirror.

ESSENTIALS

Bill Gates has written two best-selling books. In *The Road Ahead* (1995), which he wrote with two collaborators, he speculated about the technological advancements in the near and far future and how they will reshape society. *Business @ the Speed of Thought* (1999) is a book of similar ruminations about the changing business world.

Like any exceptional businessman, Gates is not shy when it comes to promoting a new product. When Gates decided that Microsoft was remiss in not joining the lucrative fray of PC gaming, he naturally did so with a splash. He introduced the Xbox at the Consumer Electronics Show in Las Vegas, Nevada, with flashy WWF superstar The Rock at his side.

The Xbox had the benefit of Microsoft's deep pockets behind it, so it could emerge as an instant competitor to Sony and Sega. The Xbox is about the size of a VCR, and Gates boasts that it the ultimate gaming experience. Gaming software is the same as DVD technology, so the device should also be able to function as a standard DVD player. It is able to do so, but only if you buy the appropriate kit to "unlock" this capability. Business is business, however.

Some have found the claims that the Xbox is three times more powerful than its competitors to be an exaggeration. Critics of Gates and Microsoft have remarked throughout the years that many of its products are released with "bugs," forcing consumers to buy an inevitable upgrade. The author of this tome has lost text when his Microsoft Windows has crashed for what the computer tells him is an <unknown> reason. (A word to the wise: Save your work often!)

Gates's current interest is biotechnology. Can a real life Data from *Star Trek: The Next Generation*, or maybe the cute kid from *AI: Artificial Intelligence* be far from fruition? In 1999 Gates and his wife Melinda established the Bill and Melinda Gates Foundation, a philanthropic organization that focuses on health issues in developing countries and other causes. Gates donated $5 billion to the Foundation in 1999.

Bill Gates, through shrewd—some say ruthless—business acumen, has changed everything about our world. Admire him or curse him, he has made an enormous impact on how we work, play, and live.

Steve Jobs

Steve Jobs (b. 1955) is the cofounder of Apple Computer, makers of the Macintosh personal computer. Along with rival Bill Gates, he brought computing and its infinite possibilities to the masses.

The Dynamic Duo

Born in San Francisco, California, Steve Jobs was an orphan. He was adopted by Paul and Clara Jobs. As a high school kid in Los Altos, California, Jobs took a summer job with the Hewlett-Packard Company. There he met Stephen Wozniak, the man who would later become his business partner. This was in the early 1970s, and as the hippie era drew to a close, Jobs took a trip to India seeking enlightenment, as was the fashion in those days.

ESSENTIALS

After high school, Jobs worked for Atari as a video game designer. Those of a certain age will remember primitive yet charming games like Asteroids, Missile Command, and Battle Zone—quaint by comparison to today's complex video games.

Returning from his pilgrimage, Jobs hooked up with his friend Wozniak, and in a Horatio Alger tale for the high-tech age, they built a computer in Jobs's parent's garage. They called it the Apple I. The computer was sold for the curiously biblical price of $666. They sold a few copies and established the Apple Computer Company in 1976.

Apple II was released shortly thereafter, and it was more user-friendly than the first. The personal computing age had begun, and it was an inexorable juggernaut that continues to infinity and beyond.

The Lisa was released in 1983. It was the first computer to introduce the now ubiquitous—and to many, indispensable—mouse. The Macintosh PC was next, with each new model becoming easier and easier for the non-nerd to use. A mouse directing a cursor to a "platform" where the programs were represented by small icons and could be opened by clicking them was an amazing innovation. It was no longer necessary to type complex codes with forward and back slashes from the c-prompt. Even Grandma could become computer literate with this system. If this sounds a lot like Microsoft Windows, which came afterward, it is.

The Big Apple

Jobs's triumph continued unchecked through the early 1980s, until financial and other problems led to his involuntary "resignation" from Apple Computer. Competition from the leviathan IBM, which entered the personal computer market in 1983 (with the Microsoft Windows platform), did not help matters.

ESSENTIALS

Jobs went Hollywood when he bought the computer division of George Lucas's Lucasfilm Ltd. in 1986 and called it Pixar Animation Studios. Pixar went on to make *Toy Story, Toy Story 2,* and *Monsters, Inc.,* and millions and millions of dollars.

The sheer might of IBM made Windows the industry standard; the concept of "cross platform" software did not exist then. They were incompatible machines. Finding himself out on his ear from the company he built, Jobs started a new computer company in 1985 called NeXT, but it turned out not to be the next big thing and it eventually closed shop.

In an example of big business irony, Apple Computer bought the technology Jobs and company had created with NeXT, and Jobs found himself functioning as a consultant for the company he had founded twenty years earlier. Within a year, Jobs was asked to resume his duties as CEO. The prodigal son had come home. Jobs turned the faltering company around. Jobs was also directly involved in the introduction of the iMac, the Mac version of the notebook computer, which was a big hit.

As a pioneer in the PC revolution, Steve Jobs is a premier example of the entrepreneurial "can-do" spirit, a Thomas Edison for the digital age. Reports say that he is also a driven perfectionist who demands the same of those around them and lets them know in no uncertain terms if they are not measuring up. Like General Patton, Jobs was not in the business of being liked. He was in the business of being the best.

Steve Case

Steve Case (b. 1958) is the man behind America Online. AOL is the most popular online service, with millions of members who have millions more screen names. It is an international Internet community, where you can do anything from check your horoscope to find your soul mate, and everything in between.

America Online began its cyber life as an Internet bulletin board called Quantum Computer Services. Case was another digital-age wunderkind and a natural entrepreneur, from managing his boyhood lemonade stand in Hawaii to becoming CEO of one of the largest companies in the history of capitalism.

Early AOL

Case was an aficionado of the early BBS (bulletin board systems), which were akin to the Internet version of the Lascaux cave paintings. Or, as Mr. Spock said in the classic *Star Trek* episode "The City on the Edge of Forever," it was like working with stone knives and bearskins in a zinc-plated, vacuum-tubed culture. User-friendly was not the watchword of the primitive online world.

Case, after a couple of failed enterprises, established his own BBS. Called Quantum Computer Services, it was designed for users of the Commodore 64 computer. It soon began to offer a graphical interface and expanded its availability to other computer models, including Apple, Tandy (Radio Shack), and eventually IBM compatibles. The main competitors in those days were CompuServe, Prodigy, and a few others. Quantum needed to make a quantum leap; it had thousands of subscribers compared to Prodigy's million.

FACTS

The late 1990s was a time of great growth for AOL, which expanded to Australia and Europe. Its stock became publicly traded, one of the first dot.coms to do so. AOL remains one of few dot.com stocks still standing after most went bust, not with a bang, but with the collective whimper of all those professionals who ended up on the unemployment line.

Case changed the company's name to America Online in 1989. Its marketing appeal was to a mainstream audience. People who would ordinarily be intimidated by the Internet were drawn to AOL because of its user-friendly format. AOL grew by the proverbial quantum leaps in the early 1990s. Mid-decade found AOL in disrepute. Customers were confronted with annoying busy signals as they tried in vain to log on, and AOL frequently crashed. AOL weathered the tough times, though, improving its capabilities and increasing its access numbers.

AOL gained millions of new subscribers yearly as the personal computer industry boomed and as the Internet began to come into its own as a valuable—and to some indispensable—alternate source for news, information, and all manner of recreation. Suddenly AOL was everywhere, gobbling up its former rival CompuServe in 1997 and a telephone company called WorldCom. In 1998 they took over Netscape, a popular Web browser and competitor to Microsoft Internet Explorer. They also bought Moviefone and its 777-FILM phone number to get movie times and to order tickets. The voices of "Mr. Moviefone" and the "Welcome" and "You've Got Mail" voice of America Online have become cult figures in their own right. Bill Gates (profiled earlier in this chapter) and Steve Case, and their respective corporate leviathans, have become the battling gladiators in the Internet Coliseum.

He's Got Mail!

In the year 2000, AOL entered into a merger that made it one of the biggest players in the entertainment industry. AOL, purchased Time Warner, and together they have become an enormous entertainment and information conglomerate. What is significant is that Time Warner, an old and established multinational corporation, was purchased by AOL, not the other way around. The fact that the new company is called AOL–Time Warner and not the reverse is an indication of just how powerful AOL has become is such a short time.

America Online chat rooms are truly a global village, where all kinds of people gather to discuss all things naughty and nice. You can make friends, network, and maybe even fall in love. But chatters beware: That "cheerleader" you think you're flirting with may actually be a forty-year-old man in boxer shorts!

Case claims that in his salad days, his goal was to "build a global medium as central to people's lives as the telephone or television . . . and even more valuable. Just as important, we were determined to build a medium that we could be proud of—one that left no one behind in the digital future we were creating." There is no doubt that he succeeded, and probably beyond his wildest imaginings. It was a long, eventful journey from Case's small shop in Tyson's Corner, Virginia, to twin towers in midtown Manhattan. Yes, as of this writing, two 70-story twin skyscrapers are being built in Columbus Circle, a few miles north of where the World Trade Center once stood.

One of the secrets of Case's success was making his service easy for the computer novice to use. While the majority of Internet users are still young guys, the bulk of AOL's users are women. Features like Instant Messaging (IM) brought together family and friends from all over the country for the price of a local phone call.

AOL's spectacular rise to the top of the international Internet community is a clear indication that a great thinker was at the company's helm. From 1992 to 1999, AOL went from 250 employees and $30 million in revenues to 15,000 employees and almost $7 billion in revenues. AOL was the first Internet company to crack the prestigious Fortune 500. And as of this writing it has 23 million members.

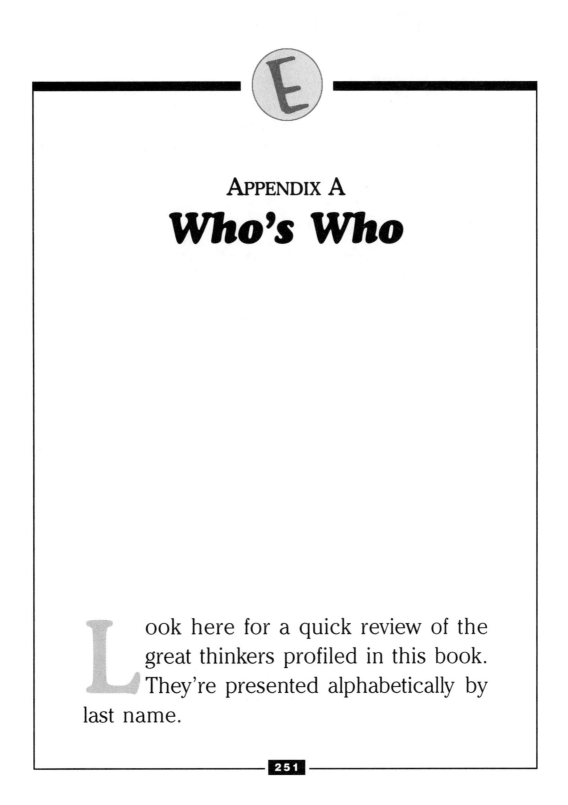

APPENDIX A

Who's Who

L ook here for a quick review of the great thinkers profiled in this book. They're presented alphabetically by last name.

John Adams

The second president of the United States, John Adams is often forgotten as a Founding Father. His failed presidency unfairly detracts from his great successes and his profound insight, unwavering patriotism, and deep philosophical and political writings.

Alexander the Great

Alexander the Great was a Macedonian king who had the advantage of being tutored by the famous philosopher Aristotle. After his father's death, Alexander assumed the throne of Macedonia and in less than three years had conquered the known world. There is a famous quote, the source of which is unclear and hotly debated: "When Alexander saw the breadth of his domain, he wept for there were no more worlds to conquer."

Dante Alighieri

Dante Alighieri was a Renaissance Italian poet and author of the classic trilogy *The Divine Comedy*, an allegorical tour through heaven and hell. He was inspired by an unrequited love for a young lady named Beatrice. Dante is proof that seemingly minor events can produce big dividends, and that a romantic devil will go to hell and back for the woman he loves.

Susan B. Anthony

She spent her whole adult life crusading for women's rights. She was also an abolitionist and temperance activist. Anthony teamed with Elizabeth Cady Stanton and exhibited a nineteenth-century version of "girl power" that eventually won women the right to vote, though neither lived to see it. They worked to change the laws, rallied other women and sensitive men around their cause, and published a newspaper called *Revolution*.

Aristotle

Aristotle studied under Plato as a student at his Academy for twenty years. Aristotle, a prodigy, was generally regarded as Plato's heir apparent. However, he disagreed with the master on several key points. Aristotle liked to walk as he philosophized, eager students in tow. His students became known as *Peripatetics,* which means "pedestrian." Aristotle is famous for the syllogism. A syllogism is a logical argument that takes two truths, connects them, and arrives at a third truth. The most celebrated syllogism is "All men are mortal. Socrates is a man. Therefore Socrates is mortal." Aristotle believed that the syllogism was the most effective and logical means to lead the mind to absolute knowledge.

The Beatles

These four lads from Liverpool did more than change the face of the music world. They changed pop culture, the phenomenon of celebrity, hairstyles, and the impact of celebrities on social and political issues. They even helped introduce American and European youth to Eastern religion in the bargain. They also made beautiful music, evolving from mop-topped bubblegum tunesmiths to profound and influential recording artists. Their records still sell extremely well, and every new anthology album released automatically goes to number one.

Anne Brontë

As little girls, Anne and her sisters, Charlotte and Emily, used their toys to create romantic adventures in fanciful kingdoms, and as young adults they turned their creativity to the art of the novel, enriching the world of literature. Anne published *Agnes Grey* in 1847, the same year that her sisters published *Jane Eyre* and *Wuthering Heights*. Anne died from tuberculosis two years later.

Charlotte Brontë

Famous for *Jane Eyre*, Charlotte was the first of the Brontë sisters to publish what has proven to be an English literature classic. The story of the naïve and innocent governess and her experiences in the employ of the brooding, secretive Rochester set the standard for all Gothic novels to follow.

Emily Brontë

Emily, the middle Brontë sister, published *Wuthering Heights* in 1847, shortly after Charlotte's success with *Jane Eyre*. This story of the passionate and preternatural love between Catherine and the Byronic Heathcliff was another instant classic. Emily died just a year later.

Giordano Bruno

Bruno was a Renaissance scientist, poet, and rebel who preached a doctrine that ultimately got him tortured and burned at the stake. He also supported the heliocentric theory and suggested that there might be life on other planets. Even if you disagree with the theory, you would probably agree that this is hardly a capital offense.

The Buddha

He began life as an Indian prince called Siddhartha Gautama circa 563 B.C. He lived a life of luxury, sequestered from life outside the palace walls. He was horrified when he was exposed to the pain and suffering endured by the majority of the people. He then took a bold step into a cruel new world and became a wandering pilgrim in search of enlightenment. He lived a monastic lifestyle of self-denial. He ended that incarnation as Buddha, which means the Enlightened One, and he added a new spiritual philosophy to the world that continues to be a predominant belief in the East and to generate interest and attract practitioners in the West.

Sir Richard Francis Burton

Burton was a Renaissance man of a decidedly macho variety. In addition to being an author, linguist, translator, and historian, he was an explorer and adventurer who braved many dangers in the quest for knowledge. What makes Richard Francis Burton a great thinker of note was his ability to translate thinking into action as well as his unorthodox and maverick personality.

Steve Case

Steve Case is the man behind America Online. He took a small Internet Bulletin Board and in a relatively short time turned it into a communications empire. From 1992 to 1999, AOL went from 250 employees and $30 million in revenues to 15,000 employees and almost $7 billion in revenues. AOL was the first Internet company to crack the prestigious *Fortune* 500. As of this writing, AOL has 23 million members.

Jesus Christ

The spiritual leader around whose life and legacy the Christian religion was formed, Jesus is perhaps the most influential figure in the history or the world. Great works have been done in his name; wars have been fought in his name. If you sift through the dogma and the many spins and interpretations and get right down to the bare bones basics, Jesus' message is a beautiful, simple spiritual message.

Winston Churchill

Churchill was the personification of his age. He was born into Victorian England, the period of the late nineteenth century when the British Empire was at the top of the great game of power and influence. He served with distinction in military and political life, fell out of favor, lived in a bitter domestic exile, and yet returned to save the day when he was needed. As prime minister during World War II he arguably saved the world by holding off the Nazi menace until the United States entered the war.

Christopher Columbus

Christopher Columbus represents another aspect of Renaissance achievement. In addition to intellectual and scientific pursuits and religious reform, there was the quest to discover new territories. Columbus changed the map of the world with his four voyages to the New World. He did a lot of terrible things along the way, but not every great thinker is a good man or woman. And we certainly cannot deny his impact on the world.

Marie Curie

Marie Curie was a chemist, who along with her husband, Pierre Curie, was a pioneer researcher in the field of radioactivity. She won two Nobel Prizes but did not profit financially from her work. Tragically, her work ultimately killed her; she developed leukemia.

Leonardo da Vinci

Leonardo da Vinci is the quintessential Renaissance man—literally. The term *Renaissance man,* refers to a person who is adept at a variety of disciplines, a jack-of-all-trades and a master of them all. Not only was Leonardo da Vinci a painter and sculptor, he was a scientist whose notes and sketches (some of which were recently purchased by Bill Gates for a reported $30 million) reveal schematics for a helicopter, submarine, and other inventions of the distant future.

The Marquis de Sade

The Marquis de Sade is one of the most misunderstood literary figures of his or any age. Born Donatien Alphonse François, he was a product of eighteenth-century France, and to this day is perceived by many as nothing more than a pervert in pantaloons and a powdered wig. De Sade lived at a time when the penalty for rattling society's cage through controversial words and deeds was being incarcerated, or worse. Even if you find him and his ideology to be bizarre and repugnant, he was an original and provocative thinker who suffered for his art.

René Descartes

This French philosopher is often called the "father of modern philosophy." He started out his career as a mathematician and is credited with discovering the concept of analytic geometry. Descartes uttered perhaps the most famous sentence in the history of philosophy. "I think, therefore I am" became the rallying cry of the modern philosophical age. Everything could be questioned, but one thing remained a fact: the thinking of the thinker. Self-awareness. You can count on at least one thing in this wacky world, according to Descartes: wherever you go, there you are.

Charles Dickens

Dickens was nothing if not prolific. He produced an enormous body of work, and most of his books are of enormous length. Some may quip that this was because he was paid by the word. Actually, most of Dickens books were serialized in the periodicals of the day, and the citizens of the English-speaking world hung on his every word, eagerly awaiting the next installment in the adventures of David Copperfield, Oliver Twist, Pip, and his many other colorful waifs.

Walt Disney

The man who gave the world Mickey Mouse was one of the most gifted animators ever produced by Hollywood. He won a record thirty-two Academy Awards, made the first feature-length cartoon (*Snow White and the Seven Dwarfs*), ventured into live-action films, and created enormously popular theme parks. The company that bears his name is one of the largest entertainment multinational conglomerates in the word. The entertainments introduced by the Disney companies are entrenched in the popular consciousness of the world.

Frederick Douglass

The life of Frederick Douglass was a true American success story. He was born a slave, escaped, and fought to help eradicate this evil from the national landscape. His autobiography is considered a classic chronicle of the times, an insider's view of the most tumultuous era in American history since the Revolutionary War.

Thomas Edison

Edison was one of the most prolific and influential American inventors. You use the items he devised every day, and you would feel a great loss if you were suddenly deprived of them. They are conveniences that have made your life infinitely more comfortable and pleasant, and you probably have no idea that one man was responsible for so many inventions. Your home entertainment center would not exist without the hard work of Thomas Edison.

Albert Einstein

Even those who know next to nothing about Albert Einstein know the visual: the old guy with the unruly white hair and bushy mustache who is dressed in a lab coat. This image has entered even the pop culture consciousness and has been lampooned in movies and cartoons for decades. Einstein's image has come to be associated with the scientist, both "mad" and otherwise. Einstein was not the eccentric crackpot sputtering incomprehensibilities in a German accent that the stereotype perpetuates. He was born in Germany but eventually became an American and was the best-known and arguably the most brilliant scientist of the first half of the twentieth century.

Elizabeth I

Elizabeth I was the Queen of England from 1558 to 1603. She was the daughter of Henry VIII and his second wife, Anne Boleyn, who got the axe (quite literally) for alleged infidelity. She was the first woman to have any staying power on the throne; the others died young of both natural and unnatural causes. Elizabeth triumphed in a man's world in the days when the glass ceiling was composed of a sturdier, far more impenetrable substance.

Benjamin Franklin

Ben Franklin was of the most amazing men of his or any age. An author, inventor, scientist, and revolutionary, he invented the bifocals and the stove. He was the first postmaster general, established the first lending library, and founded the first volunteer fire brigade. He bravely experimented with lightning, risking potentially shocking consequences. And he was a prominent voice in the American Revolution and the birth of a new nation.

Sigmund Freud

Freud was one of the most famous, influential psychologists of the twentieth century. Even those who don't know much about psychology or give much thought to the workings of the unconscious have some awareness of Freud. Two of the techniques of Freudian psychoanalysis are the interpretation of dreams and free association. Freud also came up with the infamous theory of the Oedipus complex. Oedipus was a character in a play by the Greek playwright Sophocles. Through a series of tragic coincidences, Oedipus, a king, happens to murder his father and then marry his mother. On discovering the truth, the horrified Oedipus gouges out his own eyes as penance. Freud felt that every young man goes through his internal Oedipus complex, a rivalry with his father for the attentions of his mother. Freud divided the personality into three components: the ego, the id, and the superego.

Betty Friedan

Friedan was the first president of the National Organization for Women (NOW) and is the author of the modern feminist tract, *The Feminine Mystique*, considered by many to be the document that indoctrinated the modern feminist movement. The title refers to the traditional female role of wife and mother as the ideal. To attempt to forge a destiny in a "man's world" made women somehow less than women, mutant creatures trying to be men yet lacking neither the tools nor the talent. This attitude, said Friedan, was nothing short of a global patriarchal conspiracy to keep women, as the cliché says, "barefoot and pregnant."

Galileo Galilei

Galileo was a Renaissance scientist who changed the way we look at the cosmos and our place in it. He invented the telescope and proved the heliocentric theory, meaning that Earth revolves around the Sun and not vice versa. The authorities did not warmly embrace these findings. Recall that this was not a time when people simply "agreed to disagree." People were tortured and killed for disputing established dogma. Galileo should be lauded for his courage; not faulted when, on pain of a painful demise, he recanted.

Mahatma Gandhi

This humble, spiritual man faced down the mighty British Empire and defeated it without firing a shot. His practice of passive resistance, the philosophy of nonviolent activism, makes him without a doubt one of the greatest thinkers of any era.

Bill Gates

Alternately revered and reviled, prosecuted and praised, Bill Gates has changed the way we look at the world, and the way the world can come to us. He is an inspiration to computer geeks everywhere. He is, of course, the man behind Microsoft, the computer company with whom almost all of us have had some firsthand experience.

Johann Wolfgang von Goethe

Goethe has been called the "German Shakespeare." He was a titanic literary personality in the romantic period. He was also a political figure and a scientist. Goethe's most famous work is his two-part drama, *Faust*.

Stephen Hawking

Stephen Hawking is a man who studies and speculates on things that can make the average person's brain hurt. He has spent his adult life trying to make these theories comprehensible and accessible to the general public. Not many academic eggheads can boast to having appeared on *Star Trek: The Next Generation.* Hawking played a holodeck program of himself conjured by the ever-inquisitive android Data.

Homer

The poet Homer is given credit for the two most famous adventures of the classical age, *The Iliad* and *The Odyssey*. These masterpieces were most likely composed in the eighth century B.C. Like Shakespeare long after him, Homer relied heavily on earlier source material, but he eclipsed these historical tomes with his masterful interpretation. Homer's tales were based on mythic and quasi-historic events that had been floating around the ancient world for several centuries before that.

Thomas Jefferson

Thomas Jefferson was the third president of the United States. A great thinker and a gifted writer, he wrote the Declaration of Independence. He also wrote his own obituary summing up what he wanted to be remembered for: Here was buried/Thomas Jefferson/Author of the Declaration of American Independence/Of the Statute of Virginia for Religious Freedom/And Father of the University of Virginia.

Steve Jobs

Along with Stephen Wozniak, Jobs founded Apple Computer, makers of the Macintosh personal computer, which brought computing and its infinite possibilities to the masses. Steve Jobs is a premier example of the entrepreneurial can-do spirit, a Thomas Alva Edison for the digital age. In addition to Apple, he is the man behind Pixar, the computer animation movie company that brought the world *Toy Story, Toy Story 2,* and *Monsters, Inc.*

Carl Jung

The most famous follower of Sigmund Freud, Jung's signal theory is that of the collective unconscious. This theory posits a shared memory of symbols, imagery, and memories that he called archetypes, which harken back to the dawn of human consciousness and are common in all cultures and civilizations. Jung also proposed that within every man there is an inner woman and within every woman there is an inner man. Jung was referring to feminine and masculine energy, actually, which he labeled the anima (inner woman) and animus (inner man). He believed that we have to embrace that side of ourselves and own it in order to have optimum mental health.

Immanuel Kant

Immanuel Kant was the unofficial founder of a school of philosophy and came to be known as German idealism. He sets forth his philosophy, which he called critical philosophy, in the book *Critique of Pure Reason.* Kant's area of interest was metaphysics. Metaphysics is everything out there in the world that is beyond the human mind's ability to perceive, and for many even to conceive. The philosopher, however, always has an inquiring mind and a nagging sense that there are, as Shakespeare said, "more things in Heaven and Earth." Kant called the world that we experience through our senses the *phenomenal* world and the reality beyond that the *noumenal* world. This is translated somewhat awkwardly into English as the "thing-in-itself."

Martin Luther King Jr.

King was a great social thinker who took the philosophy of civil disobedience and passive resistance that Gandhi had used in India and brought it to the United States. King changed the nation for the better by helping to end the brutal racist discrimination that afflicted black Americans in the century following the Civil War.

George Lucas

Lucas is the man behind *Star Wars*, a modern mythology and perhaps the most popular movie series of all time. The secret of Lucas's success is in no small part a result of to his keen interest in the writings of Joseph Campbell. Campbell was a mythographer who spent a lifetime studying the world mythology. He concluded that the same themes and archetypal characters recur in myths from all cultures. Lucas incorporated many of these in his *Star Wars* trilogy, and now the second trilogy, tapping into our collective consciousness.

Martin Luther

Martin Luther was a key player in the Protestant Reformation. He was a German priest who was outraged by the excesses of the Renaissance Catholic Church. He began a movement that spread across Europe and created several new offshoots of Christianity, reshaping not only religious life, but also the fabric of every aspect of life in Europe.

Niccolò Machiavelli

Machiavelli is the major political thinker to come out of the Renaissance. While Galileo was stargazing and da Vinci was sketching blueprints for the helicopter and the submarine, Machiavelli was influencing people. Unlike the other Renaissance giants who brought beauty into the world and devised mechanical marvels, Machiavelli has become the poster boy for another historical constant: the crooked politician and the sleazy businessperson. So significant is he that his name has come to describe an individual who strives to succeed by any means necessary without letting obstacles like ethics and morality get in the way.

Madonna

Madonna danced onto the music scene in 1983, and hasn't looked back. Her ability to reinvent herself—practically from album to album—has ensured her success as an entertainer and entrepreneur. Throughout her career, Madonna has tackled taboo subjects openly, usually to harsh criticism—yet she has endured. Now a wife and mother in midlife, one can only imagine what will come next.

Karl Marx

Karl Marx was the architect of what became modern communism, an ideology embraced by millions and opposed by just as many. It is a political system that went on to change the world in ways that Marx may never have imagined. A student of philosophy (in fact he called himself a scientific philosopher and sometimes a scientific socialist), he, along with Friedrich Engels, wrote *The Communist Manifesto*. Marx sought social reform to combat the injustices of the Industrial Revolution. Needless to say, this made him an unpopular figure with the European powers-that-were, and he was exiled to London. There he wrote another equally influential polemic, *Das Kapital*.

Golda Meir

Born in Russia, and raised in the United States, Golda Meir went to Palestine in 1921. She was instrumental in the foundation of Israel, where she held various offices, including ambassador to the Soviet Union, member of parliament, minister of labor, and minister of foreign affairs. She was the prime minister of Israel from 1969 to 1974. It was on her watch that Israel was attacked in 1973. Although Meir was criticized for Israel's lack of readiness to handle the surprise attack, also called the Yom Kippur War, her statesmanship and fortitude earned her the respect of friends and enemies alike.

Michelangelo

Michelangelo, along with da Vinci, is considered one of the two greatest artists of the Renaissance. Michelangelo was less of an all-around genius, but he was a more prolific painter and sculptor. Michelangelo was also an accomplished architect and, to a lesser degree, a poet. Michelangelo's great works are the sculptures *David, Moses,* the *Pietà,* and his Herculean undertaking of painting the ceiling of the Sistine Chapel.

John Stuart Mill

This British philosopher wrote eloquently on the subject of women's rights in his book, *The Subjection of Women.* He argued that a woman's lot in life was akin to slavery, and that the poor treatment of women also adversely affected men, and thus society as a whole.

Muhammad

Muhammad is the prophet who founded the Islamic religion, which is one of the three main monotheistic religions of the world. (The other two are Judaism and Christianity.) Monotheism is, of course, the belief in and worship of one God. It is really the same God, but you would never know that because of the millennia of conflict between these religions. And it is conflict that shows no signs of ending anytime soon.

Muhammad received messages from the Archangel Gabriel that he transcribed into the Qur'an, sometimes spelled Quran or Koran. This is the holy book of the Islamic faith. Muhammad conquered what is now the Saudi Arabian peninsula by less than spiritual means and made Islam the predominant religion in the region. His birthplace and his adopted home, Mecca and Medina, respectively, are the sacred cities of Islam.

Friedrich Wilhelm Nietzsche

Nietzsche was perhaps the most controversial and misunderstood philosopher. He was as much a literary figure as a philosopher. Actually Nietzsche had no formal philosophy, his rantings basically took the form of aphorisms, which are short quips and pungent observations. Some of these notions included the death of God, the advocacy of the Superman, and the theory of eternal recurrence. His main targets were Western civilization and Christianity. A sensitive soul plagued by health problems, Nietzsche ultimately descended into a madness from which he could not recover.

Camille Paglia

Camille Paglia (b. 1947) is a controversial social critic and all-around gadfly in the Socratic tradition. Her singular stance can earn the ire of both Left and Right, feminist and chauvinist. She is a courageous and envelope-pushing thinker, the Madonna of academia. Paglia tackles a variety of hot-button issues, and her opinions are explosive and acerbic wit. Paglia also has a regular column in the e-zine Salon.com. She resents being called a conservative, and thinks of herself as a libertarian Democrat. Paglia is a true original, not to everyone's taste, but as cage rattlers go, she is provocative and entertaining.

George Patton

General George S. Patton is nowadays synonymous with George C. Scott, the actor who played him in the epic film biography. Unlike many Hollywood biopics, *Patton* is an accurate depiction of this fascinating and complex man. He was the quintessential soldier and his military genius was of inestimable value in winning World War II, but his flamboyant, volatile personality often got him into trouble with his superiors.

Plato

Plato was Socrates' most famous protégé. He continued the Socratic legacy while building on it with his own theories. Plato was a firm believer in Ideas with a capital *I,* or as they are also called, Forms. Plato believed that while we can admire the beauty of a windswept beach, or the buff bodies on said beach, there exists, in the ether, the Form of Beauty.

Ron Popeil

This "king of infomercials" is one of the most influential and successful entrepreneurs in the history of capitalism. From humble beginnings and an unhappy childhood, he created a peaceful empire. He does not make weapons of mass destruction or schemes that destroy the ecosystem. He helps you "cut the fat" and "set it and forget it" with his most recent contribution to Western civilization: the Showtime Rotisserie and BBQ, and the Pasta Maker.

Ayn Rand

American novelist and philosopher Ayn Rand emigrated from Russia in 1926. Her philosophy, Objectivism, maintains that the mankind's ultimate purpose is to achieve great success. The ideal political expression of

Objectivism is capitalism, and fans of the free market economy, capitalism, libertarianism, individualism, self-responsibility, laissez-faire government, and the American dream will continue read and discuss Ayn Rand.

Wilhelm Reich

Most people have never heard of Wilhelm Reich, and those who have heard of him are probably only aware of the wealth of erroneous information that has been accepted as fact. Most of these inaccuracies are deliberate attempts to discredit and misrepresent his work. Like the great thinkers of the Renaissance who were hounded by the political and religious authorities of the day, only to have their work posthumously validated, it is likely that future generations will regard Reich the way we look at Giordano Bruno and Galileo. Men and women who are ahead of their time usually inspire criticism, and worse, when they rattle the collective cage.

Condoleeza Rice

The first African-American woman to hold a cabinet post in a presidential administration, Rice is the Chief Foreign Policy Adviser to George W. Bush. She went to work in the administration of George H. W. Bush from 1989 to 1991 as the director of Soviet and East European affairs on the National Security Council. She played a pivotal role in policy making during the days when the Soviet Union collapsed and was Bush's go-to gal regarding Russia and Eastern Europe. Today, she continues to play an active role coaching the President in foreign policy issues.

Leni Riefenstahl

Leni Riefenstahl is universally acclaimed as an arresting filmmaker. She was gifted in many ways, but she did not show sound judgment in her choice of subject matter: Adolf Hitler and his Nazi regime. She made several documentaries about Hitler and the Nazis, most notably *Triumph of the Will* (1935), which recorded the 1934 Nuremberg Rally, and *Olympia* (1938), which documented the 1936 Olympics in Berlin. *Triumph of the Will* is considered the best and most notorious propaganda film of all time.

Gene Roddenberry

This is the man who brought us *Star Trek*. Need I say more as to his credentials as a pop culture great thinker? It is often said that there are really only a handful of stories circulating in the collective consciousness and unconsciousness. Literature, drama, television, and film are infinite spins on a few finite themes. It is similar to the philosophical notion of thesis-antithesis-synthesis. Take an idea (*Wagon Train*); add a new element (science fiction) and get the synthesis of the two (*Star Trek*). This simple formula is the essence of creativity.

Eleanor Roosevelt

This First Lady changed the role of president's wife for all who followed her. She was independent, politically active, and a feminist. Although she had a privileged upbringing, at least financially, she used whatever position, power, and influence she had to fight for change in many arenas.

William Shakespeare

He is almost uniformly regarded as the English language's greatest poet and playwright. Even those who have never read of him know some of his work. Misquotes and incomplete paraphrases like "a method to his madness," "something rotten in Denmark," and "a rose by any other name" entered the vernacular and remain there.

Socrates

This dynamic, controversial Athenian spent a lifetime in the public square engaging in dialogues with the young men of the ancient Greek city-state. Socrates was the classic eccentric philosopher type: Not concerned with his appearance, by all reports not very handsome (physical descriptions have him resembling the late British actor Charles Laughton), but eager to engage in a philosophical debate anytime, anywhere. His singular method of posing questions to his intellectual quarry and drawing responses, making the unwitting upstarts think for themselves and often become acutely aware of their own ignorance, is called Socratic dialogue. This form of question and answer and the logical debate of opposing views is called dialectic. Socrates' motto should be every philosopher's raison d'être: The unexamined life is not worth living. Doing what is right is the only path to goodness, and introspection and self-awareness are the ways to learn what is right.

Steven Spielberg

Spielberg is one of the most successful directors of all time. From his first big hit *Jaws* in 1975 through 2001's *A.I. Artificial Intelligence,* Spielberg has had his fingers on the pulse of the pop culture zeitgeist as he made one hit after another: *Close Encounters of the Third Kind,* the *Indiana Jones* trilogy, *E.T., Jurassic Park, The Lost World, Schindler's List,* and *Saving Private Ryan.* Sure, there were some misfires (anyone remember *1941?*) but for the most part his track record is astounding. He won the Best Director Academy Award for *Schindler's List.*

Elizabeth Cady Stanton

A more radical thinker than many of her contemporaries, she spoke openly of reproduction rights for women, reforming the unfair divorce laws, and other topics that even some of her fellow suffragettes found extreme. She was instrumental in introducing a constitutional amendment for women's suffrage in 1878. It eventually came to life but many years after her death. Her book, *The Woman's Bible*, essentially an annotated edition of the Good Book with feminist notes in the margins, alienated most of her fellow activists.

Gloria Steinem

Steinem is a modern-day leader for women's rights who ironically began her career as a feminist with a stint as a Playboy Bunny. As a struggling journalist, she went undercover in one of the Playboy Clubs owned by Hugh Hefner of *Playboy* magazine fame. Her writing career and her feminist perspective evolved after she had a taste of what it was like to be regarded as a sex object and not as an individual with thoughts and feelings and ideas. Steinem worked with Betty Friedan and politicians Bella Abzug and Shirley Chisholm to found the National Women's Political Caucus. She also began *Ms.* magazine, a periodical devoted to women's issues.

Sun-tzu

Sun-tzu was the enigmatic Chinese figure who wrote *The Art of War*, a manual for politicians and generals on the best ways to do battle both on and off the battlefield. Modern corporate types have adapted the paradoxical teachings of *The Art of War* and applied them to the business world. After all, it is the Japanese philosophy that says, "Business is war."

Margaret Thatcher

The first female prime minister of Great Britain began her political career in 1959 as a member of the Conservative party. Thatcher brought the Conservatives into power when she became Prime Minister, serving from

1979–1990, and with U.S. President Ronald Reagan helped bring to an end the seventy-plus year reign of terror of the former Soviet Union.

Harriet Tubman

To many, Harriet Tubman is a real-life American folk hero. Her work on the Underground Railroad is legendary, and enabled her to be an effective spy for the Union Army during the Civil War. After the war, Tubman continued to fight for both racial and gender equality on behalf of all people.

George Washington

The "father of our country," Washington was a great military leader who led the troops in the Revolutionary War and served as the first president of the United States. His farsighted view and modest nature held the country together during its volatile growing pains. He rejected several entreaties to declare him a king. Had he been a more power-hungry man, America would be a very different country indeed.

Orson Welles

This literally larger-than-life American filmmaker began on the radio. He was the first person to say the famous line, "Who knows what evil lurks in the hearts of men—the Shadow knows!" And on Halloween 1938, he convinced millions of Americans that the Martians had landed in New Jersey with his radio broadcast of *The War of the Worlds*. At the age of twenty-five, he directed his first movie, *Citizen Kane*. It is generally regarded as the best movie ever made. Unfortunately he never matched that success during the rest of his long career. He was a gifted actor, director, and one of the most familiar voices in America.

Mary Wollstonecraft

Although she is perhaps better known as the mother of Mary W. Shelley, Wollstonecraft, herself, accomplished many things. She was an early feminist and author of *"A Vindication of the Rights of Women"* (1792). Wollstonecraft was a successful artist, pioneer, and political reformer.

Walt Whitman

Whitman changed the face of poetry as it was practiced going back to Homer and became one of the quintessential American literary figures of his age. He was also something of a perfectionist and a "one book writer." But what a book! He compiled one collection of verse, *Leaves of Grass*, and then spent the rest of his life editing and revising it.

APPENDIX B
Glossary

ABOLITIONISM The movement to end slavery. In this group, runaway slave Frederick Douglass found his voice and his mission as an activist and orator. The abolitionist movement was composed of escaped and free African-Americans and white supporters.

ALCHEMY The mystical medieval tradition that told of the existence of a "philosopher's stone," which could turn base metals into gold. The philosopher's stone, Americanized to the "sorcerer's stone," figures prominently in J. K. Rowling's *Harry Potter and the Sorcerer's Stone*. Johann Faust, the historical inspiration for Goethe's *Faust*, was reputed to be an alchemist. Carl Jung also wrote extensively on alchemy. He theorized that alchemists were really the first psychologists, and that alchemy was a metaphor for individuation. See also **INDIVIDUATION.**

ALLEGORY A story in which the characters are symbolic representations of universal themes. Dante's *The Divine Comedy* is an allegory.

ALLIES The American and British forces, plus a few other nations, who battled the Germans, the Italians, and the Japanese during the Second World War. See also **AXIS.**

ANIMA The "inner woman" who dwells within every man, according to Dr. Jung. He was one of the first to exhort men to get in touch with their feminine side.

ANIMUS The "inner man" within every woman, according to Dr. Jung.

APARTHEID The system of institutionalized racism in South Africa. Mahatma Gandhi lived there for twenty years and endured many indignities and hardships fighting this system. Apartheid did not end until the finish of the twentieth century, when world pressure was brought to bear on the South African government.

APHORISM Nietzsche's main technique for philosophizing; a pithy observation that can vary in length from a few lines to a few paragraphs.

A POSTERIORI Literally meaning "after." A statement, concept, or idea that is determined after the fact, based on experience or observation.

APPEASEMENT The political strategy employed by the British government of Prime Minister Neville Chamberlain. This policy allowed Adolf Hitler to carve slices out of other nations with impunity. Promising that each new invasion would be the last, Hitler was on his way to seizing most of Europe when he finally crossed the line by invading Poland and starting World War II.

A PRIORI Literally meaning "before." A statement, concept, or idea that is accepted as fact and does not need to be based on experience or observation.

AXIS The name for the alliance between Germany, Italy, and later, Japan. These three nations faced the Allies in World War II.

BLACK HOLE A collapsed star that creates a giant void in space. A black hole never goes away. It only grows larger with time, sucking in anything in its path. What happens to things that enter a black hole is not certain. Stephen Hawking has made a career out of the study of these spatial anomalies.

BOURGEOISIE The name used to describe the middle class. According to Karl Marx, this group was the sworn enemy of the workers, and the tension between the two groups would inevitably build to revolution.

CITY-STATE A city that is also in essence a nation and a self-contained government. City-states were common in ancient Greece and Renaissance Italy.

COGITO ERGO SUM Descartes's famous "I think therefore I am" proves that you can be certain of at least one reality in this crazy world: you exist because you are thinking thoughts right now.

COLLECTIVE UNCONSCIOUS Carl Jung's theory that there is a common memory for all of mankind composed of universal themes that he called *archetypes*. It is no coincidence that mythologies from diverse cultures often have identical characters and plots. Joseph Campbell wrote of the collective uncon-scious in his classic work *The Hero with a Thousand Faces*.

DACTYLIC HEXAMETER The style of verse in which the original versions of Homer's *Odyssey* and *Iliad* are written.

DEISM The religious faith that likens God to a Cosmic Watchmaker. The universe is a perfectly functioning, orderly yet impersonal cosmos. God designed it, and now it more or less runs itself. Thomas Jefferson was likely a deist. His political enemies leveled frequent charges of atheism at him.

DIALECTIC The Socratic dialogue, a series of questions and answers that helps the person discover the truth for himself or herself, rather than simply being told.

DICKENSIAN Anything that evokes the writings of Charles Dickens. Usually it refers to a rags-to-riches story in which a character from a humble background achieves success despite many obstacles.

DOGMA Rigid religious doctrine that is usually defended to the death despite scientific or other contradictory information that may come to light. In less enlightened times, those who dared defy church dogma were treated quite harshly.

ENLIGHTENMENT Also called the age of reason. The age of Voltaire and the other *philosophes,* the French word for philosopher.

EPISTEMOLOGY Another word for the theory of knowledge.

EPISTOLARY A style of fiction in which the story is told in the form of letters between the characters. Goethe's *The Sorrows of Young Werther* is an epistolary novel. The most famous such novel is Bram Stoker's *Dracula*.

ETERNAL RECURRENCE Nietzsche's proposition that we live the same life, without variation, over and over again. He probably did not mean this literally. He was suggesting that we should fashion our lives in such a way that we would not mind repeating them time and again.

EXISTENTIALISM The philosophy that life is meaningless and absurd, and the best that we can do is try to lead authentic, heroic lives in a cold and uncaring world.

FORMS Plato's doctrine that Ideas exist independently beyond their physical and mental counterparts. For example, there is a Form of Beauty, and things of beauty we see in physical reality are mere shadows of that Form.

HELIOCENTRIC THEORY The theory that the Sun is the center of the solar system and that Earth and other planets revolve around it. In Galileo's time, the church opposed this theory (now an accepted truth) and those who professed it could face the Inquisition.

HERESY Any belief or practice that opposes a religious organization. Once punishable by death, you now see all manner of heresy every time you turn on the television.

HUBRIS Extreme, overweening pride—the downfall of many a great thinker.

IDEALISM The belief that everything is "in the mind," and physical reality does not exist. Made famous by George Berkeley. Immanuel Kant was the first in the philosophical school of German idealism.

IMMANENT Something that is directly experienced. The opposite of **TRANSCENDENT.**

INDIVIDUATION Dr. Jung's phrase for the ideal human condition—a wholeness that comes from integrating the various elements of the human psyche. Balance of these elements would engender optimum mental health.

INDULGENCES Another word for reconciliation, the forgiveness of sins in the Catholic tradition. Martin Luther opposed the selling of indulgences for money to fund the building of opulent cathedrals in Rome.

INQUISITION The prosecutorial branch of the Catholic Church. It tortured and killed many heretics in its horrible heyday, among them Giordano Bruno.

IRON CURTAIN Churchill coined this phrase to refer to the separation of East and West that occurred after the World War II. Russia controlled the Eastern European countries and Western Europe and America were on the other side.

KARMA The Eastern idea of a cosmic force of order, balance, and justice in the universal. Even if you get away with bad behavior in this lifetime, you will not escape karmic justice. You will pay for your misdeeds in the next. And if you have lived a life of hardship and anguish this time around, things will be better for you the next time.

MAGUS Another name for a magician. The historical Faust was a magus who many suspected made a deal with the devil. The historical Faust was made famous in the drama *The Tragical History of Doctor Faustus* by Christopher Marlowe and *Faust, Parts One and Two* by Goethe.

MAHATMA This is a title that means "great soul." It was bestowed on Gandhi by the Indian people during his efforts to secure Indian independence through nonviolent means. W. C. Fields sometimes wrote under the pseudonym Mahatma Kane-Jeeves. This name was a whimsical take on a British aristocrat instructing his butler, "My hat, my cane, Jeeves."

MANNERISM The style of art that views the idealized male nude as the ultimate form of artistic expression. Michelangelo was the Mr. Manners of the Renaissance.

MINDSHIFT HYPOTHESIS The theory that the government knows all about the existence of extraterrestrial life and is gradually preparing the public for disclosure through pop culture and other entertainment means.

MONISTIC IMMANENTISM Giordano Bruno's belief that we are all part of a universal god-force. He meant not just humanity, but everything. See also **PANTHEISM.**

MONOTHEISM A religion that professes that one God created and presides over the universe. Judaism, Christianity and Islam are the three main monotheistic religions.

MUSE A Greek goddess who inspires creativity; also used to describe any person, usually a woman, who is a source of inspiration. Dante's muse was his beloved Beatrice. Although he loved her from afar and she died young, she still inflamed his creativity. Dante immortalized Beatrice in his masterpiece *The Divine Comedy.*

NEOPLATONISM A philosophical movement that combined the teachings of Plato with Jewish and early Christian mysticism. God is referred to as "the One."

NEW TESTAMENT The Christian religious text composed of the four Gospels of Matthew, Mark, Luke, and John, plus the Acts of the Apostles, assorted Epistles, and the Book of Revelation.

NIHILISM The ultimate in a despairing, negative worldview; utter hopelessness.

NINETY-FIVE THESES The protest documents that Martin Luther issued against the selling of indulgences. These documents started the fire that became the Protestant Reformation. Some versions have him nailing this document to a church door; other historians doubt that he actually did that.

NIRVANA The ultimate state of enlightenment that is only achieved after many lifetimes, as the soul learns and evolves on its way to spiritual bliss.

NOUMENA Kant's name for the metaphysical world, the reality that lies beyond our ability to perceive.

ORACLE In the days before the Psychic Hotlines, ancient people traveled to the temples of their particular gods to hear predictions and get advice. The oracle often spoke in cryptic rhymes that were subject to many interpretations.

PANTHEISM The belief that God is nature, not an all-powerful entity in heaven but a force that surrounds and permeates the world.

PARABLE A story that is used to illustrate a spiritual and moral message. Jesus often preached through parables. The most famous parable tells of the prodigal son.

PARADOX A seemingly contradictory concept that, upon close examination, is not contradictory at all.

PASSIVE RESISTANCE Gandhi's method to effect social change. Passive resistance bent the will of the British Empire, gaining independence for India. Gandhi was inspired by the writings of Leo Tolstoy and Henry David Thoreau, as well as by the life and teaching of Jesus Christ. Martin Luther King Jr. also used passive resistance with successful results in the civil rights movement.

PATRON A wealthy benefactor who supports an artist or other creative person. For centuries, creative types relied on the support of patrons—and the art they produced is better than anything that the National Endowment for the Arts funds these days (with your tax dollars).

PERSONA Jung's word for the face we show to the rest of the world. In fact, we have many personae. You act differently around your mother than you do at a keg party, or at least you should.

PHILOSOPHY Literally the "love of wisdom," from the Greek words *philia* and *sophia*.

PICARESQUE A novel with an ambling, episodic plot in which the protagonist encounters a variety of colorful and oddball characters. Charles Dickens's first novel *The Pickwick Papers* is a good example.

POLIS The Greek word for city-state. Athens was a city-state. The word *politics* comes from polis.

PREDESTINATION The belief that your fate is determined before you are born and that nothing you do in this life will make a difference whether you go to heaven or hell.

PRE-SOCRATIC PHILOSOPHERS The group of philosophers, also called Monists, who offered theories that the nature of reality was composed of one thing, such as water, air, fire, or numbers.

PROLETARIAT Karl Marx's name for the working class. He maintained that they do all the work yet reap none of the benefits in a capitalist society and would eventually become disgruntled enough to take to the streets in revolt.

PSYCHOSOMATIC The condition in which mental problems manifest themselves in physical disorders. Freud used psychoanalysis to identify the psychological problem in the hopes that the physical problem would be cured.

RATIONALIST The philosophy of Descartes, Spinoza, Leibniz. They believe that there are innate ideas in the mind, and not everything we know must necessarily be gathered through sensory experience.

REINCARNATION The belief that the soul returns to Earth in another body after death. Most Eastern religions, and an increasing number of Westerners, believe in reincarnation.

RELATIVISM The belief that things such as morality vary from society to society and culture to culture, and one is no better or worse than another.

RENAISSANCE MAN An overused term, it refers to someone who is talented at anything he or she tries. The original Renaissance man was Leonardo da Vinci.

SATYAGRAHA The Sanskrit word Gandhi used to describe his method of passive resistance. It conveys a deeper intensity and force than its English translation.

SHADOW Jung's version of Freud's id. The shadow is composed of the darker impulses and desires that we suppress, both out of our own discretion and because of societal influence and pressure. If we do not deal with the shadow, it will surface unbidden, which can create many problems ranging from the merely embarrassing to the dangerous.

SINGULARITY An object in space for which the normal rules of physics do not apply. See also **BLACK HOLE.**

SOCIAL CONFLICT THEORY Karl Marx believed that the inevitable tension that existed between the haves and have-nots in capitalist societies would inevitably lead the workers of the world to unite, for they had nothing to lose but their chains.

SOCIAL CONTRACT A relationship between the citizens and the people, which could be formally agreed on or an unwritten, implicit agreement. Thomas Hobbes, John Locke, and Jean-Jacques Rousseau all had versions of what they felt was the ideal social contract.

SONNET A form of poem that usually had fourteen lines, alternating rhyming lines for the first twelve with a rhyming couplet to finish it off. Shakespeare wrote 154 sonnets, which many scholars believe tell the autobiographical story of a love triangle between Shakespeare, a young nobleman, and the notorious "dark lady."

SOPHISTRY The frivolous misuse of philosophy to teach how to win arguments and sway opinions via linguistic legerdemain.

STURM UND DRANG Meaning "Storm and Stress" in English, this is a literary style in which a passionate, rebellious, and individualistic youth encounters many trials and tribulations when interacting with polite society. Goethe's novel *The Sorrows of Young Werther* is an example of this literary genre.

SUFFRAGE The right to vote, which was denied women in the United States until 1920. The feminist movement of the nineteenth century was called the Woman Suffrage movement.

SYLLOGISM Aristotle's logical argument that has two premises and a conclusion. The famous example is: All men are mortal.

Socrates is a man. Therefore, Socrates is mortal.

TABULA RASA Latin for "blank slate." Many philosophers, including John Locke and Voltaire, believed that we are born with an empty mind, ready to have sensory experiences imprinted on our brains.

THEOCRACY A government controlled by religious authorities. Unfortunately, most theocracies persecute those in the nation of a different faith. The Taliban government formerly in control of Afghanistan was the most recent example of a repressive theocracy.

THINGS-IN-THEMSELVES This is Kant's name for the **NOUMENAL** world, or the metaphysical reality that is beyond the limited reality that we can perceive, which he called the phenomenal world.

TRANSCENDENT Something beyond the realm of ordinary experience. The opposite of **IMMANENT.**

UNDERGROUND RAILROAD The network of people and safe houses that helped runaway slaves reach freedom in the North. Frederick Douglass and many of the early feminists were active in the Underground Railroad.

UNIVERSALS Aristotle's version of Platonic Forms. He believed that the Forms were within the physical object, not separate entities in another dimension.

Index

S

Sadism, 86, 87
Satyagraha, 169, 281
Science, 3
Scientific method, 46
Scientists
  Curie, Marie, 200–202
  Einstein, Albert, 210–14, 259
  Hawking, Stephen, 214–17, 262
  Reich, Wilhelm, 202–6, 269
Scientists, Renaissance, 45–50
  Bruno, Giordano, 48–50, 254
  Galileo Galilei, 46–48, 261
Secondary ideas, 18
Sexual healing, 202–3
Sexual revolution, 203–4
Shadow, the, 196–97, 281
Shakespeare, William, 72–79, 270
  blank verse of, 77
  characters of, 74–75
  comedy and, 75
  early life, 73–74
  movies and, 72–73
  plays of, 74–77
  as preeminent writer, 72–73
  sonnets of, 77–79
  writing stages of, 74
Shatner, William, 228
Siddhartha Gautama. See Buddha
Singularity, 215, 281
Slavery
  abolitionism and, 159–63, 166,
    180–81, 252, 276
  Aristotle and, 14
  Brown, John and, 161–62
  Columbus, Christopher and, 65
  Constitution and, 162–63
  Douglass, Frederick and, 159–63,
    258
  Franklin, Benjamin and, 101–2
  Jefferson, Thomas and, 120
  Tubman, Harriet and, 166, 273
  Underground Railroad and, 161,
    166, 273, 282

women's rights and, 179, 180–81
Social conflict theory, 163–64, 281
Social contract, 281
Social thinkers, 157–66, 167–73
  Douglass, Frederick, 158–63, 258
  Gandhi, Mahatma, 168–70
  King, Martin Luther, Jr., 170–73, 264
  Marx, Karl, 163–66, 265
  Tubman, Harriet, 166, 273
  See also Women's rights
Socrates, 2–7, 271
  Apology of, 5–6
  death of, 7
  on democracy, 6
  dialectic and, 3
  disavowal of knowledge, 6
  early life, 2–3
  enemies of, 4–5
  ideas and, 4
  ignorance and, 3–4
  motto of, 7
  natural philosophy of, 3
  Plato and, 7, 8, 268
  Socratic dialogue of, 3–4, 271
  trial of, 5–7
  Truth pursuit of, 3–4, 271
Socratic dialogue, 3–4, 271
Sonnets, 77–79, 281
Sophistry, 2, 281
Sophists, 2, 5–6
Sorbonne, 200, 201
Sorrows of Young Werther, 79–81
Spielberg, Steven, 231–33
  Academy Award for, 271
  films of, 232–33
  Lucas, George W., Jr. and, 231
  TV beginnings, 232
Spiritual leaders
  Buddha, 35–39, 254–55
  Jesus Christ, 27–34, 255
  Muhammad, 41–44, 266–67
Stalin, Joseph, 137
Stanton, Elizabeth Cady, 180–83, 252,
  271–72
  American Anti-Slavery Society and,
    180

first feminist convention by, 181
  suffrage amendment by, 180–81
Starr, Ringo, 234, 236
Star Trek, 227, 228–30
Steinem, Gloria, 185–86, 272
Sturm und Drang, 79, 281
Suffrage, 176, 180–83, 271–72, 281
Sufis, 44
Sun-tzu, 142–44, 272
Superego, 193, 196–97
Superman, 21, 23, 24, 267
Syllogism, 13, 253, 281–82
Synthetic judgment, 19–20

T

Tabula rasa, 19, 282
Temperance movement, 179, 180
Thales, 2
Thatcher, Margaret, 138–40, 272–273
  as Conservative, 139, 273
  European Union and, 139
  first woman prime minister, 138–39
  as "The Iron Lady", 139
The Art of War, 142–44
The Beatles, 233–36, 253
  "British Invasion" of, 234
  Elvis and, 234
  films of, 235–36
  influencers of, 234
  inventiveness of, 235
  life after, 236
  songs of, 234–35
  split-up of, 236
The Communist Manifesto, 163, 164,
  165, 265
The Feminine Mystique, 185, 260
The Fountainhead, 83–84
"The Iron Lady", 139
The Mass Psychology of Fascism,
  204
Theocracy, 282
  Christianity and, 62
  Islam as, 42–44
The Subjection of Women, 176–77

THE EVERYTHING PHILOSOPHY BOOK

By James Mannion

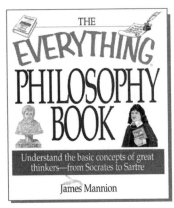

I f you've always wanted to learn about philosophy but were too intimidated to get past the first word ending in "ism," *The Everything® Philosophy Book* provides simple explanations guaranteed to make philosophic ideas and concepts easy to understand. This entertaining book offers a broad overview of many diverse schools of thought—from antiquity through the present day. *The Everything® Philosophy Book* delves into the minds of such philosophers as Socrates and Aristotle, Augustine and Aquinas, Buddha and Confucius, Voltaire and Rousseau, Russell and Sartre, and many more!

Trade paperback, $12.95
1-58062-644-0, 304 pages

OTHER *EVERYTHING*® BOOKS BY ADAMS MEDIA CORPORATION

Everything® **Dessert Cookbook**
$12.95, 1-55850-717-5

Everything® **Diabetes Cookbook**
$14.95, 1-58062-691-2

Everything® **Dieting Book**
$14.95, 1-58062-663-7

Everything® **Digital Photography Book**
$12.95, 1-58062-574-6

Everything® **Dog Book**
$12.95, 1-58062-144-9

Everything® **Dog Training and Tricks Book**
$14.95, 1-58062-666-1

Everything® **Dreams Book**
$12.95, 1-55850-806-6

Everything® **Etiquette Book**
$12.95, 1-55850-807-4

Everything® **Fairy Tales Book**
$12.95, 1-58062-546-0

Everything® **Family Tree Book**
$12.95, 1-55850-763-9

Everything® **Feng Shui Book**
$14.95, 1-58062-587-8

Everything® **Fly-Fishing Book**
$12.95, 1-58062-148-1

Everything® **Games Book**
$12.95, 1-55850-643-8

Everything® **Get-A-Job Book**
$12.95, 1-58062-223-2

Everything® **Get Out of Debt Book**
$12.95, 1-58062-588-6

Everything® **Get Published Book**
$12.95, 1-58062-315-8

Everything® **Get Ready for Baby Book**
$12.95, 1-55850-844-9

Everything® **Get Rich Book**
$12.95, 1-58062-670-X

Everything® **Ghost Book**
$12.95, 1-58062-533-9

Everything® **Golf Book**
$12.95, 1-55850-814-7

Everything® **Grammar and Style Book**
$12.95, 1-58062-573-8

Everything® **Great Thinkers Book**
$14.95, 1-58062-662-9

Everything® **Travel Guide to
        The Disneyland Resort®,
        California Adventure®,
        Universal Studios®, and
        Anaheim**
$14.95, 1-58062-742-0

Everything® **Guide to Las Vegas**
$12.95, 1-58062-438-3

Everything® **Guide to New England**
$12.95, 1-58062-589-4

Everything® **Guide to New York City**
$12.95, 1-58062-314-X

Everything® **Travel Guide to Walt Disney
        World®, Universal Studios®, and
        Greater Orlando, 3rd Edition**
$14.95, 1-58062-743-9

Everything® **Guide to Washington D.C.**
$12.95, 1-58062-313-1

Everything® **Guide to Writing
        Children's Books**
$14.95, 1-58062-785-4

Everything® **Guitar Book**
$14.95, 1-58062-555-X

Everything® **Herbal Remedies Book**
$12.95, 1-58062-331-X

Everything® **Home-Based Business Book**
$12.95, 1-58062-364-6

Everything® **Homebuying Book**
$12.95, 1-58062-074-4

Everything® **Homeselling Book**
$12.95, 1-58062-304-2

Everything® **Horse Book**
$12.95, 1-58062-564-9

Everything® **Hot Careers Book**
$12.95, 1-58062-486-3

Everything® **Hypnosis Book**
$14.95, 1-58062-737-4

Everything® **Internet Book**
$12.95, 1-58062-073-6

Everything® **Investing Book**
$12.95, 1-58062-149-X

Everything® **Jewish Wedding Book**
$12.95, 1-55850-801-5

Everything® **Judaism Book**
$14.95, 1-58062-728-5

Everything® **Job Interview Book**
$12.95, 1-58062-493-6

Everything® **Knitting Book**
$14.95, 1-58062-727-7

Everything® **Lawn Care Book**
$12.95, 1-58062-487-1

Everything® **Leadership Book**
$12.95, 1-58062-513-4

Everything® **Learning French Book**
$12.95, 1-58062-649-1

Everything® **Learning Italian Book**
$14.95, 1-58062-724-2

Everything® **Learning Spanish Book**
$12.95, 1-58062-575-4

Everything® **Low-Carb Cookbook**
$14.95, 1-58062-784-6

Everything® **Low-Fat High-Flavor
        Cookbook**
$12.95, 1-55850-802-3

Everything® **Magic Book**
$14.95, 1-58062-418-9

Everything® **Managing People Book**
$12.95, 1-58062-577-0

Everything® **Meditation Book**
$14.95, 1-58062-665-3

Everything® **Menopause Book**
$14.95, 1-58062-741-2

Everything® **Microsoft® Word 2000 Book**
$12.95, 1-58062-306-9

Everything® **Money Book**
$12.95, 1-58062-145-7

Everything® **Mother Goose Book**
$12.95, 1-58062-490-1

Everything® **Motorcycle Book**
$12.95, 1-58062-554-1

Everything® **Mutual Funds Book**
$12.95, 1-58062-419-7

Everything® **Network Marketing Book**
$14.95, 1-58062-736-6

Everything® **Numerology Book**
$14.95, 1-58062-700-5

Everything® **One-Pot Cookbook**
$12.95, 1-58062-186-4

Everything® **Online Business Book**
$12.95, 1-58062-320-4

Everything® **Online Genealogy Book**
$12.95, 1-58062-402-2

Everything® **Online Investing Book**
$12.95, 1-58062-338-7

Everything® **Online Job Search Book**
$12.95, 1-58062-365-4

Everything® **Organize Your Home Book**
$12.95, 1-58062-617-3

Everything® **Pasta Book**
$12.95, 1-55850-719-1

Everything® **Philosophy Book**
$12.95, 1-58062-644-0

Everything® **Pilates Book**
$14.95, 1-58062-738-2

Everything® **Playing Piano and
        Keyboards Book**
$12.95, 1-58062-651-3

Everything® **Potty Training Book**
$14.95, 1-58062-740-4

Everything® **Pregnancy Book**
$12.95, 1-58062-146-5

Everything® **Pregnancy Organizer**
$15.00, 1-58062-336-0

Everything® **Project Management Book**
$12.95, 1-58062-583-5

Everything® **Puppy Book**
$12.95, 1-58062-576-2

Everything® **Quick Meals Cookbook**
$14.95, 1-58062-488-X

Everything® **Resume Book**
$12.95, 1-58062-311-5

Everything® **Romance Book**
$12.95, 1-58062-566-5

Everything® **Running Book**
$12.95, 1-58062-618-1

Everything® **Sailing Book, 2nd Ed.**
$12.95, 1-58062-671-8

Everything® **Saints Book**
$12.95, 1-58062-534-7

Everything® **Scrapbooking Book**
$14.95, 1-58062-729-3

Everything® **Selling Book**
$12.95, 1-58062-319-0

Everything® **Shakespeare Book**
$14.95, 1-58062-591-6

Everything® **Slow Cooker Cookbook**
$14.95, 1-58062-667-X

Everything® **Soup Cookbook**
$14.95, 1-58062-556-8

Everything® **Spells and Charms Book**
$12.95, 1-58062-532-0

Everything® **Start Your Own Business Book**
$14.95, 1-58062-650-5

Everything® **Stress Management Book**
$14.95, 1-58062-578-9

Everything® **Study Book**
$12.95, 1-55850-615-2

Everything® **T'ai Chi and QiGong Book**
$12.95, 1-58062-646-7

Everything® **Tall Tales, Legends, and Other Outrageous Lies Book**
$12.95, 1-58062-514-2

Everything® **Tarot Book**
$12.95, 1-58062-191-0

Everything® **Thai Cookbook**
$14.95, 1-58062-733-1

Everything® **Time Management Book**
$12.95, 1-58062-492-8

Everything® **Toasts Book**
$12.95, 1-58062-189-9

Everything® **Toddler Book**
$14.95, 1-58062-592-4

Everything® **Total Fitness Book**
$12.95, 1-58062-318-2

Everything® **Trivia Book**
$12.95, 1-58062-143-0

Everything® **Tropical Fish Book**
$12.95, 1-58062-343-3

Everything® **Vegetarian Cookbook**
$12.95, 1-58062-640-8

Everything® **Vitamins, Minerals, and Nutritional Supplements Book**
$12.95, 1-58062-496-0

Everything® **Weather Book**
$14.95, 1-58062-668-8

Everything® **Wedding Book, 2nd Ed.**
$14.95, 1-58062-190-2

Everything® **Wedding Checklist**
$7.95, 1-58062-456-1

Everything® **Wedding Etiquette Book**
$7.95, 1-58062-454-5

Everything® **Wedding Organizer**
$15.00, 1-55850-828-7

Everything® **Wedding Shower Book**
$7.95, 1-58062-188-0

Everything® **Wedding Vows Book**
$7.95, 1-58062-455-3

Everything® **Weddings on a Budget Book**
$9.95, 1-58062-782-X

Everything® **Weight Training Book**
$12.95, 1-58062-593-2

Everything® **Wicca and Witchcraft Book**
$14.95, 1-58062-725-0

Everything® **Wine Book**
$12.95, 1-55850-808-2

Everything® **World War II Book**
$14.95, 1-58062-572-X

Everything® **World's Religions Book**
$14.95, 1-58062-648-3

Everything® **Yoga Book**
$14.95, 1-58062-594-0

*Prices subject to change without notice.

EVERYTHING KIDS' SERIES!

Everything® **Kids' Baseball Book, 2nd Ed.**
$6.95, 1-58062-688-2

Everything® **Kids' Cookbook**
$6.95, 1-58062-658-0

Everything® **Kids' Joke Book**
$6.95, 1-58062-686-6

Everything® **Kids' Mazes Book**
$6.95, 1-58062-558-4

Everything® **Kids' Money Book**
$6.95, 1-58062-685-8

Everything® **Kids' Monsters Book**
$6.95, 1-58062-657-2

Everything® **Kids' Nature Book**
$6.95, 1-58062-684-X

Everything® **Kids' Puzzle Book**
$6.95, 1-58062-687-4

Everything® **Kids' Science Experiments Book**
$6.95, 1-58062-557-6

Everything® **Kids' Soccer Book**
$6.95, 1-58062-642-4

Everything® **Travel Activity Book**
$6.95, 1-58062-641-6

Available wherever books are sold!
To order, call 800-872-5627, or visit us at everything.com

Everything® is a registered trademark of Adams Media Corporation.